Writing
for
Career-
Education
Students

Writing for Career-Education Students

Andrew W. Hart

James A. Reinking

St. Martin's Press   New York

Library of Congress Catalog Card Number: 76–28123
Copyright © 1977 by St. Martin's Press, Inc.
All Rights Reserved.
Manufactured in the United States of America.
09
fed
For information, write: St. Martin's Press, Inc.,
175 Fifth Avenue, New York, N.Y. 10010

ISBN 0–312–89460–0

cover design: Melissa Tardiff

Why is it that in math you are always told step-by-step how to solve a problem, but in English you are simply told to write a paper?

Gail Bartlett,
a student (*in conversation*)

To the Instructor

Writing for Career-Education Students presents a clear, step-by-step introduction to the essentials of practical writing. It is designed for students in vocational and technical programs or for courses enrolling a mixture of vocational and liberal arts students in which a strong emphasis on job-related writing is desired. It may be used for teaching freshman composition. It is also suitable for a one-term course in technical communication.

The organization of the book is simple and straightforward. Chapter 1 discusses the elements of a paragraph and ways to develop it, and chapter 2 takes the student step by step through the procedure typically followed in preparing a theme—planning, writing, and revising. These two introductory chapters are followed by five chapters on expository writing—comparison, classification, explanation of a process, definition, and description of an object—each illustrated by a number of writing models. Chapter 8 considers various kinds of letters and memorandums. Chapters 9–11 deal with three specialized types of on-the-job communication: proposals, progress reports, and investigation (or test) reports. Thus, there is a gradual shift from a general to a technical emphasis. The main body of the text concludes with chapter 12, which offers a detailed discussion of the application letter, personal data sheet (résumé), job interview, and four kinds of post-interview letters. Collectively, the twelve chapters include all the modes of writing most likely to prove useful to career-education students.

The chapters follow a consistent pattern. The opening section clearly establishes the practical value of the particular type of writing by citing several possible classroom and on-the-job assignments requiring its use. Next come the writing directions, followed by a number of student examples with discussion questions. The chapter concludes with a list of suggested writing assignments.

Following the twelve chapters that make up the main body of the text is a section entitled "English Use and Misuse" (pages 244–322). This section consists of two parts: "English Use" (pages 244–307) reviews the basic elements of grammar, punctuation, and mechanics; "English Misuse" (pages 307–322) examines the most common writing errors. A chart inside the back cover of the book lists correction symbols for the instructor's use in marking student papers. The symbols are keyed for student reference to the pertinent discussions in "English Use and Misuse."

Finally, "English Use and Misuse" is supplemented by the "Faulty Sentences for Class Discussion" on pages 323–326. These sentences, taken from student papers, can be either analyzed and corrected orally in class or assigned, a few at a time, as written work.

Writing for Career-Education Students is perhaps more student-oriented than any comparable text. In each chapter the directions for writing are presented in an easy-to-follow, step-by-step format—the mode of presentation students will encounter most frequently in their more strictly vocational courses. All of the writing examples presented are by students rather than professional writers. These models represent realistic, achievable goals and demonstrate that students can and do produce first-rate work; moreover, all the examples are directly related to students' vocational or general interests. In introducing each type of writing, we point out its importance both on the job and (when appropriate) in the student's college courses. Throughout the book we address the student directly as "you." Some instructors may regard this use of the second person as heresy in the discussion of technical writing, but we see no reason why even the most formal matters cannot be discussed informally. We all do it in the classroom every day.

These features provide a number of benefits. Students readily understand and follow the writing directions, relate closely to the models, show increased confidence in their own ability to write, and perceive the value of what they are doing. We have found that, as a result, they participate more actively in class, put more effort into their writing assignments, and produce better papers.

One further comment about our use of student examples is

in order. All too often, the professional models included in other textbooks deviate from the patterns laid down in the text itself. The student is told one thing and shown another. In this book, however, the examples clearly and consistently conform to the stipulated patterns, thus eliminating an important source of confusion and irritation. The questions accompanying the examples have been designed to reinforce important points in the discussion and good writing practice in general.

Another feature of *Writing for Career-Education Students* is its flexibility. We strongly recommend that chapters 1 and 2 be read first, but beyond those two chapters the materials in this book can be "mixed and matched" in a number of ways, depending upon the makeup of the class and the course objectives. For example, one instructor might elect to begin with the general chapters on expository writing and then proceed to more technical materials, such as business letters and memorandums, reports, and proposals. Another instructor might start right in with business letters and memorandums, letters of application and personal data sheets, and selected technical reports and then consider the expository writing modes.

In addition to being suited for the conventional classroom, *Writing for Career-Education Students* is also appropriate for an individualized study program—the "open" classroom. Its step-by-step approach allows students to proceed at their own pace. When they feel they have mastered a step, they can check with the instructor and then move on to the next step. The variety of student examples and the large number of suggestions for writing make it possible for the instructor to tailor assignments to the career interests of individual students.

We are indebted to a number of people for their encouragement and assistance. First, we would like to thank our colleagues at Ferris State College who have criticized portions of the manuscript, furnished us with models of student writing, and helped us in many other ways: John Belanger, Fred Birkam, Charles Bond, Charles Bown, Mary Braun, Richard Cronk, John Fogarty, Don Hanzek, Fred Howting, Hugh Griffith, Tom Kakonis, Shannon King, Ray MacLoughlin, Ann Remp, Jack Richards, Brandt Rowles, Richard Shaw, Elliott Smith, and Richard Young. Special thanks are due Avon Murphy. We wish to express our appreciation to the thoroughly professional staff of St. Martin's Press, and especially to Tom Broadbent and Nancy Perry. We are deeply grateful to our families for their consideration and patience during our many months of writing. Finally, our greatest debt is to the many students who have graciously allowed us to use their writing in these pages. Without their help, this book would not have been possible.

Andrew W. Hart
James A. Reinking

To the Student

No matter what career you choose, your success will be directly affected by your ability to communicate clearly and effectively in writing. In the classroom, your instructors will often evaluate your mastery of a subject by the papers and examinations you write. Prospective employers will make judgments about your qualifications and decide whether to offer you an interview on the basis of your application letter and personal data sheet. Once you are on the job, you must be prepared to write clear, accurate reports, instructions, memorandums, and letters.

There is nothing mysterious about successful on-the-job writing. It does not require a special talent, nor does it depend on inspiration. It is simply a skill, and, like any other skill, it involves a series of steps or procedures that can be learned. Once you are familiar with the steps, the more you practice the easier the task becomes.

Writing for Career-Education Students will acquaint you with the steps involved in successful writing and show you how to apply them to the specific kinds of writing you can expect to do as you pursue your career. The first two chapters, on paragraphs and themes, deal with procedures basic to all successful writing. Chapters 3–7 explain the most frequently used types of exposition: comparison, classification, explanation of a process, definition, and description of an object. Chapter 8 discusses letters and memorandums. Chapters 9–11 deal with three specialized types of on-the-job writing: proposals, progress reports, and investigation reports. Chapter 12, the final chapter, presents detailed suggestions for finding a job: preparing application letters and personal data sheets, coping with employment interviews, and writing follow-up letters.

The last section of the book, "English Use and Misuse" (pages

244–322), reviews the basic elements of grammar, punctuation, and mechanics, as well as the most common writing errors. A chart inside the back cover lists correction symbols that your instructor may use in marking your papers. For your convenience, the symbols are keyed to the specific pages in "English Use and Misuse" where you will find help in correcting the problems your instructor has pointed out.

This book has several features we hope you will find helpful. It is written in simple, everyday language. Directions are presented in an easy-to-follow, step-by-step format. Above all, the book is written directly to and for the student. In the course of your education, you have probably had the unpleasant experience of using textbooks that seemed to be designed more for instructors than for students. In preparing this book, we have tried never to forget that you, after all, are buying the book and paying for the course in which you are using it. Accordingly, we have tried to write the book as directly as possible to you.

Another feature is that all of the sample paragraphs, papers, letters, and reports have been written by students rather than by professional writers. Unlike some of the professionally written examples in other textbooks, these student examples represent realistic, achievable goals. At the same time, they are dramatic evidence that students can indeed do first-rate work. We are confident that if you learn and apply the principles presented in the following pages, you will do so, too. Here's wishing you success!

Andrew W. Hart
James A. Reinking

Contents

3 Comparison 41

4 Classification 56

5 Explaining a Process 70

9 Proposals   160

10 Progress Reports   182

11 Investigation Reports 195

12 Finding a Job 214

Writing for Career-Education Students

1

The Paragraph

Writing is a process of building larger units from smaller ones. That is, the writer uses words to make sentences, sentences to make paragraphs, and paragraphs to make a composition—a letter, report, or college theme. In this book, we deal with words and sentences at appropriate places throughout the text and in the brief handbook called "English Use and Misuse" at the end of the book. We will begin our discussion here with the paragraph.

Paragraphs help both you and your readers. Writing a paper of any kind is easier when you can focus on its separate units—the paragraphs—one by one. Your readers also benefit when a paper is divided into paragraphs, for they can grasp your main ideas one at a time and follow the progression of ideas throughout the paper in an orderly way.

To understand what is involved in writing a paragraph, you must first be familiar with five basic items:

1. one central idea
2. topic sentence
3. specific details
4. pattern of development
5. linking devices

1

In the following sections, we will discuss and illustrate each of these items.

One Central Idea

A paragraph is a group of closely related sentences that develop and clarify *one*, and *only one*, central idea. Carefully select the material you include in each of your paragraphs so that you don't stray from its central idea. Sentences that point in several different directions rather than toward a single idea will only confuse your reader.

Consider the following poorly written paragraph.

> As he crosses the parking lot, Dave notices two young men shouting and scuffling. When he opens the door to the athletic complex, he can smell the various refreshments. Once inside the gymnasium, he hears the familiar loud noises of the junior varsity basketball game. While undressing in the varsity locker room, he hears different noises.

What exactly is the writer trying to convey in this paragraph? There is no way of knowing. Each of the four sentences expresses a different idea, and none of them is developed:

1. young men shouting and scuffling
2. smells of the refreshments in the athletic complex
3. noises of the junior varsity basketball game
4. noises in the varsity locker room

For meaningful communication, each of these ideas would have to be fully developed in a separate paragraph.

Each of the following student paragraphs *does* develop and clarify one central idea.

> As he opens the door to the crowded gymnasium, Dave is blasted by the familiar noises of the junior varsity basketball game. Hundreds of voices blend together to form one huge roar, which reaches a peak whenever the home team makes a basket. Suddenly a shrill whistle silences the crowd, and then a stabbing buzzer signals a time out. With a break in the action,

the pep band strikes up the school fight song. Trumpets blare to the thumping beat of the bass drum.

While the band is playing, Dave turns and walks toward the varsity locker room, where he is greeted by different noises. The mumbling and joking of the players mix with the muffled voices of the coaches discussing the game plan in the closed office. The clanging of steel lockers as they are opened and closed blends in. Aerosol cans of skin toughener hiss as the spray is applied to tender feet. Mouse-like squeaks are heard as the nervous players pace the floor. Finally the coaches come out to give their last words of advice and encouragement.

Mike Hogan

All the sentences in the first paragraph point toward one idea—the noises in the gym during the junior varsity basketball game. No unrelated details, such as the clothes worn by the person taking tickets or the kind of refreshments being served, are included. Similarly, all the sentences in the second paragraph point toward a single, but *different*, idea—the noises of the varsity locker room. The writer signals this shift in thought to the reader by beginning a new paragraph.

Topic Sentence

The topic sentence is the most important sentence in a paragraph. Its function is to state clearly the central idea of the paragraph. All the other sentences in the paragraph build on and develop this one idea.

A topic sentence serves two purposes. First, it helps you, as the writer, to decide what to include in and exclude from your paragraph. Only information that develops or clarifies the idea stated in the topic sentence belongs in the paragraph. Information that does not do so should be excluded. Second, the topic sentence helps your reader. By providing a direct statement of the central idea, it eliminates the possibility that the reader will miss the point, and it saves the reader the trouble of having to figure out how the various bits of information in the paragraph are related.

When you formulate a topic sentence, be sure to avoid one that is too broad. The following sentence, for example, encompasses more points than can be meaningfully developed in a single paragraph. You would have to write an article or perhaps even a book to develop the idea it expresses.

> There have been great advances in technology in the twentieth century.

Here is an adequate topic sentence.

> The pocket calculator offers a number of advantages.

You could develop this idea by citing, for example, the pocket calculator's low cost, portability, versatility, and high degree of precision.

Because the topic sentence expresses the central idea developed in the paragraph, it should be placed where it can be easily recognized. Experienced writers, therefore, often start their paragraphs with the topic sentence, and you will probably find it helpful to do the same. Placing the topic sentence at the beginning not only makes the paragraph easier to write but also enables your reader to learn the subject of the paragraph immediately. Examine the following paragraph. The topic sentence is italicized.

> *The nursing station is a hubbub of activity.* Doctors are writing new orders, and their patients' charts are scattered all over the desk. Laboratory and X-ray technicians are explaining results of tests. The pharmacist brings medications and inquires about any new orders for drugs. Inhalation and physical therapists are busy checking charts for their new orders. The dietician asks why a certain patient is not eating the foods he should. Telephones ring and patients' signal lights flash continually. The members of the nursing team, all with their own duties, are trying desperately to keep up with everything that is going on, which gives them little time to spend with their patients. This pace continues through most of the morning shift.
>
> *Clare Mutter*

Here the writer clearly and immediately announces one central idea, and the rest of the paragraph develops it.

Sometimes, however, for emphasis or variety, you may want to place the topic sentence later in a paragraph. Actually, it can go anywhere. A topic sentence at the end of a paragraph, for example, can very effectively summarize or draw a conclusion from information presented in the preceding sentences. Here is a well-developed paragraph in which the topic sentence is placed at the end.

I woke up late because the alarm didn't go off. Actually, I had been so tired the night before that I had forgotten to set it; all I could think of then was the report I had stayed up until 3 A.M. typing—and how I could possibly get twenty copies ready for the sales meeting that started at 9 o'clock the next morning. When I realized that it was 8:30 and I was still in bed, I panicked. I jumped up, threw on some clothes, grabbed the report, and ran out the door. When my bus finally came along, it was so crowded that I had to stand. Not only could I not proofread the report; I also couldn't see out the window. Two blocks beyond my stop, I realized that I should have gotten off. "Stop!" I cried, then jumped off the bus and raced back up the street. When I reached the office, it was 9:15, and the meeting was already underway. Mr. Jackson, the company president, saw me as I walked by the conference room and gestured for me to come in. "One minute," I said as calmly as I could, then hurried to the Xerox machine. Without pausing, I put in the first page of the report, turned the dial to twenty copies, and pressed the print button. It was only then, as I leaned against the machine waiting for the copies to appear, that I saw the flashing sign—CALL KEY OPERATOR. The machine was out of order. The next thing I knew, Mr. Jackson was at the door, asking if the report was ready. Unable to speak, I pointed to the flashing red words. Mr. Jackson didn't say anything either. He nodded his head grimly and walked away, leaving me alone with the broken machine. *It was the worst morning of my life.*
Helen White

All the details lead up to and prepare for the last sentence. At that point, the reader can easily understand why the author of the paragraph had had the worst morning of her life.

An experienced writer will occasionally construct a paragraph in which the central idea is only implied. Although such a paragraph has no stated topic sentence, the sentences that make up the paragraph, added together, suggest a single idea which the reader has little difficulty understanding. For example, in the last sample paragraph, an experienced writer might have implied the central idea rather than stating it in a topic sentence. The combination of details—waking up late, forgetting to get off the bus at the right stop, finding the Xerox machine broken—might have been enough to make it clear that the writer had had a terrible morning. However, effective paragraphs without clear topic sentences are hard to write, and even if they are well done, they still make an extra demand on the reader. For the kind of writing you will do in the classroom and on the job, the best advice is to develop your paragraphs from clearly expressed topic sentences.

Specific Details

Most successful paragraphs contain a generous supply of specific details that develop and clarify the idea expressed in the topic sentence. Each individual detail is one piece of a larger picture. Separately, the details may mean very little, but when enough of them are properly grouped together (as described in the next section, "Pattern of Development"), the total picture emerges.

Think back to the paragraph describing the nursing station. The first detail, doctors writing new orders, means little by itself. You begin to sense the activity when you read about the laboratory and X-ray technicians. Then you see the pharmacists, the therapists, and the dietician. Finally, the nurses are described, and you have a total picture of the activity in the nursing station. The details, taken as a unit, have made the picture complete.

Now read the following paragraph and note the difference.

> There are two reasons why prices at a fast-food place like McDonald's are low. One is because the selection of food is limited. Also the franchise makes a deliberate effort to hold down operating costs.

The problem here is determining what the writer means. This short paragraph begins with an adequate topic sentence, but the writer *doesn't adequately develop it*. Instead of clarifying the main idea, the rest of the paragraph only raises questions. For example, what does the writer mean by a "limited" selection?

Are hamburgers served only with mustard? Or does the writer mean that fast-food places don't serve T-bone steaks? And what does the writer mean by "a deliberate effort to hold down operating costs"? Is it some employee's job to rush into the restroom the moment a customer vacates it and make sure the faucets aren't dripping? The writer may very well know what he or she wants the reader to understand, but the information does not appear in the paragraph. Thus the reader, instead of seeing a clear picture, gets merely a vague impression. This paragraph is obviously underdeveloped—more specific details are needed.

At this point you can see the benefits of supplying plenty of specific details. First, and most important, the reader receives the same message you intended—there is no confusion or misunderstanding. You and your reader connect. Second, specific details make your writing more vivid and interesting. (And there is an additional benefit, although it applies more to the writing you do for your courses than to the writing you will do on the job: if you provide enough details to make your ideas really clear, you will seldom have to worry about "getting enough words" for an assigned paper. When you concentrate on giving your reader a complete picture and not just a piece here and there, the length of your paper will usually take care of itself.)

When writing your rough draft, include more details than you think you'll need in the final version. It is easy to eliminate some details later if you find you have more than enough; just draw a line through them. It is much more difficult to add details later in order to make an incomplete picture complete, since you must first analyze the paragraph to determine what is missing and then decide how to fill the gap.

A frequent concern of students is "How long should my paragraphs be?" This is a good question which has no good answer. No one can give you a general rule about how many words to aim for, since the length of a paragraph depends on the amount of detail needed to develop its central idea. In writing your paragraphs, remember that the number of words you write is not your primary concern; presenting a complete picture to your reader is. When the idea expressed in your topic sentence has been fully developed, your paragraph will be long enough.

The following paragraphs by students illustrate the use of specific detail.

Hand and foot movements are critical for the snowplow operator. He uses his hands not only to steer but at the same time to raise, lower, and change the angle of the front plow. At certain points, the back plow must also be raised and lowered. Between the plow control movements, the operator's hands are busy shifting his transmission, using turn signals, flipping switches for radios and lights, and sometimes clearing fogged windshields. Meanwhile, his feet move so fast that they might appear blurry to a passenger. They are continually moving from the brakes to the clutch to the accelerator.

Jim Linscott

A program in drafting techniques acquaints students with a number of practical skills. Students first learn basic principles such as lettering, geometric construction, orthographic projection, and dimensioning. They then learn to apply product drafting to surface finish controls, geometric and positional tolerances, sections of parts, symbols used in drawing, and assembly and subassembly. During this study of the spatial relationships of lines, planes, and solids, they learn to solve layout problems by using descriptive geometry and rotational principles. Next they are taught the fundamentals of tool detailing and the basic design of tools, jigs, fixtures, dies, and molds, using standard parts such as clamps, washers, keys, locating pins, and punches. They also gain an insight into the use of drill jigs and milling fixtures, which are drawn as assemblies and then detailed into working drawings.

Richard Johnson

What is the one central idea developed in each paragraph? Express it in your own words. Now pick out the topic sentence. Why do you think it is placed where it is? Do the details help you to form a complete picture? Why or why not?

Pattern of Development

You know that a well-developed paragraph contains a generous supply of specific details. But it is not enough to present these details in whatever order they happen to come to mind. Such a method might be acceptable if you were writing in your diary, for example, because chances are that only you would read it, and you could probably follow your own ideas without a pattern. However, in paragraphs you write for someone else, pattern does matter. Your reader will have trouble understanding your meaning unless you follow a clear pattern of development. There are several common patterns a paragraph can follow; the one you use for a particular paragraph will depend on the purpose of your writing and the nature of your subject.

Five patterns of development are presented below. The first and second are basic; the last three, though listed as separate patterns, are actually special forms of the first or second.

PATTERN NUMBER ONE: GENERAL TO SPECIFIC

The general-to-specific pattern is probably the one used most frequently. The writer begins with a general statement and then moves to specific statements that explain or support it. Read again the following student paragraph, which illustrates this pattern.

> The nursing station is a hubbub of activity. Doctors are writing new orders, and their patients' charts are scattered all over the desk. Laboratory and X-ray technicians are explaining results of tests. The pharmacist brings medications and inquires about any new orders for drugs. Inhalation and physical therapists are busy checking charts for their new orders. The dietician asks why a certain patient is not eating the foods he should. Telephones ring and patients' signal lights flash continually. The members of the nursing team, all with their own duties, are trying desperately to keep up with everything that is going on, which gives them little time to spend with their patients. This pace continues through most of the morning shift.
>
> *Clare Mutter*

PATTERN NUMBER TWO: SPECIFIC TO GENERAL

In a paragraph developed by the specific-to-general pattern, specific statements are presented first. These statements explain or support a general statement, which ends the paragraph. The following student example illustrates this pattern.

> Leslie Jackson has had a number of years' experience as a secretary. Her typing is excellent—65 words a minute—as is

her steno. She is neat, punctual, and well organized, and she works well without supervision. When Leslie is given an assignment, she can be counted on to do a topnotch job. Her coworkers look to Leslie for advice, and she never fails to give them the help they need. There is no doubt that Leslie Jackson is well qualified to be an office manager.

Gloria Stillwell

PATTERN NUMBER THREE: TIME SEQUENCE

The time-sequence pattern arranges the events being described in chronological order—that is, the order in which they happen in time. Here is a student paragraph that illustrates this pattern.

I remember well the morning I had my first job interview. Before leaving home, I made certain I was neatly dressed and well groomed. It was a long drive to the interviewer's office, and more than once I thought of being rejected. Then there was the difficult time as I sat in the outer office, nervously waiting my turn. I remember tapping my feet, shifting in the chair, and trying to read several magazines. Finally, my name was called. I swallowed hard and walked stiffly into the office. The interviewer asked many questions, keeping her eyes directly focused on me all the time. After what seemed like hours, she indicated I could report for work the following Monday.

Jane Bleiler

PATTERN NUMBER FOUR: SPACE SEQUENCE

In the space-sequence pattern, specific statements are presented in an orderly arrangement that enables the reader to see how the different items relate to one another physically—that is, in space. For example, if you were describing an object such as a building, you might start at the top and work down to the bottom, describing what you see, step by step, in that order. On the other hand, you might start at the bottom and work up. This pattern of development offers many possibilities: left to right, right to left, nearby to faraway, faraway to nearby, and so on. Make sure, however, that the particular space sequence you choose is appropriate for the object being described. The paragraph below illustrates this pattern.

For many years Wilt Chamberlain, "The Big Dipper," was a familiar figure to Los Angeles Laker fans. Everybody recognized the distinctive sweatband circling his forehead, seven feet above the ground. His soft brown eyes rarely showed any anger. His neck was strong and solid, his shoulders massive. The familiar yellow number 13 jersey spanned a broad, muscular chest, which tapered sharply to a trim waist and narrow hips. His knee-length sweat socks, covering slender but rock-hard calves, were anchored in size fourteen shoes.

Janice Weitl

PATTERN NUMBER FIVE: ORDER OF CLIMAX

The order-of-climax pattern presents a series of ideas in a progression from the least important to the most important. The reader is gradually given increasingly more important information and is thus encouraged to continue reading until the main point is made. The following student paragraph illustrates this pattern.

I feel that the best compact car I can buy today is the six-cylinder Plymouth Volare (formerly the Valiant). Chrysler Corporation's television advertising has shown me that the Volare is a sharp-looking car with an excellent warranty. More important, *Consumer Reports*, an unbiased consumer magazine, has ranked the car at the top of its class. Not only does its gas mileage exceed twenty miles per gallon on the open road, but its resale value is outstanding. But what finally convinced me to go visit my local Volare dealer was the recommendation of our long-time family friend, Ted Bowles. Ted, an excellent mechanic, pointed out that the "Slant Six" engine is extremely dependable and should provide many miles of carefree driving.

Ferris Finerty

Linking Devices

Now you are familiar with some patterns of development that will give order to your paragraphs as you supply specific details to make the central idea of each paragraph clear to your reader. *Next* you must make sure that the sentences within your paragraphs are linked to one another in ways that make them flow smoothly and enable your reader to follow the progression of thought easily from sentence to sentence. *After all*, you have carefully arranged the sentences in a particular sequence to develop one continuous idea. *That is*, the idea expressed by each sentence is in some way related to the idea in the sentence before it and to the idea in the sentence after it, and they are all related, directly or indirectly, to the central idea expressed in the topic sentence. *Of course*, the relationships among the sentences are clear to you because you wrote the paragraph; *however*, they must also be made clear to your reader. This job is accomplished by the use of linking devices.

LINKING DEVICE NUMBER ONE: CONNECTING WORDS AND PHRASES

Certain words in the paragraph you just read are italicized. Each of the italicized units is an example of a commonly used connecting word or phrase. Read the paragraph again. Notice how *now*, *next, after all, that is, of course*, and *however* connect the sentences in the paragraph and relate the ideas they express to one another. To see this clearly, try reading the paragraph aloud with, and then again without, the italicized words and phrases.

Here are some of the most commonly used connecting words and phrases:

nevertheless	indeed
consequently	sometimes
furthermore	meanwhile
accordingly	as a matter of fact
moreover	in addition
hence	in conclusion
otherwise	although
then	because
subsequently	while
likewise	until
nonetheless	finally
thus	next
as a result	after
in fact	after all
for example	first

on the other hand	second
on the contrary	also
in the first place	however
now	therefore
again	again
too	if
that is	when
in other words	in this way
of course	at times
since	besides

The following student example illustrates how connecting words and phrases link the different sentences of a paragraph. The connecting words are italicized.

> The psychiatric nurse deals with dangerous mental patients, pathological personalities who have no sense of right or wrong. *For this reason*, she must be on guard at all times; she must, in effect, have eyes in the back of her head. She must *also* have a great deal of self-control. When her patient displays anger and violence, she cannot respond in kind. *On the contrary*, she must be tolerant and understanding. *Furthermore*, she must be able to recognize attempts at deception. *Sometimes* a mentally ill person, just prior to suicide, will act in a completely normal way because he or she has made the decision to die. The nurse must understand this behavior and be alert for any possible attempt.
>
> *Peg Feltman*

Notice how each sentence is related to the one before it. The connecting words and phrases make the relationships clear, linking the sentences into a continuous unit that can be followed easily.

LINKING DEVICE NUMBER TWO: REPETITION OF WORDS AND PHRASES

Repetition of key words and phrases in several sentences in a paragraph is another way of helping the reader follow the continuity of thought from sentence to sentence. Examine the following paragraph, which appeared earlier in this chapter, and notice how the repeated variations of the phrase "what does the writer mean?" help link the sentences together.

> The problem here is determining *what the writer means.* This short paragraph begins with an adequate topic sentence, but the writer doesn't adequately develop it. Instead of clarifying the main idea, the rest of the paragraph only raises questions. For example, *what does the writer mean* by a "limited" selection? Are hamburgers served only with mustard? Or *does the writer mean* that fast-food places don't serve T-bone steaks? And *what does the writer mean* by "a deliberate effort to hold down operating costs"? Is it some employee's job to rush into the restroom the moment a customer vacates it and make sure the faucets aren't dripping?

Now read the following student paragraph. Notice how the repetition of "cook" helps link the sentences together.

> Food preparation at Elias Brothers is not automated. At Elias Brothers they rely on a *cook* and his knowledge of preparing food rather than on machines and timers. There is more than one *cook* and thus more than one way that a meal can be prepared. The *cook* flips the hamburgers over, using his own judgment to decide when they are ready, and the same goes for everything else he prepares.
>
> *Tim Reid*

LINKING DEVICE NUMBER THREE: PRONOUNS AND DEMONSTRATIVE ADJECTIVES

Pronouns and the demonstrative adjectives (*this, that, these, those*) can serve as linking devices for your sentences. By pointing back to words or ideas in the previous sentence, they pull the sentences closer together and help guide your reader along a continuous path. Notice how the italicized words in the paragraph below link the sentences in a clear pattern which is easy to follow.

> There are two kinds of dental mouth mirrors. The first is made of ordinary glass and has a flat reflecting surface. With *this* mirror the dentist sees the patient's teeth just the way the patient sees them in a regular looking glass. The second, the magnifying mirror, has a concave surface that makes everything

look larger. *This* mirror gives the dentist a better view of the mouth. Both of *these* mirrors have about the same diameter as a 25-cent piece. *They* are securely mounted in circular stainless steel holders, with the rims equal in depth to the thickness of the mirrors.

Lisa Hines

Conclusion

To test your understanding of paragraphs and to review points that may have slipped to the back of your mind, reexamine each of the sample paragraphs in this chapter, and see whether you can answer the following questions:

1. What is the central idea?
2. Which sentence is the topic sentence?
3. Is the topic sentence effectively located?
4. How do the specific details help form a complete picture in the reader's mind?
5. Are there details that are not related to the central idea and would better have been eliminated?
6. Which pattern of development is used?
7. Which linking devices are used to relate the sentences to one another?

Suggestions for Writing

Write a well-organized paragraph which develops one of the following ideas. Underline your topic sentence and use the method of development you think most appropriate.

1. The one quality most necessary for success in my chosen field is _____.
2. One good example of Americans' tendency to waste is _____.
3. Proper inflation pressure prolongs tire life.
4. To me, the most attractive career would be _____.
5. The best (or worst) thing about fast-food restaurants is _____.
6. The most difficult part of being an X-ray technician or dental hygienist (or substitute another occupation) is _____.

7. The college course I find most useful is _____.

8. The quality I most admire in a person is _____.

9. One reason licensing of auto mechanics is a good (or bad) idea is
_____.

10. Fixing a leaky faucet (or substitute another task) is (or is not) a difficult job.

11. Concentration (or substitute your own term here) is an important part of a successful golf game (or substitute your own sport).

12. The primary value of using dental floss regularly is _____.

13. A draftsman must have a good math background.

14. The key to being a successful nurse (or substitute another occupation) is _____.

15. What I most enjoy doing in my spare time is _____.

16. A key punch operator or an auto mechanic (or substitute another occupation) must have great manual dexterity.

2

The Theme

In the course for which you are using this book, your instructor will probably ask you to write a number of themes (also known as essays, compositions, or sometimes merely "papers"). Writing themes is good training for many kinds of writing you will have to do in college and on the job. Nevertheless, the announcement that a theme will be due is one that many students dread.

Much of this anxiety about writing themes stems from a mistaken idea about the writing process—the idea that good themes are dashed off in a burst of inspiration by "born writers." Students themselves often help promote this notion by claiming that their topnotch papers were cranked out in an hour or so of spare time. Such claims may be true now and then—and natural ability and even "inspiration" may help. But the fact is that most successful themes are simply the result of following a systematic, orderly series of steps. When you see a well-written paper, you see only the final product; what you don't see is the careful step-by-step process the writer used to develop that product.

This is not to say that there is one particular plan, one fixed order of steps, that automatically produces a well-written paper. Some experienced writers follow one plan, some another, often combining certain steps as they proceed. Moreover, specialized types of writing, such as those you'll be dealing with later in this book, require special procedures. However, it is possible to lay out a basic series of steps that will serve you well, not only for themes but for most other writing you will do. Once you know these steps, you too may wish to combine some of them as you write. For now, however, your best guarantee of a successful paper is to take the following steps one by one.

1. understanding the assignment
2. choosing your topic
3. determining your qualifications
4. establishing a specific focus
5. writing your thesis statement
6. brainstorming your subject
7. organizing your information
8. writing the first draft
9. polishing your theme

Each of these steps is discussed below.

Understanding the Assignment

In assigning a theme, your instructor may give you a specific topic, a choice among several topics, or an entirely free choice. Themes are usually relatively short, ranging from about three hundred to perhaps a thousand words; your instructor may assign an approximate length or leave the length entirely up to you. Whatever the case, be sure you clearly understand the assignment before proceeding any further. Surprisingly, many students overlook this vital first step.

Think of it this way. If your employer asked you for a report on a particular subject—let's say on how working conditions should be improved—and you responded by turning in a report on some entirely different subject—such as how your company could make its advertising more effective—would you expect your employer's approval? Or in class, if you answered an examination question with a well-written discussion that was totally unrelated to the question, would you expect to receive an A?

In short, if you are uncertain about how much freedom you have in choosing a topic, or if a specific topic has been assigned and you don't understand it clearly, don't leave the classroom imagining that you'll be able to figure it out later. Ask your instructor then and there to clarify the assignment for you. Chances are that your instructor will admire your determination to "get it right."

Choosing Your Topic

If you have been assigned a specific topic and you clearly understand the assignment, you are ready to move on to the next step. However, if you have been given either a limited or free choice of topics, you need to do some careful thinking. Very often, the instructor has the class explore a general subject, through outside reading or classroom discussion or both, and then asks the students to write a theme on any topic related to that general subject.

For example, suppose that your class has been reading or talking about the trend toward shorter work weeks and the increased amount of leisure time that employees will enjoy. The classroom discussion then turns to the ways the new leisure time may be profitably and enjoyably used. Members of the class suggest participation in various hobbies and sports. You are asked to write a two- or three-page theme on a topic of your own choice related to this general subject. You decide to write on some aspect of participation in sports.

Obviously, sports is too large a subject for two or three pages. Although you have ruled out the viewing of sports and decided to focus on participation, your subject still cannot be covered in so little space. Even if you narrow the subject to one sport— say, tennis—your subject is too large; whole books are written on tennis. Your problem, in short, is to establish a specific topic that you can deal with thoroughly and interestingly in only two or three pages. If your theme is to be successful, your topic must meet the following requirements:

1. It must be clearly related to the assigned general subject.
2. It must be something you know about (or can learn enough about in the short time you have).

3. It must be limited enough to be adequately developed in the small space you have.
4. It must interest you; if you're bored with your topic, you will write a boring paper.

If you are lucky, a topic that meets all these requirements will occur to you immediately. More often, however, you will arrive at a suitable topic only after some careful consideration and perhaps after jotting down many ideas and then eliminating those that seem least promising.

Occasionally, you may find yourself "blocked"—unable to come up with anything that seems right. This happens to most students at one time or another. An excellent way to break such a block is to talk the general subject over with others: classmates, friends, members of your family, or even—if you need to—your instructor. Discussion can "open up" a subject, exposing a variety of aspects that might not have occurred to you. Furthermore, knowing how others feel about a subject will sharpen your awareness of how you feel about it.

This increased awareness is perhaps the best way of avoiding what is sometimes called "the terror of the blank page": that feeling you get when you sit, pen in hand, but the right words won't come. The only thoughts that go through your mind are "I don't know what to write about" or "I don't know anything about the subject." Discussion can end all that.

Determining Your Qualifications

One of the most important keys to writing a successful theme is to choose a topic you are qualified to write on. Being qualified means that you are both interested in and well acquainted with the topic. These two almost always go hand in hand.

There are three basic types of qualification for selecting a subject. The first—and most useful—is *personal participation*. When you write about your own experiences, you already have a variety of beliefs, feelings, and facts to discuss in specific detail. For example, to return to the sports theme, if you don't know a birdie from a bogey, you should not write about golf unless you have the time and interest to learn something about it first. On the other hand, if you played on the high school tennis team for three years, you might consider writing about tennis. When you are interested in your topic, your theme will probably interest your reader. After all, you are writing to communicate, to share your ideas, not merely to complete an assignment.

If you can't write about personal experience, there is a second type of qualification to fall back on, *observation.* You can write about something that you have seen or heard, even though you haven't actually participated in it. Surely there are things you have observed at work, on television, at the movies, in classroom discussions, and at plays, concerts, and athletic events that interest you and that you know a good deal about. One of these might serve as the topic for your theme.

The third type of qualification is *reading.* Anything you have read in trade publications, shop manuals, magazines, technical journals, newspapers, novels, or textbooks can provide interesting material for a theme. However, students seldom rely exclusively on knowledge gained through reading. Instead, they usually combine that knowledge with details acquired through participation and observation.

Keep in mind that the most important person in your life is you. Subjects you are personally well acquainted with and interested in are the ones on which you will write most informatively and interestingly.

Establishing a Specific Focus

Once you have selected a topic you are qualified to write on, the next step is to establish a specific focus for your theme—that is, to narrow the topic down to a segment that is small enough to be developed in detail in the space you have.

Suppose that because of your experience on the high school team you decide to write your sports theme on tennis. Already you have started to focus, since tennis is only one of many possible sports topics. However, additional focusing will be necessary. Consider, for example, the following aspects that could be included in a theme on tennis:

1. its increasing popularity today
2. major tournaments

3. different court surfaces
4. equipment needed
5. tennis scoring
6. tennis terminology
7. different rackets
8. different grips
9. tennis strategy (singles)
10. tennis strategy (doubles)
11. playing the net
12. topspin strokes
13. backspin strokes
14. different serves
15. return of serve
16. proper body position
17. importance of footwork
18. special shots: the lob
19. special shots: the drop volley
20. special shots: the overhead

This is only a partial list, but it does show the importance of zeroing in. To cover all these aspects in a relatively short paper would be impossible. You would be able to write only one or two sentences about each aspect, and no clear picture of anything would emerge. In addition, the problem of organization would be enormous.

On the other hand, if you focus on *one* aspect of tennis—such as playing better singles—you can develop each of your main points in a paragraph or more. This is what focus is all about. Above all else, it involves saying more about less. It involves concentrating on one aspect of a subject in some depth rather than treating many aspects superficially.

How narrowly and in what direction you focus depends on two factors. First, consider the assigned length of your paper. The shorter the paper, the narrower your focus must be. For a three-hundred-word theme, you might focus on some of the conditioning exercises necessary for a singles player. For a five- to six-hundred-word theme, you might discuss conditioning exercises, concentration, and consistency.

Second, consider the type of reader you will be writing for.

This reader is your audience. Keep in mind that your writing should communicate ideas your reader can understand. You must focus on an aspect of your topic that will be meaningful to your audience. Notice, for example, how your audience would affect the focus for the tennis theme. If you were writing for the beginning player, you might focus on equipment needed and scoring. For the intermediate player, you might focus on conditioning, concentration, and consistency, and for the advanced player, on special shots. Unless you are writing in your diary, you must always consider your reader. On some occasions, you may be asked to write for a particular audience, while on others you may be asked to choose your own. The important thing is to have a definite reader-audience in mind.

Although at times you may want to name your intended audience in the paper itself, generally it is not necessary to do so. If you write with a definite reader in mind, your intention should be clear.

Writing Your Thesis Statement

Once you have established a specific focus, the next step is to develop your thesis statement. To do this, think carefully about the following questions: "What exactly do I hope to accomplish by writing this paper? What is my specific reason for writing?" The answers to these questions should be reflected in one carefully considered thesis statement. The thesis statement is usually a single sentence, though occasionally, especially for a long paper, it may be necessary to write two or three sentences.

You will recall that the topic sentence clearly states the central idea of a paragraph. It also helps you decide what information to include in and exclude from the paragraph. (You may want to review pages 3–6.) What the topic sentence does for a single paragraph, the thesis statement does for an entire theme.

Because you can't proceed any further with your writing without knowing exactly what you hope to accomplish, it is necessary to compose your thesis statement at this point. After all, if you don't know why you are writing the theme, your reader won't either. Spend some time thinking about it. Then, when you have a clear thesis statement in mind, *write it down*. Don't assume you'll keep it in your head; ideas sometimes slip away. In addition, having your thesis statement in written form will make the next two steps—brainstorming and outlining—much easier.

The thesis statement can be written in two forms: specific and general. In the specific form, one statement clearly spells out the main points the theme will discuss. Such a thesis statement for your tennis theme might be: *Three keys to playing better tennis singles are conditioning, concentration, and consistency.* Now you have a point-by-point guide to follow when you develop your paper. You can discuss each of these keys in a paragraph or more. When you decide which to discuss first, second, and third, you have a general outline for your theme. Moreover, with a specific thesis statement, your reader knows precisely the points to look for in later paragraphs and thus will be able to follow your discussion with ease.

Sometimes writers prefer to leave the thesis statement more general. A general thesis statement for your tennis theme might be: *If you are really serious about playing better tennis singles, there are several ways you can improve your game.* Note, however, that in this example neither the writer nor the reader has a clear guide to the points that will follow. The reader must wait to find out what they are. For certain kinds of writing the general thesis statement may be desirable, but for most theme writing and for the writing you do on the job the specific thesis statement is almost always the better choice.

Notice that both thesis statements are broad enough to include the central ideas—and therefore the topic sentences—of all the paragraphs.

Another important hint about your thesis statement: you may decide to alter it slightly or even change it completely if you run into difficulties developing your paper. If this happens, write out your new thesis statement before you proceed further. Otherwise you run the risk that your thesis statement will point in one direction and the rest of your theme will go off in another.

Brainstorming Your Subject

Guided by your thesis statement, you are now ready to start brainstorming your subject. This involves jotting down everything you might possibly use to develop your theme: facts, ideas, examples, illustrations—in short, the *specific details* that will enable you to communicate your ideas fully and clearly to your reader. (You may wish to review the discussion of specific details in chapter 1, page 6.) Jot down your details as they occur to you; the order in which you list them makes no difference at this stage.

Here again is the proposed specific thesis statement for the tennis paper: *Three keys to playing better tennis singles are conditioning, concentration, and consistency.* Below is a possible list of details you might jot down to develop it.

1. always keep ball in play
2. don't try foolish shots
3. place the ball so opponent runs
4. stay in good condition yourself
5. running
6. jogging
7. skipping rope
8. keeps you on your toes
9. keep your mind only on the game
10. personal distractions
11. courtside distractions
12. temper distractions
13. don't continually drive ball with power
14. two-on-one drill
15. lob ball over their heads
16. return a down-the-line passing shot
17. don't try spectacular overhead
18. chance for opponent to make mistake
19. game of percentages
20. most games are lost, not won

Notice that these items are not necessarily expressed in complete sentences. Some of them might not even make sense to anyone but you, the writer. There's nothing wrong with this. The list is for your own benefit; if you understand its meaning, that's all that's necessary.

Look closely and you will see how some thoughts have led to others during the brainstorming. For example, item number one, consistently keeping the ball in play, leads naturally to the next item, avoiding foolish shots. Item three, placing the ball so the opponent runs, leads to item four, staying in good condition yourself, which in turn leads to items five, six, and seven—and so forth.

As you organize and write your theme, some of the items in your list will probably be omitted, some combined, and some modified. Chances are that you will think of others to add as well. For now, though, you have a good start on the supporting material.

One final note is in order. If you have trouble preparing your brainstorming list, perhaps your topic isn't as interesting or as promising as you originally thought. Sometimes all you need is to take a break and then try again. But if you continue to have trouble, don't hesitate to modify or even completely change your thesis statement and start a new list of details to support this statement. Now—not later—is the time to redirect your efforts.

Organizing Your Information

Once you have listed your details and ideas, the next step is to organize them in some meaningful pattern. This pattern will guide your writing, and later it will help your reader to understand your ideas.

If you have ever listened to a disorganized speaker spill out ideas in no particular order, you probably recall that it was hard to keep your attention focused on the speech, let alone make sense of it. The ideas may have been valuable; but, if you couldn't follow them, how would you really know? A garbled listing of ideas serves no one; an orderly presentation is essential for communication.

For large projects—for example, a library research paper or a technical manual—order is achieved by following a formal outlining procedure. In a formal outline, the main divisions are indicated by Roman numerals, and the various subdivisions are indicated (in decreasing order of importance) by capital letters, Arabic numbers, small letters, and so forth. However, a simpler, less formal written plan is usually sufficient to guide you in writing a relatively short theme. The important thing is to draw up a *written* plan; don't try to carry it only in your head. Ideas have a way of becoming hazy or slipping away entirely. The plan provides the pattern for your theme—the way you'll group your ideas and the order in which you'll present them—and putting it in writing insures that you won't overlook any part of it.

When you draw up your plan, first determine the main points you want to make. If you chose the specific form of thesis statement, you already know them. If you chose the general form, however, you will have to decide on your main points now. In any case, write each point at the top of a separate sheet of paper. For the tennis theme, the three points—or headings— would be:

1. conditioning
2. concentration
3. consistency

Under each heading list those items from your brainstorming list that will develop and support the point. When completed, your three sheets should look something like this:

Conditioning

stay in good condition yourself (4)
running (5)
jogging (6)
skipping rope (7)
keeps you on your toes (8)
two-on-one drill (14)
lob ball over their heads (15)
return a down-the-line passing shot (16)

Concentration

keep your mind only on the game (9)
personal distractions (10)
courtside distractions (11)
temper distractions (12)

Consistency

always keep ball in play (1)
don't try foolish shots (2)

place the ball so opponent runs (3)
don't continually drive ball with power (13)
don't try spectacular overhead (17)
chance for opponent to make mistake (18)
game of percentages (19)
most games are lost, not won (20)

At this stage you should consider how you will arrange your three main headings. Which one will come first? Second? Third? An answer might be suggested by recalling some patterns of paragraph development—time sequence, space sequence, and order of climax (see pages 8–11). These patterns will work as well for complete themes as for single paragraphs. In the case of the tennis theme, you could not use space sequence, but you could use either time sequence or order of climax.

Assume you choose order of climax. You might write down the following sequence:

1. conditioning (important)
2. concentration (more important)
3. consistency (most important)

Once you have decided on this sequence, prepare a more detailed plan showing what you hope to discuss in each paragraph of your theme. Such a plan is illustrated below. As you examine it, notice that the plan is not definite. Your outline should always remain flexible and subject to change. For example, at this stage you can't know with certainty whether one or two paragraphs will be needed to develop each of the three main headings. A quick glance at the number of items under each heading suggests two paragraphs for conditioning, one for concentration, and two for consistency, but until you are actually writing you won't know for sure. Here is the plan:

FIRST PARAGRAPH: introduction (this will be discussed in the section entitled "Polishing Your Theme")

SECOND PARAGRAPH: discuss conditioning

THIRD PARAGRAPH: continue to discuss conditioning *or* start to discuss concentration

FOURTH PARAGRAPH: discuss concentration

FIFTH PARAGRAPH: continue to discuss concentration *or* start to discuss consistency

SIXTH PARAGRAPH: discuss consistency

SEVENTH PARAGRAPH: discuss consistency

EIGHTH PARAGRAPH: conclusion (this will also be discussed in "Polishing Your Theme")

Now for a word of encouragement. Strange as it may seem, the greater part of your work is now behind you. Writing might be called a "front-end loaded" process; that is, most of the steps occur before you actually start writing. So don't feel discouraged because you have little to show for much planning. The finished product—a well-organized paper—will amply repay your efforts.

Writing the First Draft

Writing the first draft—your next step—should be relatively easy. After all, you have a familiar topic, a specific thesis, enough information to support the thesis, and a pattern to follow. Sometimes, however, you may have a bit of difficulty actually getting started. When you sit down to write, the words won't come, and all you can do is doodle or stare at the blank page.

Perhaps your delay is caused by trying to write the introduction—your opening paragraph. Students often find that this is one of the hardest parts of a theme to write. They want to get off to a good start but simply can't think of the proper way to begin. If this happens to you, just skip the introduction for the time being. Once you have some of your ideas on paper, an effective opening will come to you more easily.

A good way to begin is to place your thesis statement and written plan in front of you. They will start you thinking. To actually get words on paper, you may find it helpful to rewrite your thesis statement at the top of the page.

Now turn to the first main heading of your plan. For the tennis theme, it is conditioning. After you look over the items under this heading, prepare a suitable topic sentence for what will be your second paragraph. (The first, of course, will be your introduction.) Such a sentence might be: *Since you will be continually running, conditioning is necessary.*

Next, think back again to the different patterns of paragraph development discussed in chapter 1. Would it be best to organize this discussion of conditioning according to the general-to-specific pattern? Time sequence? Order of climax?

Perhaps the best choice will be time sequence. You decide that preliminary conditioning exercises off the court should come first, followed later by specific tennis exercises on the court. In fact, you now decide that your explanation is likely to call for two paragraphs, one for off-court exercises and one for on-court exercises. That's all right; as we said, the plan is supposed to be flexible.

At this point you are ready to develop the paragraphs with the specific details listed in your plan under conditioning. Write on every other line and leave wide margins so that you will have room to add things later when you polish the draft. As you write, expand the sentence fragments from your plan into complete sentences. *Don't*, however, spend a lot of time trying to write smooth sentences. *Don't* pause to polish each sentence after you write it. These delays could cause you to lose your train of thought, and you might end up doodling or staring again. If your first draft contains fragments, loosely worded sentences, or other errors, you can correct them later. The object right now is to get your ideas and supporting details on paper in the right sequence.

Sometimes a specific point can be adequately explained in a single sentence; at other times two or more sentences will be needed. Perhaps other related details, facts, or examples that are not on your list will occur to you. By all means, include them. If they later prove unnecessary, you can simply cross them out.

When your first draft of these two paragraphs on conditioning has been completed, it might look something like this. (At this point the sentences have not been polished.)

Since you will be continually running, conditioning is necessary. This must start before one gets to center court. A lot of running in place or jogging 5 miles a day will help you build up your endurance for a 3 or 5 set match. Remember, there's no one out there to help you and there will be very little rest time. Jumping rope is also excellent. It teaches you to stay on your toes and not be flatfooted.

That's not the whole story on conditioning. Later, when you're ready to take to the court, some tennis drills will help you. These include the two-on-one drill and shadow drill. All these movements help prepare you for the actual conditions of a game. If you practice them now they'll come naturally during a game.

Now that you have finished the first draft of the conditioning paragraphs, write the concentration and consistency paragraphs in the same manner. When you have completed these and start to write the conclusion, you may experience the same difficulty you had with the introduction. If you do, skip the conclusion, too, until later.

At this point you are finished (except, possibly, for your introduction and conclusion) with your first draft. That's enough work for now. Put the draft aside and take a break. This break is not merely a rest; it is an important part of the writing process.

Polishing Your Theme

Your last major step—polishing your theme—calls for a careful inspection of your first draft. This inspection involves examining what you have written word by word, sentence by sentence, paragraph by paragraph, and making whatever improvements are needed.

To do an effective job, you should wait at least a half day before you start. Unless you have put your writing aside for a while, you will not see it with a fresh eye and will overlook errors you would otherwise notice; that is, you will read what you *think* you have written rather than what you *actually have* written. An excellent way to catch many problems you might overlook is to read your theme out loud. You will be much more likely to notice errors such as word omissions, excessive repetition, clumsy sentences, and sentence fragments if you hear what you have written.

Polishing involves three main tasks: making your language clear, editing your paragraphs, and correcting any misuse of English. Don't try to do all these things at once. Instead, go through your draft carefully several times, watching for a different set of problems each time. In addition, if you haven't written your introduction and conclusion or come up with a title, you will want to fill these gaps now. Each of these tasks is discussed below.

MAKING YOUR LANGUAGE CLEAR

Clarity is the ultimate goal in all writing, and you should examine all your words and sentences to make sure that your reader's job will be as easy as possible. As you check for clarity, consider these questions:

1. Are my sentences written in clear, simple language?
2. Am I sure of the meaning of the words I use?
3. Have I carelessly left out any words?
4. Have I become "windy," cluttering the theme with excess words?
5. Have I used punctuation appropriately to prevent confusion or misreading?
6. Have I explained the meaning of terms that my reader might not understand? (For example, to a card player "deuce" means two, but to a tennis player it means a tie at 40–40.)

One of the most effective ways of achieving clarity is to use vivid, precise words to express your ideas. After all, words are your primary means of communicating with your reader. Examine the two paragraphs below. Both describe the early morning actions of a student's roommate; the difference is the writer's choice of words.

> Coffee cup in hand, she *moves* toward the bathroom. The coffee is spilled *noisily* on the tile floor as she *reaches* for the light switch and *turns* it on. After *looking* briefly at the face in the mirror, she *walks* toward the bathtub.

> Coffee cup in hand, she *stumbles* toward the bathroom. The coffee she spills on the tile floor makes *a slapping sound* as she *gropes* for the light switch and *flips* it on. After *squinting* briefly at the face in the mirror, she *shuffles* toward the bathtub.
>
> *Jeanne Thorpe*

The italicized words in the first paragraph are general and imprecise, while those in the second are vivid and specific. The second version allows the reader to picture exactly the actions being described; the first creates no such picture because the words are indefinite.

Do not confuse precise, concrete words with "fifty-cent words"—those that are complex and pretentious. (Most likely there are no words in the second paragraph above that are not in your vocabulary.) Words should promote, not block, communication.

EDITING YOUR PARAGRAPHS

After you have checked for clarity, turn to editing your paragraphs. To edit, simply apply what you learned in chapter 1. Examine the paragraphs one by one, asking yourself these basic questions about each paragraph and correcting any shortcomings you find.

1. Does it have one, and only one, central idea?
2. Does it have a topic sentence (stated or implied)?
3. Does this topic sentence help to develop the thesis statement?
4. Does each sentence within the paragraph help to develop the topic sentence?
5. Does the paragraph contain an adequate supply of specific details?
6. Does the paragraph follow an appropriate pattern?
7. Are the sentences within the paragraph connected by appropriate linking devices?

Linking devices are useful for connecting the paragraphs of the theme, as well as the sentences within the paragraphs. These devices serve as insurance, helping to guarantee that your reader will be able to follow the development of your ideas from start to finish. Be sure to add them wherever they are needed.

Examine the following three paragraphs (which were the first three paragraphs of this chapter) and notice how the second paragraph is linked to the first, and the third paragraph to the second, by the repetition of key words, phrases, or ideas (printed here in italics).

In the course for which you are using this book, your instructor will probably ask you to write a number of themes (also known as essays, compositions, or sometimes merely "papers"). *Writing themes* is good training for many kinds of writing you will have to do in college and on the job. Nevertheless, the announcement that a theme will be due is one that many students *dread*.

Much of *this anxiety* about *writing themes* stems from a mistaken idea about the writing process—the idea that good themes are dashed off in a burst of inspiration by "born writers." Students themselves often help promote this notion by claiming that their topnotch papers were cranked out in an hour or so of spare time. Such claims may be true now and then—and natural ability and even "inspiration" may help. But the fact is that most successful themes are simply the result of following *a systematic, orderly series of steps*. When you see a *well-written paper*, you see only the final product; what you don't see is the *careful step-by-step process* the writer used to develop that product.

This does not mean that there is *one particular plan, one fixed order of steps*, that automatically produces a *well-written paper*. Some experienced writers follow one plan, some another, often combining certain steps as they proceed. Moreover, specialized types of writing, such as those you'll be dealing with later in this book, require special procedures. However, it is possible to lay out a *basic series of steps* that will serve you well, not only for themes but for most other writing you will do. Once you know these steps, you too may wish to combine some of them as you write. For now, however, your best guarantee of a successful paper is to take the following steps one by one.

CORRECTING MISUSE OF ENGLISH

Finally, check your writing for correctness. Since correctness defies brief explanation, the errors commonly found in student themes are discussed in a separate section at the end of this book. These writing errors include, among others, misuse of the apostrophe, faulty pronoun reference, dangling modifiers, misplaced modifiers, nonparallelism, faulty comparisons, sentence fragments, comma splices, and run-on sentences.

Spelling deserves special mention, since carelessness in spelling is likely to make your reader think you are careless in your thinking, too. A good way to check for spelling errors is to examine your theme backward, carefully, from the last word to the first. You can then concentrate only on the spelling of individual words, and content will not interfere.

THE INTRODUCTION

If you have delayed writing your introduction, this is the time to write it. It need not be very long; for a five-hundred-word theme, an introductory paragraph of three or four sentences should be enough. Your thesis statement may be placed anywhere in the paragraph, but often it is especially effective at the end. Positioned there, it not only indicates your reason for writing but also serves as a clear link to the second paragraph.

Writers frequently use the opening sentences of the introduction to attract the reader's attention. This can be done in several ways. You may, for example, make an arresting statement, mention a personal experience, or present specific details related to the topic of the theme. The following openings from student themes illustrate these approaches.

A picnic with either half-raw or burned black chickens is both unappetizing and wasteful. However, if you can follow written directions, you can serve your guests delicious chicken halves, grilled to a golden brown perfection. (*arresting statement*)

Joe Fowler

Having worked in hospitals as a nurse for several years, I have known nurses in many different specialties who are dedicated and well qualified. (*personal experience*)

Peg Feltman

Analysis of furnace flue gas for carbon dioxide (CO_2) is one of several ways of testing a heating unit to be sure it is operating at peak efficiency. When a furnace is operating normally, the CO_2 content of the flue gas will be 8–10 percent. A lower reading may denote an air leak in the furnace, the wrong type of fuel oil, a defective nozzle, an air shutter that is open too far, a flame with the wrong shape, or any of several other undesirable conditions. (*specific details*)

Charles Finnie

It is not always necessary, however, to use an attention-getting device in your introductory paragraph. Sometimes, particularly in technical papers, merely stating your purpose will be enough. The decision depends on who your reader will be, how much interest the reader already has in the subject, and how much the reader knows about the subject and about your qualifications to write on it.

THE CONCLUSION

Most themes will require a conclusion. Like the introduction, it can be relatively short—two or three sentences in most cases. An adequate conclusion summarizes or supports the main idea your theme has developed; that is, it reinforces the significance of the discussion that has come before. Since your conclusion is your final chance to communicate with your reader, you should try to present it as effectively as possible.

An effective conclusion can be achieved in several ways. You may, for example, briefly summarize your discussion, make a prediction based on your discussion, or use some emphatic ending that will stick in the reader's mind. The following excerpts from student themes illustrate these techniques.

> Grilling chickens is quite simple if you use quality meat, select a high-grade cooking oil, and baste and turn the meat regularly. (*brief summary*)
>
> *Joe Fowler*

> The doctor, then, is skilled in human anatomy, and the auto mechanic is skilled in automobile anatomy. Since we are undergoing a gradual shift to a service-oriented economy, perhaps the day isn't too far off when the auto mechanic will get the recognition and respect he deserves. (*prediction*)
>
> *Eric McArthur*

> The elimination of trapping would subject fur-bearing animals to fierce competition for their dwindling habitat, and starvation would be widespread. Do we humans want this? (*emphatic ending*)
>
> *William Ewald*

Perhaps the most common type of ineffective conclusion is the one that is not related to the paper's main idea. A conclusion that veers off in a completely new direction or introduces an entirely new topic can be worse than no conclusion at all. Imagine the effect, for example, if the writer of a carefully developed theme on playing better tennis were to end by saying, "Some of these suggestions can also help improve your handball game." Suddenly the reader is being asked to consider an entirely new topic, which is then left totally undeveloped.

Another type of ineffective conclusion might be called the "midnight special." The hour is late, and the writer, trying to finish quickly, jots down the first couple of sentences that come to mind. For example, the tennis theme writer might abruptly conclude by saying, "All in all, these things will improve your game." This conclusion is faulty because it states weakly what has already been stated more forcefully throughout the theme. It fails, that is, to reinforce the significance of the theme, and so it leaves the reader without any strong impression. In fact, it suggests that the writer lost interest in the subject.

THE TITLE

Unless a title pops into your head as you are writing, it is usually best to finish your theme before choosing one. A good title is both specific and accurate. A specific title suggests the theme's exact focus rather than its general topic. For example, "The Three C's of Better Tennis Singles" is more effective than simply "Tennis." You aren't writing about the sport in general, but about ways of playing better singles. An accurate title is one that is not misleading. Your reader must see the connection between what the title promises and what the theme delivers. For example, "Tennis Singles: Moving to the Top" would be inaccurate; it suggests that you will explain how to become a champion (perhaps a professional) when in fact this aspect of the topic is never discussed.

The title of a nontechnical paper can be either common or catchy. A common title simply tells the reader what to expect, while a catchy one attempts to arouse the reader's curiosity. Here are some examples of possible titles for student themes.

COMMON: "Handling Your Hangover"
CATCHY: "The Mourning After"

COMMON: "McDonald's and Elias Brothers: How They Differ"
CATCHY: "Big Mac vs. Big Boy"

COMMON: "How to Grill Hamburgers"
CATCHY: "From Butcher to Bun"

Technical papers almost always have common titles.

The Finished Product

If you followed the steps discussed in this chapter, your tennis theme would look something like the following student theme. As you read the theme, pay careful attention to the marginal notes, which point out some of the key writing elements. (The thesis statement, topic sentences, and some of the linking devices are printed in italics.)

Title: specific, accurate, catchy

The Three C's of Better Tennis Singles

Introduction: arresting statement

In the last few years tennis has enjoyed a rise in popularity unequaled by any other sport. *As a result,* many players are trying to improve their game. *Three keys to playing better tennis singles are conditioning, concentration, and consistency.*

Linking device

Thesis statement

Topic sentence, with links to preceding paragraph

Since a singles match requires endurance, proper conditioning is necessary. This conditioning should begin before you arrive at the court. Jogging three to five miles a day and running in place are both excellent exercises for increasing your stamina. *They* help insure that, in a deciding third set, you will not lose the match because of exhaustion. Jumping rope, *another good exercise,* conditions you to stay on your toes rather than play flat-footed. You'll have a much better chance of reaching and returning your opponent's shots if you start toward them from your toes.

Specific details: jogging, running in place, jumping rope

Linking device

Linking device

Topic sentence, with links to preceding paragraph

When you arrive at the court, a good conditioning exercise is the two-on-one drill. Have two of your friends stand at the net and

Specific details	hit the ball to you in the opposite backcourt.
Linking device	Ideally *they* should place the shots just out of your reach so you are continually running,
Specific details: lob, drive, etc.	chasing the ball. On your return shots, alternately try to lob the ball over their heads, drive it between them down the middle of the court, attempt a down-the-line passing shot, or drill the ball low and hard directly
Linking device	at the net players. With *this continual running* and *these four returns*, you will be preparing for the actual conditions of your next match.
Topic sentence, with links to preceding paragraphs	*As you play this match, you should work on developing the ability to concentrate—the second key to improving your game.* Concen-
Term defined	tration involves focusing your attention only on the game at hand and not allowing anything else to distract you. Courtside and personal distractions are the two most common among tennis players. Courtside distractions include watching players in the next court, talking to a friend outside the court, and joking with your opponent between points. Personal distractions include such things as worrying about a test, mulling over a personal problem, and thinking about the refreshments
Linking device	after the game. *All of these distractions* result in poorly hit balls and lost points. All good tennis players are able to discipline themselves to concentrate only on the game.
Topic sentence, with links to preceding paragraphs	*Probably the most important key to improving your game is consistency.* Steady placement of your shots is much more effective than occasional brilliance. Many players
Specific details: spectacular shots, power strokes, blast, overpower, etc.	make the mistake of trying spectacular shots and using power strokes rather than playing a steady, consistent game. For example, don't try to blast a spectacular pro-style overhead

or continually overpower your opponent with hard, driving shots. These attempts will lose more points for you than they will win.

Topic sentence

Linking device (links to preceding paragraph)

Specific details

Tennis is a game of percentages. The *consistent* player keeps the ball *steadily* in play so the opponent is more apt to make a mistake. Hitting the ball away from your opponent with average speed is percentage tennis; drilling the ball with power is not. All experienced players realize that very often matches are not won, but lost.

Conclusion (prediction)

If you follow these suggestions, don't expect to successfully challenge Jimmy Connors or Chris Evert. Do expect, however, to start beating some of the players who used to beat you.

Ferris Finnerty

The marginal notes above point out only some of the elements that contribute to the effectiveness of this student theme; any attempt to indicate all of them would have made the notes confusing. The most important point to be made about this theme could not be noted in the margin, and it is the one with which this chapter opened: the theme is successful because the writer followed an orderly series of steps in arriving at an appropriate topic, establishing a specific focus, making a written plan, and writing and polishing the draft.

3

Comparison

Hardly a day goes by when you don't use comparison in some way. You may evaluate two different job offers, for example, or consider two health insurance plans, or explain two methods of wallpapering a room. Whenever you examine two items and note their similarities and differences, you are comparing.

Comparison is also an effective method of presenting written material, one you will use often in the writing you do both for your classes and on the job. Your instructor may ask you to discuss, in an examination or report, the basic similarities or differences between two machines or principles—for example, the conventional gasoline engine and the Wankel engine or preventive dental care and restorative dental care. Your employer may ask you to evaluate two different proposals for improving working conditions or to report on the performance characteristics of two X-ray machines, lathes, typewriters, or other pieces of equipment. These assignments, which involve explaining or evaluating two different items, call for papers of comparison.

Comparisons do not have to be limited to only two items: the conventional gasoline engine can be compared to both the Wankel engine and the diesel engine. You will have less difficulty with comparisons, however, if you first master the techniques of comparing only two items. After all, it is always easier to focus your attention on two things than it is to deal with three or more.

Writing a paper of comparison involves five basic steps:

1. choosing your topic
2. establishing your focus
3. developing your thesis statement
4. selecting your details
5. selecting your method of organization

Each of these steps is discussed below.

Choosing Your Topic

If you are asked to choose the items to be compared, make sure that there is some basis for meaningful comparison between the items you choose. The two items must have something in common. For example, you could compare two golfers on their driving ability off the tee, putting ability, and sand play, or two cars on their appearance, gas mileage, and manufacturer's warranty. But you could not very well compare a golfer with a car, for no basis for meaningful comparison is evident.

Be sure, too, that the items you select will provide an interesting comparison. This is rarely a problem for comparisons you write on the job, for the subject of your comparison is usually determined by a particular work situation, and you can assume that your reader—your employer, a coworker, or perhaps a customer or client—will be interested. But for papers you write in class or for a general audience, you should try to choose items that will enable you to give your audience new information or, if the items are familiar to the audience, give the audience a fresh way of thinking about them.

For example, it would be very hard to write an interesting paper comparing a pencil and a ball-point pen. There certainly is a basis for comparison—both are used for writing—and obviously there are similarities and differences that could be described at some length. The problem is that the similarities and differences *are* obvious; they would already be thoroughly familiar to anyone who might be likely to read such a comparison. It would be difficult to give the reader new information or a fresh way of thinking about the items.

On the other hand, it certainly is possible to write interestingly about commonplace objects, as long as the reader can learn something. For instance, it would be possible to write an interesting and useful comparison of two different types or brands of ball-point pen. Type A is a better buy than the more widely advertised Type B because, although Type A costs twice as much, it lasts three times as long. What's more, Type A can be refilled when it runs out, but Type B must be thrown away. Type A writes more sharply and is less likely to skip because it has a magnesium-alloy rather than a stainless-steel ball. Type B is inclined to leak; Type A does not—and so forth.

A comparison such as this meets all the requirements for choosing a topic. The items have enough in common to provide a basis for comparison, yet they are not so similar that the discussion of one merely echoes the discussion of the other. The similarities and differences are not too obvious to be interesting; on the contrary, they provide opportunities for a comparison that enables the reader to learn something or see the items in a new way.

Establishing Your Focus

When you have two comparable items in mind, you are ready to start thinking about the particular points of comparison you will discuss—in other words, your focus. The focus you choose is determined by your *reason for writing* (purpose) and the desired *length* of your paper. The importance of these two considerations can be illustrated by the following example. Suppose you were in charge of the record and tape department of a local department store, with two excellent salespeople working for you. The manager of your store has told you of plans to open a branch store in a suburban shopping center and asked you to submit a brief written report—"just a page or two"—comparing the qualifications of your two salespeople for the job of managing the record department in the new branch store.

In this example, the items to be compared have already been chosen for you: the two salespeople. Your reason for writing is also clear: to help the store manager decide which of the two salespeople should be offered the new position. Moreover, the manager has asked that the report be *brief*, and even if no restriction on length had been stated you would have understood that the manager was very busy and not the sort of person to appreciate a report that was any longer than necessary.

Now, in order to see plainly how your reason for writing determines the proper focus for your comparison, consider how many possible points of comparison between the two salespeople you could think of if you did *not* have a clearly established reason for writing. Here is just a partial list:

1. clothes
2. religion
3. hobbies
4. sense of humor
5. eye color
6. mathematical ability
7. hair style
8. sales skills
9. use of tobacco
10. bowling ability
11. musical knowledge
12. social activities
13. attendance habits
14. interest in current affairs
15. cooperativeness
16. food preferences
17. smile
18. political views
19. knowledge of ordering and accounting procedures
20. ability to deal with customers

Obviously, many of the characteristics listed above have nothing at all to do with either person's suitability to manage a record department. When you think about your reason for writing, you can strike many items off the list—for instance, eye color, religion, and bowling ability. As you do this, you are establishing your focus.

But even after you have narrowed the list down to the characteristics that are somehow related to your reason for writing, you may have more points on the list than you can develop adequately in a *brief* report of "just a page or two." If you tried to cover all of them, you would have space for no more than one or two sentences about each. Questions would be raised but not answered, and your reader would probably fail to get a clear impression of the two individuals being compared. Since your report must be brief, you would do much better to limit the focus of your comparison to just the few points that are most essential and then develop each of these points with specific details in a paragraph or more.

Here again your reason for writing can help you: since your purpose is to help your reader choose between the two salespeople, it will be most useful to focus mainly on differences rather than similarities. For instance, if *both* people are cooperative and have satisfactory attendance habits, you can eliminate these points. However, you may feel that sales skills are so important to the new job that, even though both salespeople are highly skilled, you should include that one important similarity in your comparison. The most significant differences between the two people as candidates to manage the record department, you decide, are in their musical knowledge and their knowledge of ordering and accounting procedures. Now you have established the focus for your comparison.

Notice an important feature of the three points of comparison just mentioned—sales skills, musical knowledge, and knowledge of ordering and accounting procedures. These are separate points; that is, they do not overlap. If, on the other hand, you had chosen sales skills and ability to deal with customers, essentially you would have been discussing one point of comparison instead of two, since ability to deal with customers is a sales skill. Whenever you choose points of comparison, make sure that they do not overlap.

Developing Your Thesis Statement

Once you know your purpose and have established your focus, you are ready to formulate your thesis statement. This statement will serve as a checkpoint, helping you maintain your focus as you write your paper. If you were comparing the two salespeople mentioned above, your thesis statement might be: *Although Pat and Lee are both excellent salespeople, I believe Pat would be the better choice for manager because of her wider knowledge of music and her greater knowledge of ordering and accounting procedures.* This statement does three things:

1. names the two items under discussion
2. states the specific points that will be discussed
3. shows whether the paper will point out similarities, differences, or both

The thesis statement for every comparison paper you write, regardless of the topic, should do these same three things.

Selecting Your Details

Merely stating that two items are similar or different is not enough; you must show your reader *how* they are similar or different. This is done with well-chosen specific details and examples.

Specific details give your reader a clear picture of what you are trying to convey. If you merely say that both Pat and Lee are excellent salespeople, you have no way of knowing that your reader will understand the statement in the same way you meant it. On the other hand, if you develop the statement in a paragraph with specific details—how both Pat and Lee are cheerful even with difficult customers, know what is in stock and where to find it, are careful to keep the stock in good order, consistently get extra sales by suggesting additional purchases related to their customers' interests, and so forth—you have given your reader a clear picture. Guesswork is eliminated, and communication succeeds.

Again, it is a good idea to jot down the specific details and examples that will help develop your thesis statement rather than trying to keep them in your head. You may find it useful to use the brainstorming technique described in chapter 2, pages 24–26. For each point of comparison, list all the supporting ideas that come to mind. And because you will be writing about two items, you should make a separate list for each. This procedure may seem cumbersome now, but later you'll be glad you followed it. With separate lists for each item, giving details for each point of comparison, you will be able to write your paper easily, no matter which method of organization you choose.

Selecting Your Method of Organization

At this point the only major decision left to make is how to organize your paper. Basically there are two possibilities for a comparison paper: the *block method* and the *alternating method.*

In the block method, the basic organization is provided by the items being compared. In other words, the writer first presents —in one block—*all* of the information about one item and then— in another block—*all* of the information about the other item. Within each block the individual points usually are discussed in the same order. The paper comparing Pat and Lee, organized according to the block method, would follow a pattern such as this:

   I. Introduction
  II. Specific details about Pat
      A. Pat's sales skills
      B. Pat's musical knowledge
      C. Pat's knowledge of ordering and accounting procedures
 III. Specific details about Lee
      A. Lee's sales skills
      B. Lee's musical knowledge
      C. Lee's knowledge of ordering and accounting procedures
  IV. Conclusion

You should use the block method only if your paper is short, that is, if it includes only a few points of comparison. With a short paper, your reader will be able to keep all the points in the first block clearly in mind while reading the second block. This would be difficult for the reader of a lengthy paper to do.

If your paper is long—that is, if it includes numerous points of comparison—it is better to use the alternating method. In the alternating method, the basic organization is provided by the points of comparison rather than by the items being compared. In other words, the writer brings up each point and compares the two items on that particular point before bringing up the next point. Usually, clarity is best achieved if the items being compared are presented in the same order for each point. Organized according to the *alternating method,* a paper comparing Pat and Lee would follow a pattern such as this:

I. Introduction
II. Pat's and Lee's sales skills
   A. Pat's sales skills
   B. Lee's sales skills
III. Pat's and Lee's musical knowledge
   A. Pat's musical knowledge
   B. Lee's musical knowledge
IV. Pat's and Lee's knowledge of ordering and accounting
   procedures
   A. Pat's knowledge of ordering and accounting procedures
   B. Lee's knowledge of ordering and accounting procedures
V. Conclusion

Generally, the alternating method is easier for your reader to understand. Because a specific comparison is completed at each point, the reader never has to pause in the middle of the paper and look back in order to grasp a similarity or difference.

Once you've decided upon your method of organization, you are ready to write your first draft. The first draft of a comparison paper is written and polished like any other theme. Simply follow the procedure described in chapter 2.

STUDENT EXAMPLES

Two Men at the Controls—One Airborne, One Grounded

(1) If you were to drive by the Kent County airport viewing area on almost any winter day, you would probably see several people watching the various aircraft departing and landing. But have you ever seen a crowd observing the operation of a modern snowplow? This is a snowplow that is equipped with both front and back plows, four-wheel drive, and two-way radio. Most people recognize the coordination and skill required of a pilot, but few realize that the snowplow operator has similar demands made upon his physical and mental powers.

(2) The pilot uses his hands and feet constantly. His hands are used to turn and adjust all the radio controls and flight instruments, to alter the angle of bank, and to change the aircraft's

longitudinal axis with reference to the horizon. While he is airborne, the pilot's feet move in coordination with his hands to bank and turn the plane; on the ground, his feet actually steer the taxiing aircraft.

(3) Hand and foot movements are also critical for the snowplow operator. He uses his hands not only to steer but at the same time to raise, lower, and change the angle of the front plow. At certain points, the back plow must also be raised and lowered. Between the plow control movements, the operator's hands are busy shifting his transmission, using turn signals, flipping switches for radios and lights, and sometimes clearing fogged windshields. Meanwhile, his feet move so fast that they might appear blurry to a passenger. They are continually moving from the brakes to the clutch to the accelerator.

(4) Accompanying the high level of physical skill required of the airplane pilot and the snowplow operator is a considerable amount of mental strain. The pilot's duties include a great deal of preflight planning, during which he must consider the weather, the weight and balance of the plane, and the flight path. In the air, he must constantly sort out the picture presented by his radio and instruments and think continually of the safest way to handle any problems that arise.

(5) The snowplow operator usually begins work in the early hours of the morning. He must allow for the limitations of the equipment while he works, considering, for example, extremely cold weather and brittle parts, both of which may impair efficiency. The operator must also work under time pressure, calculating every movement so that the work is accomplished in the least amount of time. He knows that in a few short hours traffic will increase and his efficiency will then decrease.

(6) At the end of a flight and after the route has been plowed, both individuals will be physically and mentally drained, but at the same time they will feel a sense of satisfaction from executing the duties of their occupations.

Jim Linscott

Discussion Questions

1. Identify the thesis statement and discuss its effectiveness.
2. Discuss the function of specific details in paragraphs 2 and 3.

3. Is this paper organized by the block method or the alternating method?
4. What is accomplished by the sentence in paragraph 1 that begins, "This is a snowplow that is equipped . . ."?
5. Do you think the student has chosen an appropriate title? Why or why not?

The "People Doctor" and the "Car Doctor"

(1) In our society a doctor is considered a professional person and an auto mechanic is considered a service person. Most people have much more respect for a doctor than they do for an auto mechanic. But how often do people recognize some of the similarities of these two occupations? If you consider the following resemblances, perhaps you will develop a bit more respect for your neighborhood mechanic.

(2) The first similarity is procedural. A patient comes to the doctor because something is not functioning properly in his body. The first thing the doctor does is ask the patient what is wrong. Second, the doctor investigates the cause of the symptoms. This can be done by physical or X-ray inspection or by various laboratory tests. Finally, the doctor diagnoses the patient's ailment.

(3) A mechanic follows basically the same procedure as the doctor. A customer comes to the mechanic because something is not functioning properly in his car. The mechanic first listens to the customer's description of the symptoms. Then he investigates the causes by a visual, an auditory, or an electronic inspection. After the inspection, he diagnoses the car's problem.

(4) The second similarity is that both the doctor and the mechanic deal with extremely complex systems. For example, in checking the human heart the doctor is confronted with intricate passages and valves which control the distribution and pressure of blood throughout the body. Among these are the pulmonary valve, aortic valve, and ventricular valve.

(5) Now consider the mechanic who repairs automatic transmissions. The main operational unit in the transmission, the valve body, also has intricate passages and valves, which control the distribution and pressure of oil throughout the transmission. Some of these valves are the manual valve, pressure regulator

valve, reverse and modulator boost valve, and intermediate boost valve.

(6) A third important point of similarity is the manual dexterity required of both the doctor and the mechanic. When checking for a hernia, for example, the doctor palpates the lower abdominal wall. This involves gently feeling the area. Failure to exercise sufficient gentleness could cause the patient severe pain and perhaps aggravate an already serious condition.

(7) Similarly, the mechanic replacing a dashboard light must exercise precise hand control. The dash conceals a jungle of electrical wiring. Unless skilled hands make the replacement, the car's entire electrical system could be shorted out. Manual dexterity is also needed when the mechanic installs metering rods in the carburetor for regulation of gas flow. This must be done by precision touch, since the rods are inside the carburetor.

(8) The doctor, then, is skilled in human anatomy and the auto mechanic is skilled in automobile anatomy. Since we are undergoing a gradual shift to a service-oriented economy, perhaps the day isn't too far off when the auto mechanic will get the recognition and respect he deserves.

Eric McArthur

Discussion Questions

1. In this theme the student discusses three points of similarity. What are they? Do they overlap or are they separate?
2. What type of organization is used here—the block method or the alternating method?
3. Notice the student's use of concrete details to illustrate the points of similarity. The paragraphs on the auto mechanic are generally a bit longer and include more details than those on the doctor. Why?
4. Discuss the importance of this sentence in paragraph 6: "This involves gently feeling the area."

Different Shifts, Different Actions

(1) The nursing team in a small hospital is directly concerned with meeting the routine and special daily needs of the patients. The team leader is usually a registered professional nurse, and members of the team may include registered and

practical nurses, nurse's aides, and attendants. Although all nurses care for patients, the duties and working conditions of the nursing teams on the morning shift and the afternoon shift are quite different.

(2) The morning shift begins at 7:00 A.M., when patients are awakened and prepared for any laboratory tests, X-rays, or medications the doctors have ordered. Temperatures, pulses, and respirations are taken, and such things as enemas or preoperative injections are given. Breakfast is prepared and served, and then medications—for example, pain pills—are given.

(3) By this time the doctors have arrived to see each of their patients. The nursing station is a hubbub of activity. Doctors are writing new orders, and their patients' charts are scattered all over the desk. Laboratory and X-ray technicians are explaining results of tests. The pharmacist brings medications and inquires about any new orders for drugs. Inhalation and physical therapists are busy checking charts for their new orders. The dietician asks why a certain patient is not eating the foods he should. Telephones ring and patients' signal lights flash continually. The members of the nursing team, all with their own duties, are trying desperately to keep up with everything that is going on, which gives them little time to spend with their patients. This pace continues through most of the morning shift.

(4) The afternoon team members usually are able to devote more attention to the personal needs of their patients. Preparing for supper, for example, usually consists of clearing tables of miscellaneous items such as flowers or cards, washing faces and hands for those unable to do so, and positioning patients for eating comfort. After supper, visitors arrive, and when they leave, the team members have time to spend with their patients, teaching them about their conditions and how to care for them- selves when they are discharged. For example, diabetic patients are shown how to administer insulin injections, what foods to eat and how to prepare them, and how to care for their skin.

(5) Patients are then prepared for the night—beds are straightened or changed, and back rubs and last medications are given. At 10:00 P.M. most patients are asleep. The nursing station is calm, with only two or three nurses doing their charting. This involves recording how their patients have tolerated treatment

and medication. Everything is in its place and, except for an occasional signal light from a patient, everything is quiet.

(6) Although both shifts have the same responsibilities—the care and welfare of their patients—afternoon team members usually work in a much more relaxed atmosphere. Because there are fewer people around, the pace is slower and the treatment is more personalized.

Clare Mutter

Discussion Questions

1. The thesis statement is the last sentence in paragraph 1. Does it meet the three requirements for a thesis statement of a comparison paper? Explain your answer.
2. Identify and discuss the specific details that you think are most effective in giving the reader a clear picture of the two shifts.
3. Which method of organization does the student use—the block method or the alternating method?
4. If you were to compare two different work shifts of a job you are familiar with, which job would you choose? What individual points would you select for comparison?

Tie-Dyeing and Batik

(1) Ours is an age of self-expression, with more and more people attempting to develop their creativity through a variety of art forms. Tie-dyeing and batik represent two popular means of personal expression. The processes have similar origins and are based on a common principle, but they utilize different materials and yield different results.

(2) Batik and tie-dyeing are ancient arts that date back many centuries before Christ. Tie-dyeing probably originated in Asia, although it was used in one form or another by almost all ancient civilizations. Batik likewise originated in Asia and until recently was practiced only in that area.

(3) Both techniques are forms of resist dyeing, which involves doing something to a fabric to prevent dye from penetrating certain areas. In tie-dyeing, string, twine, or rubber bands are bound tightly around portions of a cloth, thus prevent-

ing the dye from soaking into the compressed areas. In batik, resistance is obtained by painting areas of the cloth with wax, which soaks into the fibers and keeps the dye out. In both cases, the design on the finished product is produced by the patterns of the undyed areas.

(4) Of the two techniques, tie-dyeing is much easier and much more widely practiced. It is especially popular among young people, who use it to decorate T-shirts, blue jeans, curtains, pillow cases, and the like. The procedure requires only a few materials: dye, a container to hold it, string or some other binder, and, of course, the item being dyed. The person winds the cloth around a finger or stick, then ties a string around the resulting bulge. Variations in pattern can be obtained by tying objects in the cloth, clamping the cloth between pieces of wood, or covering portions with plastic bags. These techniques result in abstract patterns made up of irregular patches of light color on a dark background. Precise pattern control is impossible, since the arrangement of wrinkles under the ties determines the outline which is produced.

(5) Batik, commonly used for framed pictures and wall hangings, is much more difficult and less widely practiced than tie-dyeing. The materials and equipment needed—besides the cloth—are dye, a dye container, a frame, thumb tacks, a brush, wax, a double boiler, a source of heat, paper towels, and an iron. The cloth is first stretched over and tacked onto the frame. Melted wax is applied everywhere that dye is not wanted, and the cloth is then removed from the frame and placed in the dye. Once the dyed cloth is dry, more wax can be applied, and the cloth can be dyed again. This procedure can be repeated as often as is desired. Finally, the cloth is placed between layers of paper towel and heated with the iron so that the wax is melted and soaked up by the paper towel. Although batik involves considerable time and effort, the results amply justify the work. Patterns vary from the completely abstract to precise compositions resembling intricate tapestry.

(6) Combining the two techniques can produce interesting effects. A batik pattern can be superimposed on a tie-dyed background, or a cloth can be waxed before it is tie-dyed. As with any art form, the chief limit is the person's imagination.

student unknown

Discussion Questions

1. In this paper, does the student focus on similarities, differences, or both?
2. Has the student chosen an appropriate topic for a comparison paper? Explain.
3. Are there sufficient details to give you a clear picture of the similarities and differences between tie-dying and batik? Discuss, citing specific examples.
4. Specifically, what is accomplished by paragraph 6?

Suggestions for Writing

Write a comparison paper on one of the following topics. The paper may point out similarities, differences, or both. Use whichever method of organization seems more appropriate.

1. Two types of travel accommodations
2. Two types of music
3. Something natural and something artificial
4. Two auto mechanics (or substitute some other skilled occupation)
5. Single life and married life
6. Television detectives or policemen and real-life detectives or policemen
7. The physical or mental demands of two jobs
8. Two types of parents
9. Two methods of studying
10. Two advertisements
11. Two athletes
12. Two employers
13. Business, residential, or slum districts of two different cities
14. A favorite social spot during the day and during the evening
15. Two acquaintances who have different political views
16. Two types of leadership
17. Two sportscasters or news commentators
18. Two techniques for doing something in your own field
19. Two devices used in your field
20. The working conditions of two jobs

4

Classification

Classification is a useful way to explain a large, complex, or hard-to-grasp topic. In classifying, you divide a topic into separate categories and then discuss the categories one at a time. The explanation is thus simplified, for you deal with the topic not all at once but in small, manageable parts.

You will use classification frequently in your written work, both for your classes and on the job. In the classroom, your instructor may assign a paper classifying carburetion systems, computer languages, drawing pens, furnaces, light-measuring instruments, oscilloscopes, respirators, or spectrographs, to name only a few possibilities. If you are employed by a manufacturing engineering laboratory, you may be asked to test and classify major types of refrigeration feed systems to determine which system best meets the specifications for a particular job. Or as a sanitary engineer, you may classify the different types of water filtration systems to show which is best suited to insure the quality of a particular community's water. Whatever your career may be, you will make countless uses of classification.

Classification is a natural way for the mind to deal with many subjects. It is more difficult to grasp a large or complex topic when it is considered as a whole than it is to grasp that topic when it is grouped into separate categories. This is true not only for the writer but for the reader as well. Think how much more readily your reader could comprehend the broad topic of less-than-full-size cars if you classified these cars as subcompacts, compacts, and intermediates.

Specifically, classification makes the overall subject easier to grasp by allowing the reader to understand two things more clearly:

1. the separate categories
2. the way these categories relate to one another

Thus, a paper which classifies cars as subcompacts, compacts, and intermediates might help the reader better understand:

1. the size, seating capacity, maneuverability, price, or other distinctive features of typical vehicles in each category
2. how these factors vary from category to category

Because classification is one of the most useful ways of presenting a subject, it is important for you to learn what is involved in this method. Essentially, there are five basic steps in writing a classification paper:

1. choosing your topic
2. establishing your focus
3. avoiding overlapping categories
4. developing your thesis statement
5. organizing and writing your paper

These steps are discussed in the sections that follow.

Choosing Your Topic

When you write on the job, you will rarely need to choose a topic; the demands of your occupation will provide your writing assignments. For example, you might need to classify the different services your particular department performs. In the classroom, however, you may often be asked to choose a topic.

Choosing a topic for a classification paper should present no serious problems, for almost any subject that can be divided or grouped into categories is a possible topic. For example, you might classify members of the dental work team into the categories of dentist, dental hygienist, dental assistant, and dental laboratory technician; secretarial positions into the categories of legal, medical, and executive; or drill presses into the categories of upright, radial, gang, and multiple. Your best bet is to choose a topic with which you are familiar, perhaps one related to your career.

Establishing Your Focus

Once you've decided upon a topic, you are ready to select one specific focus. Special care is necessary in selecting the focus of a classification paper because most topics can be classified in a number of ways. To write a successful paper you must center on and develop just one.

For example, consider some of the possible ways to classify customers at a fruit market. One way these customers can be grouped is by age—young people, middle-aged people, and older people. A second way is by the amount they purchase—those who buy one or two items, those who buy several items, and those who buy large quantities. A third way is by the different types of undesirable behavior they exhibit. These examples are not merely random listings of customers. Rather, in each case, customers are grouped into separate categories based on one particular characteristic.

Once you have chosen a basis for classification, you must decide whether your focus will include all categories or only selected categories—those that are most important, given your reason for writing. For example, if your purpose is to give the reader a *comprehensive* view of undesirable fruit market customers, some of the many types you would discuss include those customers who return apples to the orange bin, handle the produce excessively before they buy, continually complain, cheat the market, taste the fruit, and allow their children to run wild. On the other hand, if your reason for writing is to describe those customers that annoy you the most, you might focus on just three types: those who handle the produce excessively before they buy, those who continually complain, and those who cheat the market. Frequently your writing assignments will require you to focus only on selected categories.

Avoiding Overlapping Categories

When you have a specific focus in mind, check to make sure that the categories you have chosen do not overlap. In other words, each category must be a separate grouping that does not extend into the "territory" of another grouping. Think back to the example of less-than-full-size cars at the beginning of this chapter. As we noted, these cars can be classified as:

1. subcompact cars
2. compact cars
3. intermediate cars

This is a *proper* classification because none of the three categories overlaps into the "territory" of the others. Each is a separate grouping.
   Now consider another classification of cars:

1. American small cars
2. European small cars
3. Japanese small cars
4. sports cars

This is an *improper* classification because some cars—the British Triumph, for example—are both European small cars *and* sports cars. Similarly, some Japanese and American small cars are sports cars too. None of the categories is a separate grouping. This classification, therefore, would result in confusion—the very thing classification is supposed to clear up.

Developing Your Thesis Statement

At this point, write down the purpose of your paper. This purpose, or a rephrasing of it, will be your thesis statement, which serves as a checkpoint to help you develop the proper categories as you write.

The thesis statement of a classification paper should tell your reader two things:

1. the topic—what you are classifying
2. the central idea—what you want your reader to grasp

Thus, the thesis statement for the paper classifying undesirable fruit market customers might be: *Undesirable customers at a fruit market fall into three main categories, and when you meet them all in one day you have one big headache.* The reader of this statement knows immediately that the paper is going to classify undesirable customers and point out the problems these customers create.

Organizing and Writing Your Paper

Once you have come this far, organizing your paper will not be difficult. All you have to do is decide on an effective order—which of your categories you will discuss first, which second, and so on. The arrangement you choose depends on your reason for writing, your subject, and the categories you are focusing on.

In a paper classifying undesirable fruit market customers, you might first discuss those who create small problems, then those who create worse problems, and finally those who create the worst problems of all. The number of paragraphs needed to describe each category will depend on how much you have to say.

Thus, the overall plan for a paper organized in the above way might look something like this:

FIRST PARAGRAPH: introduction

SECOND PARAGRAPH: discuss customers who handle produce excessively

THIRD PARAGRAPH: discuss customers who complain about the quality of the produce

FOURTH PARAGRAPH: discuss customers who complain about the service they receive from the employees

FIFTH PARAGRAPH: discuss customers who cheat the market

SIXTH PARAGRAPH: conclusion

Your paper could, of course, contain more than six paragraphs if you wished to discuss any of the categories more thoroughly.

Now develop each category by adding a generous supply of specific details. These details are what will make the distinctions among the various categories clear to your reader and give your reader a clear image of each kind of customer. For example, with details added, one type of undesirable customer might be described as follows:

> "Charlie Cheater" knows all the tricks of cheating. He will add berries onto an already full basket. He will take 6/79¢ oranges and tell you they're the 6/59¢ ones. He will put expensive grapes in the bottom of a sack and add cheaper ones on top. Then he'll tell you that they are all the cheaper variety.
>
> *Clarence DeLong*

By using specific details such as these to explain every category, you will succeed in communicating effectively with your reader.

STUDENT EXAMPLES

Fruit Market Customers

(1) You will find almost as large a variety of customers at a fruit market as you will find fruits and vegetables. The undesirable ones seem to fall into three main categories, and when you meet them all in one day you have one big headache. Perhaps you will recognize these people as I describe them.

(2) "Sammy Squeezer" is the least annoying of these undesirables. He wants to make sure that everything he buys is "just right." He pokes his thumbs into the top of a cantaloupe. If they penetrate very deeply, he won't buy this particular specimen, considering it to be overripe. He squeezes the peaches, plums, nectarines, and any other fruit that he can get his hands on. After ten of these people squeeze one piece of fruit, it will surely be soft, even if it wasn't originally. Moving on to the corn, Sammy carefully peels back the husk to examine the kernels inside. If they don't suit him, he doesn't bother to fold the husk

back to protect the kernels; he simply tosses the ear back into the basket. The problems he creates for the employees are primarily physical—removing the damaged items after he leaves.

(3) A more annoying customer is "Betty Bitcher." She is never satisfied with the quality of the produce: the bananas are too green, the lettuce has brown spots, the berries are too ripe, and the potatoes have green spots. Sometimes you wonder if Betty would have been satisfied with the fruit grown in the Garden of Eden.

(4) The produce has no monopoly on her complaints, however. Betty also finds fault with the service she receives from the employees. Talking to other customers or directly to the clerks, she can be heard saying such things as "Why is this the only place I ever have to wait in line? They must have trouble getting good help here." Even as she leaves the market, which is none too soon, she must make one last complaint: "You mean I have to carry my own potatoes to the car?" The problems she creates for the employees are primarily mental—she can make your nerves quite active.

(5) Perhaps the most annoying customer of all is "Charlie Cheater." You have to keep your eye on him constantly because he knows all the tricks of cheating. He will add berries onto an already full basket. He will take 6/79¢ oranges and tell you they're the 6/59¢ ones. He will put expensive grapes in the bottom of a sack and add cheaper ones on top. Then he'll tell you that they are all the cheaper variety. Likewise, he will put expensive nectarines in a sack, place a few cheaper peaches on top, and try to pass them all off as peaches. If he is caught, he usually says, "I don't know how that happened. My little girl (or boy) must have put them in there." The child usually looks dumbfounded.

(6) The problem Charlie creates for the market is twofold: financial and legal. If you don't catch him, your profits suffer. If you do catch him, you almost have to prosecute, usually for amounts of only a dollar or two, or you'll have every Charlie in town at your door.

(7) Did you recognize any of these customers? If you didn't and would like to see some of them in action, stop in at Steve's Fruit Market. That's where I work, and that's where I meet them.

Clarence DeLong

Discussion Questions

1. What is the student's reason for writing? Point out specific evidence to support your answer.
2. What pattern has the writer selected to organize his paper?
3. Do any of the three categories the writer has chosen overlap?
4. If you were to classify customers at some business establishment, how would you categorize them?

The Technical Drafting Curriculum—What to Expect

(1) Technical drafting involves many areas of study. Students who enter this field will find that three of the most important areas they will study are drafting techniques, mathematics, and machine shop processes. Unless students master these three areas, they cannot hope to succeed in their later work.

(2) When they study drafting techniques, students first learn basic principles such as lettering, geometric construction, orthographic projection, and dimensioning. They then learn to apply product drafting to surface finish controls, geometric and positional tolerances, sections of parts, symbols used in drawing, and assembly and subassembly. During this study of the spatial relationships of lines, planes, and solids, they learn to solve layout problems by using descriptive geometry and rotational principles. Next they are taught the fundamentals of tool detailing and the basic design of tools, jigs, fixtures, dies, and molds, using standard parts such as clamps, washers, keys, locating pins, and punches. They also gain an insight into the use of drill jigs and milling fixtures, which are drawn as assemblies and then detailed into working drawings.

(3) The second area of study is mathematics. Students study algebra to learn ratio and proportion, which are used in planning weights and sizes for jobs involving kinematics, hydraulic mechanics, and pulley and gear ratios of machines. They also learn how to formulate the size of screw threads, determine cutting speeds and feeds, and measure the pressures of fluids and gases that are used in mechanics. In plane and spherical trigonometry they learn to measure the sizes and shapes of tapers, polyhedrons, spheres, and gears.

(4) In a third area of study, machine shop processes, students learn to use the shaper, milling machine, lathe, grinder, handsaw, drill press, planer, file, hand tap, micrometer, height gauge, and vise, and they make precision parts according to blueprint specifications. They study welding to learn various types of joint design, welding symbols, and methods of inspection and testing of welds. They study metallurgy to learn heat and structural properties of ferrous and nonferrous metals and methods of nondestructive testing. They study kinematics to learn how cams and gears operate. They study physics to learn about series and parallel circuits, Ohm's Law, magnetism, electrical measurement, chemical effects of electricity, electrical generation and transformation, and motor principles such as capacitance and inductance.

(5) These are not the only areas of study drafting students will encounter, but they are the most basic ones. If students are able to master these three, they are well on their way to success.

Richard Johnson

Discussion Questions

1. Notice that in paragraph 1 the writer mentions "drafting techniques, mathematics, and machine shop processes." Considering what follows in the rest of the paper, would it have made any difference if he had said "mathematics, machine shop processes, and drafting techniques"? Explain.
2. What is the student's reason for writing?
3. If you were to classify areas of study in your own field, what would your categories be?

Meeting a Special Challenge

(1) Having worked in hospitals as a nurse for several years, I have known nurses in many different specialties who are dedicated and well qualified. However, the four specialties that I consider the most demanding in the profession are surgical nursing, psychiatric nursing, emergency care, and terminal care.

(2) The surgical nurse is highly skilled in the postoperative care of patients. She knows how to run complex equipment such as suction and ventilating machines. She knows how to respond to her patients so that they feel the operation was a success. For

example, she helps the patient who has just undergone a radical mastectomy to see that the surgery was for her overall good. In response to an obvious apprehension, she reassures the patient that she is just as much a woman as before. The surgical nurse must have a special gift for winning the trust of her patients.

(3) The psychiatric nurse deserves a medal for courage. She deals with dangerous mental patients, pathological personalities who have no sense of right or wrong. For this reason, she must be on guard at all times; she must, in effect, have eyes in the back of her head. She must also have a great deal of self-control. When her patient displays anger and violence, she cannot respond in kind. On the contrary, she must be tolerant and understanding. Furthermore, she must be able to recognize attempts at deception. Sometimes a mentally ill person, just prior to suicide, will act in a completely normal way because he or she has made the decision to die. The nurse must understand this behavior and be alert for any possible attempt. Perhaps the most trying part of being a psychiatric nurse is never being able to relax. For this reason, these nurses often work a few years in a psychiatric hospital and then take a year off to work in a general hospital.

(4) The emergency room nurse must have analytical talents and must remain calm in the face of disaster. She has to assess the patient, determine how serious the situation is, and respond with the correct treatment. For example, she must know that a patient brought in short of breath and cyanotic in color probably has congestive heart failure. Immediately she must establish an airway and administer oxygen, while appearing calm and serene to avoid the snowballing effect of panic. It's not an easy job to deal with the public when they or one of their loved ones is in a life-threatening situation. This nurse sees many horrible sights, such as the victims of motorcycle accidents. Sometimes the body is brought in first and then a part, such as a finger, is brought in later. Perhaps the most trying part of being an ER nurse is the sudden personal identification with a patient. If a seriously injured five-year-old boy is brought in and the nurse has a little boy at home, there is bound to be a bond of identification and pity. She must suppress this natural emotion because her alert actions quite possibly can keep the patient alive until the doctor arrives. Most nurses don't care for ER duty, but the ER nurse

feels she can do the most good there because someone's tomorrow may depend on her. It's a great feeling when she saves a life.

(5) Perhaps the nurse I admire most of all is the one who is able to care for the terminally ill patient. To be in constant contact with someone who is about to die takes a tremendous amount of courage, stamina, and tact. The basic foundation of all nursing is the care and welfare of the patient, but this nurse must face the fact that she can't ultimately help her patient. She can't bring out the element of hope as other nurses do. She must be honest and yet always tactful. She is often confronted with the horrible question, "Am I going to die?" She can respond by pointing out that everyone will die some day or by engaging the patient in a discussion. She can, for example, say, "Do you think you're going to die?" If the patient answers "yes," she can then ask why he thinks so. By this discussion she is helping the patient face the inevitable. She must be honest and not promise that he will recover, but she must also avoid saying bluntly that he will die. Even though this is the way the terminal care nurse "helps" her patient, her recognition of inevitability runs counter to the entire nursing philosophy.

(6) Nursing is never easy, and we should all be grateful to the people who choose this demanding profession. But the four types of nurses I have described deserve exceptional praise for meeting a special challenge.

Peg Feltman

Discussion Questions

1. Has the student selected interesting categories for her classification? Explain.
2. What is the purpose of the following phrase in paragraph 1: "Having worked in hospitals as a nurse for several years"?
3. Does the student develop each of her categories effectively with specific details? Discuss, pointing to several examples.
4. If you were to classify the specialties in some profession, what would your categories be?

Direct Expansion Refrigeration Systems

(1) The three most important types of direct expansion refrigeration systems are the capillary tube system, the automatic

expansion valve system, and the thermostatic expansion valve system.

(2) The capillary tube system consists of a compressor, a condenser, an evaporator, a temperature-sensing element (thermostat), and possibly a condenser fan motor. The special parts include a filter drier and a capillary tube flow control. The refrigerant is released from the compressor through the high side (or outlet) as a high pressure gas. It flows through the condenser, where it is cooled to a high pressure liquid. It then flows into the liquid line and from there to the filter drier, where all contaminants are removed. The refrigerant reaches the capillary tube flow control as a high pressure liquid.

(3) This flow control is located in the middle of the system. Its job is to meter the refrigerant so as to maintain a pressure difference between the high side (inlet) and the low side (outlet). The metering is done while the compressor is operating. After the refrigerant is metered through the capillary tube and changed to a low pressure vapor, it absorbs heat from the refrigerated space while moving through the evaporator coils. From there it moves through the suction line and back to the compressor. This cycle is repeated until the desired temperature is reached.

(4) The automatic expansion valve system (A.E.V.) consists of the same parts as the previous system with two exceptions. The A.E.V. uses a liquid receiver, and it has an automatic expansion valve instead of the capillary tube flow control. The refrigerant flows from the compressor as a high pressure vapor to the condenser, where it is cooled. After being cooled it turns from a gas into a high pressure liquid and goes to the liquid receiver. Here the refrigerant is stored until it is needed. At that time it flows through the filter drier and to the metering device, which in this case is the automatic expansion valve. This valve automatically determines whether refrigerant will flow through it to the evaporator. If the pressure is low enough in the evaporator coil, refrigerant is allowed through the valve. When the refrigerant reaches the outlet of the valve, it is sprayed into the evaporator coil and, because of the low pressure, boils rapidly, absorbing heat from the refrigerated space. The refrigerant flows back to the compressor to repeat the cycle until the desired temperature is reached.

(5) The thermostatic expansion valve system (T.E.V.) con-

sists of the same parts as the A.E.V. system except for a different control valve. The refrigerant flows from the compressor through the condenser, liquid receiver, and filter drier, and finally to the thermostatic expansion valve. The operation of this valve is controlled by three forces: the pressure in the evaporator coil, the pressure of the control bulb, and the spring pressure in the valve. The control bulb is a thermal element that is mounted on the evaporator coil outlet and connected to the valve by a capillary tube. The pressure in the coil must be low and the temperature of the bulb must be above the desired temperature before the valve will open. The warmer the evaporator, the wider the valve will open, and the faster refrigeration will take place. The valve will close once the desired temperature is reached.

(6) Because these are the three most common and important direct expansion systems, beginning students of refrigeration and air conditioning must be thoroughly familiar with all of them.

Charles Finnie

Discussion Questions

1. What is the student's reason for writing?
2. The student has discussed three categories (types) of refrigeration systems. Do you find that the three discussions follow a consistent pattern? Explain.

Suggestions for Writing

Write a classification paper on one of the following topics.

1. Pocket calculators
2. Auto mechanics
3. Types of exams
4. College courses
5. Police work
6. Computer languages
7. Newspaper columnists
8. X-ray machines
9. Tennis players (or golfers, swimmers, or some other athletes)
10. Drawing pens
11. Carburetion systems

12. Water filtration systems
13. Eating places
14. TV detectives
15. Areas of a hospital
16. Sports announcers
17. Popular magazines

5

Explaining a Process

Explaining a process is one of the most widely used types of written communication. A paper that explains a process presents step-by-step directions for doing something or tells how a procedure is or was carried out.

Whatever your field of study may be, you will find the ability to write a process paper essential. To mention just a few examples, you would use a process paper to explain how to test an automobile engine, administer cardiopulmonary resuscitation, give an insulin injection, take fingerprints, program a computer, develop an X-ray film, measure air contaminants, charge a refrigeration unit, or analyze a chemical compound. Since you so often will find it necessary to explain a procedure to others, it is essential that you become skilled at this type of writing.

There are seven basic steps involved in writing a process paper:

1. choosing your topic
2. developing your thesis statement
3. writing your introduction
4. discussing the theory

5. listing and ordering your steps
6. developing your steps
7. writing your conclusion

Each step is discussed below.

Choosing Your Topic

For the writing you do on the job, topic selection is seldom a problem since your topic is dictated by some particular work situation—the need to explain a procedure to your coworkers, for example, or perhaps to a customer or client or even the boss. In the classroom, however, you may often be asked to choose a topic. As we have noted in earlier chapters, the topic you select for any paper should be one you are qualified to write on. Especially in the case of the process paper, the best qualification is personal experience. If, for example, you have never grilled hamburgers, you certainly should not try to explain the process to someone else. However, if you did the outdoor cooking for your family all last summer, grilling hamburgers might be an excellent topic. You would know the steps involved very well and be able to explain them clearly and completely.

Be careful not to choose a topic that is too simple or too complex. This is an especially important consideration when you are writing a paper of an assigned length. If you try to explain how to light a match, for example, you will soon run out of things to say. On the other hand, how to overhaul an automobile engine might be a fine topic if you have unlimited space, but it could not be explained adequately in a paper of only a few hundred words. In short, the topic you choose should be simple enough to be explained fully within the assigned length yet complex enough to provide material for an interesting paper.

Developing Your Thesis Statement

Once you have chosen your topic, you are ready to develop your thesis statement. The thesis statement, as you know, controls the direction of the entire paper. It indicates one specific focus and helps you decide what to include and exclude as you write.

Consider the following example: *Grilling hamburgers on an outdoor charcoal grill is a simple process that almost anyone can master.* One specific focus is quite apparent here. When the writer says *grilling,* you know the paper will not explain broiling or pan-frying. When the writer says *hamburgers,* you know the paper will not discuss pork chops or meatloaf. When the writer says *outdoor charcoal grill,* you know the paper will not deal with gas grills, electric grills, or open campfires. In addition, you know that grilling hamburgers is *a simple process,* one you can easily follow. If, on the other hand, the thesis statement were *Making a meal properly involves following a step-by-step process,* the focus would not be specific. The writer would have no clear guideline for developing the paper, and the reader would have a less-than-adequate idea of its content.

Writing Your Introduction

As soon as you have formulated a thesis statement, it is a good idea to write the rest of your introductory paragraph. Although we noted in previous chapters that introductions can be written after the body of a paper is completed, the introduction for a paper explaining a process is somewhat different. In this type of paper, the introduction includes information that you need to keep in mind while developing the rest of the paper. Writing the introduction first lessens the chance that you will overlook an important point.

The introduction should, if possible, include a list of all the items needed to carry out the process. If the required items would result in too extensive a list, they can be introduced at appropriate points later in the paper, but ordinarily the items are listed at the start. For a paper explaining how to grill hamburgers, for example, the list might read as follows:

> You will need a clean grill, charcoal briquets, charcoal lighter fluid and matches, hamburger meat, a plate, a spatula, and some water to put out any flame caused by fat drippings.
>
> E. M. Przybylo

This list should include not only necessary items but also anything —such as the water—that *might* be needed for the process. And if the purpose of some item—again, the water—is not immediately clear, you should indicate briefly what that purpose is.

In addition to the list of equipment and materials, the introduction often must include other information. If there is any question whether the reader will understand the value of the process, the introduction should tell the reader why the process is useful. Further, if a process requires special conditions, you must say what these conditions are. For example, the exterior of a building can be painted only if the temperature is above a certain point. Therefore, if you were explaining how to paint a house, you would note this condition in your introduction. Similarly, if a person must have special training in order to carry out a process, this fact must be mentioned in the introduction. Thus, if a chemical procedure requires some special ability not every chemist has—for example, the ability to operate an X-ray spectrograph—then the introduction must specify this.

An introductory paragraph for the hamburger grilling paper might look something like this:

> Grilling hamburgers on an outdoor charcoal grill is a simple process that almost anyone can master. Before starting, you will need a clean grill, charcoal briquets, charcoal lighter fluid and matches, hamburger meat, a plate, a spatula, and some water to put out any flame caused by fat drippings. The sizzling, tasty patties you will have when you finish are a treat that almost everyone will enjoy.
>
> *E. M. Przybylo*

Discussing the Theory

With some technical papers, it may be helpful to state the theory on which the process is based before explaining the process itself. The theory, usually discussed briefly in a separate paragraph, should come immediately after the introduction.

Do not confuse the theory with the reason why a process is carried out. *Theory* means the basic principle or principles underlying a process. Suppose you are explaining the process for making oxygen in the laboratory from a mixture of potassium chlorate and manganese dioxide. You might state the theory somewhat as follows:

This process is based upon the fact that potassium chlorate decomposes to form oxygen when heated. The manganese dioxide does not supply oxygen but rather acts as a catalyst which promotes the decomposition of the potassium chlorate at a lower temperature.

Phyllis Jedele

The reason for carrying out the process—for example, to obtain oxygen for a variety of combustion experiments—would be mentioned elsewhere in the paper, probably in the introduction.

Unless there is some clear principle underlying the process, do not give a theory. Thus, an explanation of how to change a flat tire requires no theory. A scientific procedure, on the other hand, is usually based on a theory, and you should acquaint your reader with it before you explain the procedure.

Listing and Ordering Your Steps

Once you have written your introduction and, if necessary, stated the theory, make a list of all the steps involved in carrying out the process. Although you are well acquainted with these steps, always assume that your reader is not. Only if you explain the procedure clearly and completely will your reader be able to understand and follow it successfully.

Perhaps the greatest danger in explaining a process is leaving out a step that is obvious to you but would not be to your reader. To avoid this danger, list on a separate sheet of paper all the steps you can think of. Above all, don't try to carry the steps in your head.

Your first list of the steps in grilling hamburgers might look something like this:

1. remove grill rack
2. prepare charcoal
3. light charcoal
4. make hamburger patties
5. replace grill rack
6. place patties on it
7. shortly flip them over
8. remove patties from grill when done to suit your taste

Now examine these steps to see whether anything is missing. You will soon find you have forgotten to tell your reader to wait about thirty to forty-five minutes after lighting the charcoal before putting the hamburgers on. By then the briquets will have turned an ash-white color—an indication that they are at their hottest. You know from experience to allow the briquets time to heat up. Your reader, however, may never have grilled hamburgers and therefore will not know that it is necessary to wait. Realizing your omission, simply insert the missing step in the proper place.

Once you are satisfied with the steps you have listed, arrange them in a proper order. (Consider what would happen, for example, if you told your reader to place the patties on the grill before lighting the charcoal.) The steps in a process paper are arranged in one or two ways: fixed order or order of choice.

Fixed order means that there is basically only one correct way of arranging the steps: step one must be completed before step two is started, step two before step three, and so forth. Changing an automobile tire is an example of a fixed-order process. The car must be jacked up before the flat tire is removed, and the flat tire must be removed before the spare tire is put on.

Not all processes, however, must be performed in a fixed order. Sometimes there are several possible ways to arrange the steps. When you grill hamburgers, for example, it doesn't make much difference whether you light the charcoal before or after you gather the ingredients or whether you make the patties before or after you light the charcoal. But since some order is necessary for your explanation, present the steps in the order that has worked best for you. Arranging the steps in this way is known as *order of choice.*

If your paper is nontechnical, once you have arranged your steps you are ready to begin your explanation. In technical papers, however, it is usually desirable to list at least the major steps in a single sentence before taking them up in individual paragraphs. In such cases, this list is placed immediately after the discussion of theory. For two examples, see the second paragraph of "Hand Developing X-Ray Film" (page 83) and the second paragraph of "Compression Pressure Testing of an Automobile Engine" (page 84).

Developing Your Steps

Now you are ready to discuss your steps in detail. Because you want the reader to see them as separate actions, present the main steps in separate paragraphs or groups of paragraphs. Then develop the paragraphs with enough specific details to make the process clear.

Whenever possible, try not to overburden your reader with numerous steps. If a process involves a considerable number of steps, see if you can combine related-small steps into main steps that your reader can follow more easily. For example, of the items in the preliminary list for the paper on grilling hamburgers, you could combine in a single statement the steps of removing the grill rack, preparing the charcoal, and lighting the charcoal. Similarly, you could combine replacing the grill rack, placing the patties on it, and shortly flipping them over. (Sometimes you may find that what you considered a step is actually a comment upon or an explanation of the step just before or after it. In this case, the comment or explanation belongs with the step that it refers to.) Your main concern, however, should always be clarity. If combining steps would result in confusion, use as many separate steps as are necessary to make the process clear to your reader.

The first main step in grilling hamburgers—removing the grill rack, preparing the charcoal, and lighting it—might be developed somewhat like this:

> The first step is to get the fire going. Remove the grill rack and stack about twenty charcoal briquets in a pyramid shape in the center of the grill. Stacking allows the briquets to burn off one another and thus produce a hotter fire. Next squirt charcoal lighter fluid over the briquets. Wait about five minutes before tossing in a lighted match so that the fluid has time to soak into the charcoal. The flame will burn for a few minutes and then go out.
>
> When the flame goes out, allow the briquets to sit for another fifteen minutes so the charcoal can start to burn. Once the burning starts, do not squirt on any more lighter fluid. A flame could quickly follow the stream back into the can, causing it to explode. As the briquets begin to turn from a pitch-black to an ash-white color, spread them out with a stick

so they barely touch one another. Air can then circulate and produce a hot, even fire—the type that makes grilling a success.

E. M. Przybylo

Note that all of these directions are written in the form of commands. Instructions are almost always written in this form because it is the most straightforward and the easiest for readers to follow.

When you discuss the steps, be sure—unless the reason is obvious—to indicate the purpose of each action as well as how to perform the action. This was done at several points in the paragraphs just quoted. The reader who has this information will work more intelligently and efficiently and be less inclined to skip tasks that seem unnecessary.

If all or part of a step is especially hard to carry out, warn the reader and indicate how to overcome the difficulty. In addition, if there is a chance that an action might be performed improperly, caution the reader against varying the set procedure. This is especially important if an improper action can cause dangerous results. Thus, when explaining how to start the briquets, the writer of the paragraphs above warns his reader not to add lighter fluid once the briquets are burning.

Occasionally, two or more steps of a process must be performed simultaneously. In such a case, be sure to point out, before you describe the first of these steps, that the steps must be performed at the same time.

Writing Your Conclusion

Once you've presented the final step, do not end your paper abruptly—your reader may feel "cut off." A few brief closing remarks will help your reader see the total process more clearly. Thus, in a concluding paragraph, you could (1) summarize the process, (2) evaluate the results, or (3) discuss the importance of the process. Write whichever type of conclusion you think will be most appropriate for the paper and most helpful to your reader.

Other Types of Process Papers

So far this chapter has explained how to write directions for someone to follow. Sometimes, though, you will be writing not to tell your reader how to perform a process but simply to explain how a process is carried out. And sometimes you may be reporting on how a particular process *was* performed. These latter types of explanations are written in just the same way as a set of directions, except for two differences: the list of materials and equipment is sometimes omitted, and the writer presents the steps not in the form of instructions for the reader to follow but merely as facts for the reader to understand. In the three examples that follow, you can see how the three methods of explaining a process differ. Note that the first paragraph gives directions, the second simply explains how a process is performed, and the third reports on how a process was performed.

To begin step one, slowly turn the intensity knob clockwise until a spot of light appears on the screen. Adjust the focus control to make the spot as small and sharp as possible. Next, turn up the horizontal gain control until there is a horizontal line about eight divisions long on the screen. Adjust the intensity so the line is just bright enough to be seen plainly, and readjust the focus for the finest possible line.

Glenn Jones

To prepare a bacterial smear for staining, a drop of distilled water is first placed on a clear glass microscope slide by means of an inoculating loop. The loop and the opening of the tube containing the bacterial culture to be examined are next passed through a Bunsen burner flame to sterilize them. A small bit of culture is then removed with the loop, and the loop is rubbed in the drop of water on the slide until the water covers an area 1½ inches long and approximately the width of the slide. Next the opening of the culture tube is reflamed to prevent contamination of the culture and then replugged. The smear is allowed to air dry, and the slide is passed, smear side up, through the flame of the burner until it is warm to the touch. The dried smear should have a cloudy, milky-white appearance.

student unknown

The analyzer was adjusted so the scale read zero and connected to the short sampling tube which had previously been inserted into the smoke stack. The sample was taken by depressing the bulb the requisite number of times, and the results were then read and recorded. The procedure was repeated, this time using the long sampling tube and sampling through the fire door.

Charles Finnie

STUDENT EXAMPLES

How to Grill Hamburgers

(1) Grilling hamburgers on an outdoor charcoal grill is a simple process that almost anyone can master. Before starting, you will need a clean grill, charcoal briquets, charcoal lighter fluid and matches, hamburger meat, a plate, a spatula, and some water to put out any flame caused by fat drippings. The sizzling, tasty patties you will have when you finish are a treat that almost everyone will enjoy.

(2) The first step is to get the fire going. Remove the grill rack and stack about twenty charcoal briquets in a pyramid shape in the center of the grill. Stacking allows the briquets to burn off one another and thus produce a hotter fire. Next squirt charcoal lighter fluid over the briquets. Wait about five minutes before tossing in a lighted match so that the fluid has time to soak into the charcoal. The flame will burn for a few minutes and then go out.

(3) When the flame goes out, allow the briquets to sit for another fifteen minutes so the charcoal can start to burn. Once the burning starts, do not squirt on any more lighter fluid. A flame could quickly follow the stream back into the can, causing it to explode. As the briquets begin to turn from a pitch-black to an ash-white color, spread them out with a stick so they barely touch one another. Air can then circulate and produce a hot, even fire—the type that makes grilling a success.

(4) After the briquets are spread properly, start making the hamburger patties, but first set aside a small ball of hamburger to use for greasing the grill rack. For each patty, take about a quarter of a pound (about two ice cream scoops) of hamburger in your hand and shape it into a ball. Then flatten the ball with your hand and compress the meat to insure extra firmness, since hamburgers sometimes fall apart on the grill.

(5) The thickness of the patties is up to you. Do not, however, make them too thick; you may end up with patties well cooked on the outside and still raw inside. One inch in depth by five inches in diameter will do nicely. These dimensions allow for shrinkage, and the patties will fit your hamburger buns perfectly. As you make the patties, place them side by side on a plate, not on top of each other. Stacking causes them to stick together.

(6) Now check the heat of the briquets. Hold the palm of your hand over them at the height the meat will be cooking—six inches is perhaps average. When you can barely count "one Mississippi, two Mississippi, three Mississippi" before the heat forces you to jerk your hand away, the coals are just right for grilling.

(7) Before replacing the grill rack, take that small ball of hamburger and rub the rack where the patties will be cooking. This will prevent your patties from sticking to the grill.

(8) Now put the rack on the grill at the desired height—the bottom notch if you want the meat to cook quickly, the top notch if you want it to cook more slowly. Use the spatula to place the patties on the rack, spacing them evenly above the charcoal to insure uniform grilling. After a minute or two, turn the patties with the spatula and expose the raw sides to the heat. This will sear the meat and lock in the flavor.

(9) After both sides have been seared, grill the patties to your own individual taste. If you like them rare—red inside and juicy—cook them about six to eight minutes on each side. If you like them well done—brown inside and not juicy—cook them about twelve to fifteen minutes on each side.

(10) When you remove the patties from the grill and place them on buns, you are ready to enjoy a mouth-watering treat that you will long remember.

E. M. Przybylo

Discussion Questions

1. Reread the following clause and sentences:
   "since hamburgers sometimes fall apart on the grill" (paragraph 4)
   "Stacking causes them to stick together." (paragraph 5)
   "This will prevent your patties from sticking to the grill." (paragraph 7)
   "This will sear the meat and lock in the flavor." (paragraph 8)
   What does each of these accomplish?
2. Notice the phrase within parentheses in paragraph 4. Why has the writer included this information?
3. What is the purpose of the second sentence of paragraph 5?
4. If you were to write a paper explaining how to prepare one of your favorite foods, which one would you select? What would be the main steps in the process?

The Mourning After

(1) How to handle a hangover is a problem many people share. Since the discovery of the grape, man has dedicated himself to the imbibing of alcoholic beverages. This imbibing often causes us to awaken to the rumbling of a thousand horses galloping across our foreheads and a volcano-like condition in our stomachs. But worry not—a remedy is as near as the kitchen.

(2) Once awake, chances are good you may want to die, but chances are even better that you'll survive. The first and most difficult task on the road to recovery is to pry your head off the pillow and firmly plant both feet on the floor. Don't despair if this seems impossible at first, since it sometimes takes four or five attempts. Now cautiously shuffle your feet toward the kitchen. Stay close to the wall and try not to jar the object on your shoulders that feels as though it's hosting the Stanley Cup Playoffs.

(3) The kitchen should bring a slight degree of relief as you sense that the soothing potion is near at hand. Locate a juice pitcher or any container that has a lid. Remove the lid and pour a third of a glass of concentrated lemon juice, the kind used for cooking, into your container. Add two-thirds of a glass of soda water, if available, or tap water. The next step requires the most finesse. Take a bottle of Tabasco sauce and ever so gently shake a dash into the cure. Add two Alka-Seltzer tablets and a half dozen cubes of ice. Your remedy is now ready to be mixed. Place

the lid on the container and shake it vigorously for ten to fifteen seconds (this sometimes happens without your initiating the motion).

(4) The potion is now ready to be consumed. Pour it into a large drinking glass and place two aspirin in your mouth. The moment of truth is at hand. Drink this exhilarating remedy in one sustained motion and feel the soothing coolness of your pipes as the wonder mix works its way to your stomach. As the aspirin sends relief to your banging head, the Alka-Seltzer, lemon, and Tabasco will revitalize your stomach.

(5) As you sit and read the morning paper, you'll feel your senses being restored. Your head will stop throbbing, your pipes will cool, and your burning stomach will experience relief. The price you'll pay today for what you bought last night will be a bargain with this magic elixir. You can now ready yourself for the day and hope all matters of consequence can be avoided until noon.

Charles Case

Discussion Questions

1. Comment on the effectiveness of the title the student has given his paper.
2. In paragraph 3, what does the student mean when he says "this sometimes happens without your initiating the motion."
3. Are the steps in this paper in fixed order or order of choice?
4. Three types of conclusions were mentioned earlier in this chapter. Which does the writer use in this paper?

Hand Developing X-Ray Film

(1) X-ray film development is a procedure whereby the invisible, latent image on exposed film is converted to a visible image by treating the film with a developer solution. The special equipment needed to perform this process includes an exposed X-ray film, a film hanger, three solution tanks, and a dryer. The solutions needed are developer, fixer, and water, each in a separate tank at 68° F.

(2) The process is based on the fact that an alkaline developer transforms exposed (ionized) silver bromide crystals on the

film into clumps of black metallic silver that form an image. The unexposed (nonionized) silver bromide is not affected by this treatment. The complete development process consists of five steps: (1) developing, (2) rinsing, (3) fixing, (4) rerinsing, and (5) drying the film.

(3) The exposed film is first removed from the cassette and attached to the hanger. The film is then suspended in the developer solution for about five minutes. This solution softens and swells the gelatin on the outside of the film, then reacts with the ionized silver bromide crystals to reduce them to metallic silver.

(4) When the film is developed, it is placed in the rinse water tank, which contains running water, for thirty seconds. Running water insures that the film is rinsed properly. It removes the alkaline part of the developer so it will not neutralize the acidic fixer.

(5) Next the film is placed in the fixer solution for ten minutes. This solution clears the film of nonionized silver bromide and hardens the gelatin emulsion, thus increasing its resistance to damage.

(6) The film is then returned to the rinse water tank. It is allowed to remain there for twenty-five minutes so that the fixing salts will be removed, since residual fixer would cause the image to discolor and fade.

(7) Finally, the film is removed from the rinse water tank and the excess water is allowed to run off. The film is then placed on the dryer, generally a type of rack. During the drying process, the film can be easily damaged. Since dirt from the air may become embedded in the film or the film may become scratched, extreme care is taken to protect the film at this stage.

(8) Drying takes approximately fifteen minutes. The dried film is a permanent, finished radiograph that helps diagnose a suspected condition.

student unknown

Discussion Questions

1. Has the student chosen an appropriate process to explain? Discuss.
2. What is the purpose of the last sentence in paragraph 1?
3. Where is the theory discussed? Why is it desirable to include the theory for this process?

4. Why has the student given the purpose for each step? In what way is this information helpful?
5. Are the steps in fixed order or order of choice?
6. Earlier in this chapter we mentioned three types of process papers: those giving directions, those merely explaining how a process is performed, and those reporting on how a process was performed. Which type does this paper illustrate?

Compression Pressure Testing of an Automobile Engine

(1) Compression pressure testing is a process that indicates the compression ratio of an automobile engine. Here is a simple, accurate procedure for determining engine compression. The tools needed to carry out this process include a spark plug wrench, a large screwdriver, a remote-control starter switch, and a compression pressure gauge.

(2) The process is based on the fact that if the head gasket and piston rings are in good condition, the combustion chamber will be tightly sealed during the compression stroke. If a gauge is inserted in place of the spark plug, the amount of compression can be measured. A high gauge reading indicates a good seal while a low reading indicates a poor seal. The three basic steps in the procedure are: (1) preparing the engine for testing, (2) pressure testing, which includes inserting the gauge into each cylinder and recording the readings, and (3) comparing the pressure readings to one another and to the engine compression specifications.

(3) To prepare the engine, first remove the spark plug wire located at the top of each plug. Next, remove the plugs from the block with the spark plug wrench. Connect the remote-control starter switch to the starter solenoid terminals. To prevent the car from starting, disconnect and ground the ignition-coil tower wire located at the distributor. Finally, block open the carburetor throttle with the large screwdriver. This will prevent gas from overflowing.

(4) To pressure test the engine, force the end of the gauge into the number one spark plug hole. Make sure the rubber tip of the gauge completely seals the hole, or inaccurate readings will result. Depress the remote-control starter switch until the engine cranks seven complete compression strokes. Observe and record

the compression reading and the number of the cylinder tested. Remove the gauge and test each of the remaining cylinders in the same way.

(5) In order to interpret the results of the pressure tests, the readings must be compared with one another and with the engine compression specifications. First, compare the individual cylinder readings. They should be within 20 percent of one another. A greater variation indicates that excessive wear has caused an unbalanced engine, which cannot be corrected by mere tuning. The second comparison, between the average of the readings and the known engine compression specification, shows the amount of engine wear. If the average is within 20 percent of the specification, the engine is considered mechanically sound. If the average is more than 20 percent below the specification, the engine is excessively worn and should be rebuilt. If the average is more than 20 percent above the specification, the engine has heavy carbon deposits and needs to be decarbonized. Low pressure reading in two adjacent cylinders may indicate a faulty head gasket.

(6) Periodic compression tests will indicate the condition of an auto engine and alert the owner to any needed repairs or adjustments.

student unknown

Discussion Questions

1. Notice that paragraph 2 lists the three major steps involved in the procedure. How is the reader helped by this list?
2. At one point the writer warns the reader against performing a procedure improperly. Locate the warning.
3. Cite two places in paragraph 3 where the writer indicates the purpose of an action.
4. If you were asked to explain a technical procedure with which you are familiar, what procedure would you select? What would be the main steps in your explanation?

Suggestions for Writing

Write a paper explaining one of the following processes. Be sure that you include all the necessary steps, select an appropriate order, and develop each step with sufficient details.

1. How to install a manual throttle
2. How to prepare a blood smear for microscopic examination
3. How to program a computer
4. How to grow a specific type of fruit or vegetable in your home garden
5. How to use dental floss
6. How to monitor the atmosphere for air contaminants
7. How to record with a tape recorder
8. How to assemble or repair some common household device
9. How to obedience train a dog (or how to train another pet)
10. How to charge a refrigeration unit
11. How to perform the Schilling test for pernicious anemia
12. How to change the oil in an automobile
13. How to sew a zipper in an article of clothing
14. How to administer cardiopulmonary resuscitation (CPR)
15. How to clean and gap spark plugs
16. How to repaint a car
17. How to clean teeth or apply fluoride treatments to teeth
18. How to serve a tennis ball
19. How to install, modify, or overhaul a particular type of air-conditioning or refrigeration unit
20. How to carry out a process related to your field

6

Definition

As you write for your classes and on the job, you will often have to clarify the meaning of some term for your readers. The term may be unfamiliar, it may be used in an uncommon sense, or it may mean different things to different people. Whenever you clarify the meaning of a term, you are defining. A definition may be a phrase or sentence, or it may require several pages, depending on your purpose, your reader, and the complexity of the thing being defined.

At times, a brief definition like those found in dictionaries will be satisfactory. Thus, in writing for a general audience about heating systems, it would probably be sufficient to define *furnace plenum* by explaining that it is "an air compartment maintained under pressure and connected to one or more ducts." Similarly, a paper for nonspecialists about treating wounds might briefly explain the special medical meaning of *proud* by a simple paren- thetical phrase, as in this example: "the proud (excessively swollen and granulated) flesh surrounding the typical wound." The first of these examples defines an unfamiliar term; the second, a term used in an uncommon sense. Both definitions, though brief, probably would provide all the information the reader needs.

Often, however, brief definitions are not sufficient. This is especially true when you are dealing with new or abstract terms. Think of the vast number of new terms that have come into use in recent years as a result of technological developments—*diode, lunar module, nuclear reactor,* and *supersonic jet transport,* to name only a few. In addition, social and political developments have produced countless new terms such as *environmentalism, consumerism,* and *transactional analysis.* When you use new and unfamiliar terms such as these in your writing, it is often necessary to explain them in detail. Your audience may never have heard of the concept, and a dictionary definition—even if you can find one—will not provide enough information.

Terms such as *consumerism* and *transactional analysis* are not only new but highly abstract. An abstract term stands for an idea, an attitude, a condition, a quality—something, in short, that we cannot feel, see, or otherwise experience with our senses. *Jealousy, generosity, power, liberalism, love,* and *sadness* are but a few examples. Because abstract terms stand for intangible things, a short definition often gives your reader only a hazy notion of your intended meaning.

Suppose, for example, that you define *power* as "the ability to achieve noticeable results." You have in mind people who can make far-reaching decisions within an organization. Your reader, however, thinks of a drop forger or a giant earth-moving machine. Communication has obviously failed. In order to make yourself understood, you must expand your definition.

Concrete terms—such as *house, pocketknife,* and *swim*—stand for objects or actions we can clearly perceive with our senses. Unlike abstract terms, most concrete terms can be adequately explained with dictionary definitions. For example, if you say that a *pocketknife* is "a small knife with blades that fold into slots in the handle," your reader will probably have little difficulty understanding what you mean.

Some concrete terms, however, can mean different things to different people. *Drug pusher* is one example. To many people, a drug pusher is anyone who illegally sells any narcotic substance. Others limit the term to sellers of heroin, cocaine, and other hard drugs. Obviously, if you write a paper recommending stiff sentences for drug pushers, you must clearly define what you mean by the term. Otherwise, your reader might misunderstand your position.

Sometimes, as in the previous example, a brief definition is needed to clarify a particular term within a paper. At other times, an entire paper may be an extended definition. Your instructor, for example, may ask you to define a technical or social term like *weather satellite* or *urban sprawl* or an abstract term like *hope* or *despair*. Your employer may ask you to define a procedure for new employees, the safety program followed in the plant, or the essential features of a new product. This chapter will show you how to develop such an extended definition.

Writing a paper of extended definition involves four basic steps:

1. choosing your topic
2. establishing your formal definition
3. expanding your definition
4. writing your introduction and conclusion

Each step is discussed below.

Choosing Your Topic

When you are working, the duties of your job, not personal choice, will determine what definitions you write. In the classroom, however, your instructor may give you several topics and ask you to define one of them. First, pick something you know about or can learn enough about in the time available. Your knowledge can be the result of personal experience, observation, reading, or any combination of these. Be certain, also, that the topic interests you. If you ignore these guidelines, your writing will go very slowly, and the paper you produce is likely to prove both inaccurate and boring.

Establishing Your Formal Definition

Once you have chosen your topic, your next step is to prepare a one-sentence formal definition. This definition does two things. (1) It places the item being defined in a broad category. (2) It tells how this particular item differs from others in the same category. Consider the following example: "A catbird is a small American songbird with a slate-colored body, a black cap and tail, and a catlike cry." This definition places the catbird in the category of American songbirds, then distinguishes it from others in that category by its color, markings, and cry.

There are certain pitfalls to avoid when you prepare your formal definition. First, your definition should not be too broad. If you define a *rifle* as "a firearm used mainly for hunting large game," you are committing this error. Rifles are not the only firearms used for this purpose; shotguns are used as well. To narrow the definition, you might say, "A rifle is a firearm that has spiral grooves inside its barrel and is used mainly for hunting large game."

The opposite extreme—an overly narrow definition—is the second pitfall to avoid. "Motor oil is a liquid petroleum product used to lubricate automobile engines" is an example of this type of error. The definition is too narrow because it fails to indicate that motor oil is used to lubricate other engines as well. To expand the definition, simply add the missing information: "Motor oil is a liquid petroleum product used to lubricate the engines of automobiles, motorcycles, lawn mowers, and the like."

Circularity, the third pitfall, occurs when the term being defined, or a form of the term, is repeated as part of the definition. Nothing is clarified when you define a *puritanical person* as "one with puritanical beliefs." If your reader doesn't know what a puritanical person is, he obviously won't know the meaning of "puritanical beliefs" either. You must define the term with words that will be meaningful to your reader—for example, "A puritanical person is one with extremely strict moral and religious views."

The use of "is where" or "is when" is the fourth pitfall in writing formal definitions. "A hospital is where sick and injured people are cared for" and "Procrastinating is when a person habitually delays taking necessary action" illustrate this error. Both of these definitions are faulty because neither one explicitly *names* a category to which the item being defined belongs. Notice the improvement when the "is where" and "is when" phrases are eliminated: "A hospital is an institution in which sick and injured people are cared for" and "Procrastinating is the habitual delaying of necessary action."

The last pitfall is using language that your reader is not likely to understand. Dr. Samuel Johnson's definition of a *network* as "anything reticulated or decussated, at equal distances, with interstices between the intersections" is an often-cited example that violates this principle. Its failure to communicate stands in marked contrast to the clarity of "A network is an arrangement of cords, wires, or rods that cross at regular intervals and are fastened together at the points where they intersect."

In applying this principle, do not assume you must avoid all technical terms when writing a formal definition. For example, in defining *crustaceans* for advanced biology students, it might be entirely appropriate to state that these creatures possess a "chitinous or calcareous exoskeleton." These terms, however, would be meaningless to most general readers; it would be better to tell such readers that crustaceans have "a hard outer shell."

Expanding Your Definition

Once you have established your formal definition, the next step is to expand it. This expansion can be accomplished by any of the writing methods discussed in previous chapters—for instance, comparison or classification. The method you choose will depend on your topic and purpose. As in all good writing, a generous supply of specific details is essential in a definition paper.

Comparison is often helpful in defining a new or unfamiliar object or device. This method involves pointing out resemblances and/or differences between the new item and one your reader is familiar with. Several approaches are possible. You may, for example, focus on physical properties, construction, mode of operation, size, power, or efficiency. In the paragraphs below, the student compares the means by which cooling is accomplished in a liquid-cooled engine and in the less familiar air-cooled engine.

> In conventional liquid-cooled engines, the heat from the burning air-fuel mixture passes through the walls of the cylinder and into a coolant in a jacket surrounding the cylinders. The heated coolant is pumped through a radiator, where it is cooled

by an air stream blowing past the thin-walled tubes or cells through which it passes. It is then returned to the jacket to absorb more heat.

In air-cooled engines, heat is absorbed directly by a stream of air passing over the outside of the engine. The outside cylinder walls have metal fins to increase the amount of surface from which engine heat is lost, and the cylinders may also have spaces between them for better air circulation. To provide the great volume of air needed for proper cooling, a fan or blower may be utilized. Special cowlings and baffles may also be placed around the engine near the cylinders to increase the flow of air.

Edward Daley

Classification, another writing method that is useful for developing a definition, involves dividing a topic into separate categories and then discussing the categories one at a time. The following excerpt from a paper on air contamination uses classification to expand the definition of *respirators*.

Three major types of respirators—air-supplied devices, self-contained breathing devices, and air-purifying devices—are utilized for protection against air contaminants. Air-supplied devices consist essentially of a mask, hood, or suit connected by a hose to a stationary tank of air. With self-contained breathing devices, air is supplied from a tank carried by the user, or oxygen is generated in a chemical canister. Air-purifying devices are equipped with filters or chemical canisters which remove contaminants from incoming air before the wearer breathes it.

Alice Ludo

Process explanation is an especially versatile method of developing a definition. You may use it, for example, to explain what a device does or how it is used, how a product is made, how a procedure is carried out, or how a natural event takes place. The paragraph below, from a paper defining *cardiopulmonary resuscitation*, explains how a procedure is carried out.

The first step in carrying out cardiopulmonary resuscitation is to open the airway. This is done by hyperextending the neck and pulling the lower jaw forward. When a person is unconscious, the tongue falls to the back of the throat and blocks the air passage. With the head hyperextended, the tongue is pulled from the back of the throat, allowing the air to pass. Pulling the jaw forward opens the passage further and facilitates breathing. Once these measures have been taken, the victim may begin to breathe spontaneously. If he does not, the next step, artificial breathing, must be started.

Karen Bateman

Illustration—that is, use of specific incidents, events, or examples—is especially effective for defining an abstract term or for tracing the changes in the meaning of a term. In the excerpt below, the student utilizes illustration to help develop a paper defining *fear*.

Once I started school, I developed a great fear of tests, term papers, and speaking in front of the class. Formal speeches were especially hard for me. Heart pounding, cold sweat beading my forehead, I would suffer acute mental agonies as I stammered my way through my talk. This "academic fear syndrome" lasted until my junior year in college.

Diane Trathen

When you are defining events, conditions, or problems, it is often desirable to describe their causes. The following paragraph, part of a paper defining *crib deaths*, shows the use of cause.

In a March 1975 *Science Digest* article, Dr. R. C. Reisinger, a National Cancer Institute scientist, links crib deaths to the growth of a common bacteria, *E. coli,* in the intestines of newborn babies. The bacteria multiply in the intestines, manufacturing a toxin that is absorbed by the intestinal wall and then passes into the bloodstream. Breast milk stops the growth of the organism, whereas cow's milk permits it. Therefore, Dr. Reisinger believes, bottle-fed babies run a higher risk of crib death than breast-fed babies.

Trudy Stelter

Negation is a technique that involves showing what a term does *not* mean. It is especially useful for defining events and occurrences and for correcting popular misconceptions. Notice how the student uses negation in the excerpt below.

Researchers do not know what crib death is, but they do know what it is *not.* They know it cannot be predicted; it strikes like a "thief in the night." Crib deaths occur in seconds, with no sound of pain, and they always happen when the child is sleeping. Suffocation is *not* the cause, nor is aspiration or regurgitation. Researchers have found no correlation between the incidence of crib death and the mother's use of birth control pills or tobacco or the presence of fluoride in water.

Trudy Stelter

Although each of the above methods represents one possible way of expanding your definition, few papers are developed by a single method. The way you organize your material will depend on your topic and on the aspects of it that you consider.

Writing Your Introduction and Conclusion

As we have noted earlier in this book, the introduction and conclusion are often written after the first draft of the paper has been completed. For papers of definition, the introduction and conclusion should present no serious problems. Ordinarily, a few sentences will be sufficient for each.

The introduction can do any of several things: attract attention with an arresting statement or question, present a brief case history, or comment on the importance of the item being defined. In addition, the introduction contains the formal definition of the term.

The conclusion generally summarizes the paper's main points, comments on the significance of the information, presents results, or makes a prediction.

STUDENT EXAMPLES

TM

(1) Merv Griffin, Clint Eastwood, Joe Namath, and many other celebrities practice it. So do Americans of every personality type from carefree to compulsive and of every age from nine to ninety. This relatively new passion is Transcendental Meditation,

or TM for short. TM is a technique for relaxing that involves silently repeating a "mantra" in order to increase awareness and relieve tensions. Not long ago it was only a student cult, but now it has caught on with businessmen, housewives, and others. As a result, public interest in the origin, nature, effects, and methods of practicing TM has mounted steadily.

(2) TM was introduced in the United States during the 1960s by Maharishi Mahesh Yogi of India. He studied it himself for thirteen years in the Himalayas before bringing it into the open. TM originally was a Hindu practice, but it is neither a religion nor a philosophy. The practice of TM requires no change in life-style, no kind of expertise, and no special diet. After the initial instruction, which sometimes takes place in a group, one practices TM alone and in private. It does not interfere with any established moral, social, or religious beliefs. It is just a new psychological experience.

(3) TM produces a physiological state of deep relaxation, even though the subject remains awake and aware of what is going on about him. The subject repeats the technique daily to prepare mind and body for everyday activity. Although little is known about how the process works, articles in scientific journals indicate that the TM technique lowers the meditator's metabolic rate, breath rate, blood lactate concentration, and blood pressure, while improving reaction time, perceptual abilities, and other health indicators.

(4) TM does not require intense concentration or any form of rigorous mental or physical control. The technique is taught by trained and qualified instructors and is easily learned in a few lessons. The subject then practices it twice daily, each time for fifteen to twenty minutes. To practice TM, the subject sits in a comfortable position with eyes closed and silently repeats, or meditates on, a "mantra"—a word without meaning which allows the attention to shift inward, producing relaxation. The mantra is one of many sounds which have proved to be especially harmonious when applied to the right type of personality. The instructor selects the word each individual uses, and the individual should never reveal this word to another person, or supposedly it loses its potency.

(5) Since TM reduces tensions and prepares the body for daily activity, the subject practices it twenty minutes before

breakfast to get the body set for the day ahead and twenty minutes before the evening meal to recharge the body for the evening. TM and a full stomach do not mix but instead produce unhappy reactions such as nausea and indigestion.

(6) Transcendental Meditation is not a fraud. Thousands of Americans claim that it really works for them, and their enthusiasm is creating thousands of converts each month.

Terri Klamer

Discussion Questions

1. Identify the formal definition in paragraph 1 and indicate what it accomplishes.
2. What purpose is served by the other sentences in paragraph 1?
3. In what paragraph does the student use negation as a method of development?

Robbing the Cradle

(1) Jane and Dick Smith were proud, new parents of an eight-pound, ten-ounce baby girl named Jenny. One summer night, Jane put Jenny to bed at 8:00. When she went to check on her at 3:00 a.m., Jane found Jenny dead. The baby had given no cry of pain, shown no sign of trouble. Even the doctor did not know why she had died, for she was healthy and strong. The autopsy report confirmed the doctor's suspicion—the infant was a victim of the "sudden infant death syndrome," also known as SIDS or "crib death." SIDS is the sudden and unexplainable death of an apparently healthy sleeping infant. It is the number one cause of death in infants after the first week of life and as a result has been the subject of numerous research studies.

(2) These studies have uncovered several facts about crib death victims. First, most die during the cold months between November and February. Boys seem to be more susceptible than girls. A disproportionate number of victims are from nonwhite families and from families of low socioeconomic status. Premature infants are more likely to die than those carried full term. Finally, the death rate appears to be highest among the three-month-old babies.

(3) Although researchers do not know what SIDS is, they do know what it is *not*. They know it cannot be predicted; it strikes like a "thief in the night." Crib deaths occur in seconds, with no sound of pain, and they always happen when the child is sleeping. Suffocation is *not* the cause, nor is aspiration or regurgitation. Researchers have found no correlation between the incidence of SIDS and the mother's use of birth control pills or tobacco or the presence of fluoride in water. Since it is not hereditary or contagious, only a slim chance exists that SIDS will attack twice in the same family.

(4) As might be expected, researchers have offered a variety of theories as to the cause of crib death. In a March 1975 *Science Digest* article, Dr. R. C. Reisinger, a National Cancer Institute scientist, links crib deaths to the growth of a common bacteria, *E. coli*, in the intestines of newborn babies. The bacteria multiply in the intestines, manufacturing a toxin that is absorbed by the intestinal wall and then passes into the bloodstream. Breast milk stops the growth of the organism, whereas cow's milk permits it. Therefore, Dr. Reisinger believes, bottle-fed babies run a higher risk of crib death than breast-fed babies.

(5) Another theory has been advanced by Karl J. Kadlub, a Battle Creek clinical psychologist, and his son, K. Gregory Kadlub, a premedical student. Their theory, as presented in the December 1, 1975, *Grand Rapids Press,* holds that crib deaths are triggered by infant feeding. After the infant is placed in its crib for the night, a large bubble of gas is forced from its stomach into the air passages, which may already be partially blocked due to the child's sleeping position. The bubble becomes trapped in the windpipe, prevents air from entering, and causes the child to suffocate.

(6) The loss of a child through crib death is an especially traumatic experience. Parents often develop feelings of guilt and depression, thinking they somehow caused the child's death. To alleviate such feelings, organizations have been established to help parents accept the fact that they did not cause the death.

(7) Many researchers are at work seeking an explanation and preventative for SIDS. Meanwhile, all we can do is hope that an infant who is dear to us does not fall victim to the killer.

Trudy Stelter

Discussion Questions

1. Identify the formal definition in paragraph 1. Does it meet the requirements for a formal definition? Support your answer.
2. Examine the opening paragraph. Which of the introductory techniques mentioned earlier in the chapter does the student use in this paragraph?
3. If you were to define a common cause of death, which one would you choose? How would you develop your definition?

Voiceprints

(1) A voiceprint is a graphic record of an individual's voice characteristics. The graph consists of a complicated pattern of wavy lines. As is true of fingerprints, no two voiceprints are alike.

(2) A voiceprint is made by using a sound spectrograph, an instrument that records the energy patterns of the spoken word. Voice readings are affected by such physiological characteristics as the configuration of the lower respiratory tract and the contours of the vocal cavities, as well as by the movements of the vocal cords, lips, and tongue. These factors, taken together, make each voiceprint unique. To obtain a voiceprint, the subject speaks into a microphone, and the voice is recorded on a magnetic tape. This tape runs around a cylindrical drum, where an electronic scanning device picks up the information. A pen then records the information on paper as a graph.

(3) The medical profession has utilized voiceprints in a number of studies. One study, reported in the March 1974 issue of *Scientific American,* investigated the cries of infants. The findings showed that a distress cry is louder, longer, and noisier than a hunger cry and tends to be irregular, with more interruptions and gagging. This same study also showed that abnormal cry characteristics appear to be associated with certain physical defects. In one instance the researchers discovered that an apparently normal infant with an especially shrill cry had no cerebral cortex. Generally, abnormal infants had higher-pitched cries than those with no physical impairment. These findings suggest that voiceprints may have value as a diagnostic tool.

(4) Diagnosing infant problems is not the only medical use of voiceprints. Psychiatrists have used them to determine emo-

tional stress in patients, and they have aided surgeons in repairing cleft palates.

(5) Law enforcement agencies rely heavily on voiceprints to identify bomb hoaxers, individuals making obscene phone calls, and other persons using telephones for illegal purposes. A voiceprint is taken during the phone call, held until a suspect has been apprehended, and then compared with the suspect's voiceprint. This technique has helped the police obtain numerous convictions.

(6) The use of voiceprints in criminal proceedings has not been without controversy and setbacks, however. In a number of instances, appeals courts have reversed convictions obtained through use of voiceprints, holding that the prints were unreliable. Also, some early studies showed that the percentage of voiceprints mistakenly identified could range as high as 63 percent, thus raising serious doubts about the validity of voiceprints as evidence. More recently, though, (see the January 10, 1972, issue of *Time* magazine) a massive study comparing 34,000 voiceprints has led to the conclusion that they do constitute a reliable means of identification.

(7) With this type of comprehensive evidence, the use of voiceprints in medicine and the courts seem assured for some time to come.

Terri Chapman

Discussion Questions

1. Identify the formal definition sentence in paragraph 1.
2. What is the primary method of development in paragraph 2?
3. Examine the closing paragraph. Which of the concluding techniques mentioned earlier in the chapter does the student use?

Suggestions for Writing

Write a definition paper on one of the following topics. Make sure that your paper includes a formal definition. Expand your topic by the method(s) you consider most appropriate.

1. Urban sprawl
2. Exurbia
3. Salesmanship

4. Feedback
5. Charisma
6. Anesthesia
7. Handgun
8. Viscosity
9. "Grease monkey"
10. Radiation
11. Loyalty
12. Water table
13. Erosion
14. Pitch
15. Encounter group
16. Drag race
17. Refrigeration
18. Police science
19. Hospitality
20. Nutrition
21. Consumerism
22. Preventive dentistry
23. Restorative dentistry
24. Secretary
25. Some term from your field of study

7

Description of an Object

As a student, and later on the job, you may often find it necessary to write a description of an object. An instructor may ask you to describe a pizza cutter, T-square, surveyor's range pole, or some other device. Your employer may call on you to describe a newly developed machine for the shop or factory; the floor plan, heating system, or wiring system of a building; or a dam, TV broadcasting tower, or similar facility. All such descriptions follow a similar pattern of development. For purposes of explanation, however, we will focus on descriptions of relatively small devices.

To write a successful description, you must be thoroughly familiar with the device you are describing. If it can be taken apart and put together again, do so—preferably several times. If manufacturer's literature is available, read it carefully. Learn and use the proper names for the various parts of the device. Finally, have the device on hand so you can check it while you are writing.

A description of an object is made up of three parts:

1. introduction
2. description of major components or functional parts
3. conclusion

These parts are discussed in the sections that follow.

Introduction

The introduction, generally one paragraph long, differs somewhat from the type written for most other papers. In a paper describing an object, the introduction does three things:

1. defines the device being described
2. provides an overall description
3. lists the major components or functional parts

If the definition of the device doesn't make its function clear, a brief explanation of this function should follow the definition.

Ordinarily, a one- or two-sentence definition is adequate. This definition names the device; it places the device in a larger category; and it tells how the device differs from others in the same category. A zipper, for example, might be defined like this:

A zipper is a fastener made up of two rows of metal or plastic teeth that are meshed and separated by a slide.

This sentence shows that the zipper falls into the larger category of fasteners but differs from other fasteners—snaps, hooks, or buttons—in appearance and method of operation.

Like the definition, the explanation of function may be only a sentence or two in length. The function of a zipper might be explained as follows:

It is used to fasten or unfasten adjacent pieces of fabric, as in garments and tents.

The overall description should enable the reader to visualize the device clearly. In writing this portion, be sure to consider every important feature of the device, such as its dimensions, shape, color, weight, and materials of construction. The features that are important, of course, will vary depending upon the particular object. If you are describing a toothbrush, for example, weight is not important. However, weight is an important feature of a portable vacuum-pressure tester and should not be ignored.

When you describe a *particular model* of a device and include dimensions and weight, you must give them exactly. Thus, if you describe an Acme Model 41 rolling pin, you must give the exact length of that model. If, on the other hand, your topic is rolling pins in general, a range of lengths and weights is all you need provide.

You can often make a description clearer by comparing the shape of the device to that of a familiar object. A T-square might be likened to the capital letter "T," for example, or a crescent wrench to a rod with a "C"-shaped opening at one or both ends.

The major components or functional parts should be listed in a sentence or two and numbered if there are more than three. Several logical arrangements are possible. If the parts operate one after the other, you might logically list them according to their order of operation. If the actual function is performed by just one part, you might list that part first. If some parts are concealed from view, you might first list the external parts and then the internal parts.

The following is a typical introduction for a paper describing a device—a dental mouth mirror. As required, the paragraph defines the device, explains its function, describes its appearance, and lists its major components.

> A dental mouth mirror is an instrument used by dentists, dental hygienists, and dental assistants to look inside the mouth and view the patient's teeth. The mirror makes it possible to see tooth surfaces in areas of the mouth that are beyond the range of direct vision. Besides providing increased illumination, it is also a useful retractor of the patient's cheeks and tongue. The glass and metal instrument somewhat resembles a coin with a rod welded at an angle to the edge. It consists of two major parts, the mirror and the handle.
>
> *Lisa Hines*

Description of Major Components or Functional Parts

Once you have listed the major components or functional parts, you are ready to describe them. Except where the information is obvious, you must explain the purpose of each component or part and note any important features—size, shape, materials of construction, and the like. In addition, you must make clear the position of each component or part in relation to the others. Indicating position precisely is sometimes harder than it appears.

For instance, if you describe a T-square, it is not enough to note that the blade is centered to the head at right angles; you must also note the amount of overlap and whether or not the blade is inset into the head. Here is a description of one component of a dental mouth mirror.

> The handle is connected to the mirror by a small screw which extends ½ inch from the edge of the holder and is set at an angle to the plane of the mirror. This screw threads into a socket in the end of the handle. The thick part of the handle is called the shank. It is approximately 2¼ inches in length, with a diameter of ¼ inch. The thinner portion is 2 $\frac{11}{16}$ inches long and has a diameter of ⅛ inch. The handle is made of brushed aluminum or steel.
>
> *Lisa Hines*

In most cases, each part is discussed in a single, separate paragraph. However, with complicated parts that consist of two or more elements, additional paragraphs are often needed.

Conclusion

The conclusion of your paper, usually one paragraph long, can present several kinds of information. One common way to end is to tell the reader how to use the device. For example, a description of a dental mouth mirror might conclude with an explanation of the mirror's use.

> Held with a modified pen grasp and inserted into the mouth, the dental mouth mirror is used to detect cavities and obtain a general idea of the patient's dental needs. It provides immeasurable assistance in detecting stains and deposits on the teeth as well as in locating spots of decay.
>
> *Lisa Hines*

Another kind of conclusion explains how a device operates. This is especially appropriate for a mechanism in which some or all of the functional parts are concealed from view.

Still another effective conclusion emphasizes a particular advantage or feature of the device. For instance, if the device is more efficient, powerful, or economical than some similar device, this type of conclusion may be the most appropriate.

Illustrations

A drawing or photograph of the object or one or more of its parts often accompanies the description. An illustration allows you to write a shorter description and at the same time to convey a more precise impression of the device to your reader. Consider, for instance, how difficult it would be to create an accurate word-picture of a scissors or the head of a claw hammer. With a drawing or photo, conveying this image would not be a problem. Illustrations do not, however, adequately indicate the materials of construction, finish, or use of the device. These you must make clear in your written description.

For external views, both drawings and photographs are suitable. Photographs provide a truer likeness than drawings, but they make no distinction between important and unimportant details. If emphasis is important, it is possible to retouch or crop a photograph to accent desired features. Photographs can rarely be used, however, to show the inside of a device. A drawing is usually needed.

Internal details may be shown with either a cutaway or exploded-view drawing. A cutaway drawing omits part of the casing, allowing the viewer to see the internal parts and their arrangement. An exploded-view drawing shows the device disassembled, with the parts arranged in the same relative position they occupy when it is together. Cutaways are generally used for large devices and exploded views for small, complex ones. Exploded views are especially effective for showing how devices are assembled.

A schematic diagram is a special drawing used to depict electronic and mechanical systems. It differs from other illustrations in that the parts of the system are represented by symbols rather than drawn realistically. For example, a series of alternating long and short lines stands for a battery and a zig-zag line for a resistor. Without schematic diagrams, many systems could not be drawn understandably. Pages 109, 111, and 114 show several types of illustrations.

Although on-the-job writers seldom need to prepare finished drawings, they must often draw the preliminary sketches from which the technical illustrator works. Students, however, must prepare any drawings needed for their papers.

STUDENT EXAMPLES

Toothbrush

(1) A toothbrush is a device for manually cleaning the teeth. The ordinary toothbrush is made of plastic and resembles a miniature clothes brush. It consists of two parts: a handle and a large number of bristles.

(2) The handle holds the bristles and provides a grasping place for the user. It is approximately five-and-one-half inches long, one-half inch wide, and one-fourth inch thick, and it has the same general shape as a Popsicle stick. The bristles are mounted at one end of the handle, and occupy an inch-long section of one surface. A hole is drilled through the handle at a point about one-half inch from the end opposite the bristles. This can be used for hanging up the brush.

(3) The bristles of the toothbrush do the actual cleaning. They are made of stiff nylon or some similar material. Each bristle is about one-half inch long and perhaps one-one hundredth inch in diameter. The bristles are arranged in clumps, and the clumps in turn are arranged in rows. The number of bristles per clump, as well as the number of rows and the number of clumps per row, varies with different brands of brushes. By using different-length bristles in different clumps, it is possible to contour the surface of the bristle section to provide better cleaning action.

Janice Weitl

Discussion Questions

1. Indicate the significance of the following phrases:
   "resembles a miniature clothes brush" (paragraph 1)
   "the same general shape as a Popsicle stick" (paragraph 2)

2. Is the writer describing toothbrushes in general or one particular model? How can you tell?
3. Examine the conclusion. What type of information does the writer present here?

The United States Flag

(1) The United States flag is a banner that symbolizes our nation and its ideals of freedom, liberty, and justice. As such, it is displayed in many different places and on many different occasions. For example, it is displayed routinely in classrooms, courts, and in front of public buildings, as well as on special holidays by business establishments and private citizens. It is also carried in military parades and used to drape caskets at military funerals.

(2) Flags vary greatly in size. All, however, are rectangular, with a width of 1 unit and a length of 1.9 units. These proportions hold regardless of the flag's size. The flag is usually made of nylon or cotton cloth, although it is sometimes imprinted on plastic or metal. It consists of two parts: the union, or star field, and the field of stripes.

(3) When the flag is properly hung in the horizontal position, the rectangular union is in the upper left-hand corner. The union, positioned so that its long dimension runs parallel to the long dimension of the flag, has a length of .79 units and is .5385 the width of the flag. The union contains fifty white stars on a dark blue background. Each star is five-pointed, measures .0616 the width of the flag between opposite points, and is positioned with one point directly upward. The stars are arranged in nine horizontal rows spaced an equal distance apart; the odd-numbered rows contain six stars and the even-numbered rows contain five. The stars are staggered so that each one in the even-numbered rows is directly below the center of the gap between two stars in the odd-numbered row immediately above. Within all rows, adjacent stars are spaced an equal distance from one another.

(4) The field of stripes contains seven red and six white horizontal stripes of equal width, arranged in an alternating pattern with a red stripe uppermost. The top seven stripes extend from the right end of the union to the right edge of the flag. The bottom six stripes extend the entire length of the flag.

(5) Not only the entire flag but also its individual elements have symbolic significance. Thus the thirteen stripes represent the thirteen original states, while the fifty stars represent the fifty states which comprise the nation today.

Shirley McCall

Discussion Questions

1. Identify the definition sentence in paragraph 1 and indicate what it accomplishes.
2. What is the function of the other sentences in paragraph 1?
3. What is accomplished by the following sentence in paragraph 2? "These proportions hold regardless of the flag's size."
4. Why is the first sentence of paragraph 3 necessary?

Imhoff Cone

(1) The Imhoff cone is a measuring device which determines the total amount of settleable solids in one liter of sewage. The sewage sample is placed in the cone and then left undisturbed for one hour, during which time the settleable solids fall to the bottom and can be measured. The device has an overall height of 23 inches, is made of cast iron and Pyrex, and weighs about 5 pounds. It consists of two functional parts: the metal support stand and the cone itself.

(2) The support stand has a rectangular cast iron base 10 inches wide, 6 inches deep, and 1 inch thick. Inserted into the base, equidistant from each side and 2 inches from the end, is a ½-inch solid steel rod which extends 22 inches vertically. Two inches below the top of this rod and extending over the base is a horizontal steel rod 2 inches in length which terminates in a circular steel loop with an inner diameter of 4½ inches. The support stand weighs 4 pounds.

(3) The cone weighs 14 ounces, is 18 inches in height, and is made of clear Pyrex. It resembles a cone used for holding ice cream. The opening at the top is 4¾ inches in diameter, and 1 inch below this opening a horizontal line has been etched into the glass. When the cone is filled to this mark, it contains one liter of sewage sample. At the pointed end is a graduated scale made up of forty units, with every tenth unit indicated by a numeral.

IMHOFF CONE AND SUPPORT STAND

Scale — ⅜″ = 1″

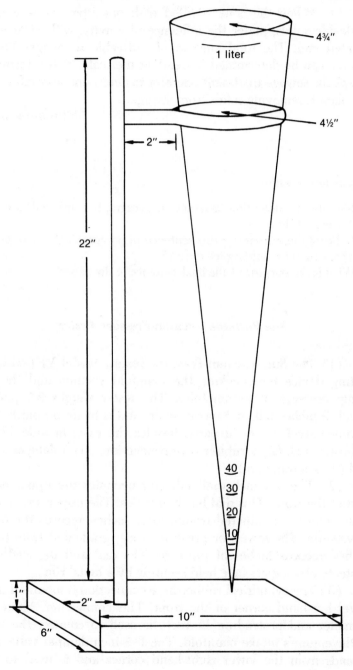

This scale indicates, in milliliters, the amount of solids that has settled.

(4) When the cone is filled with one liter of sewage, the settleable solids, under the influence of gravity, will settle to the pointed end. The total amount of settleable solids per liter of sewage can be determined by reading the scale. This information allows the sewage treatment operator to determine how effectively the plant is removing solids from sewage.

Philip Boesenecker

Discussion Questions

1. Identify the definition sentence in paragraph 1 and indicate what it accomplishes.
2. Indicate the purpose of this sentence in paragraph 3: "It resembles a cone used for holding ice cream."
3. What is the purpose of the final sentence of the paper?

Sun Portable Vacuum-Pressure Tester

(1) The Sun Vacuum-Pressure Tester, Model VPT-212, is a testing device for checking the manifold vacuum and the fuel pump pressure of automobiles. The tester weighs 2.5 pounds, stands 9 inches tall, is 5 inches wide, and is made primarily from stamped steel. Its main parts, besides the case, include (1) an indicator dial, (2) a rubber-hose connection, (3) a damper valve, and (4) a sensing unit.

(2) The 3¾-inch dial indicator occupies the upper center part of the front. This dial has two scales. The upper, or vacuum, scale, which is graduated from 0 to 22 inches, records the inches of vacuum. The lower, or pressure, scale, graduated from 0 to 7 inches, records inches of pressure. The dial and its needle are protected by a glass face held securely by a metal rim.

(3) The cylindrical rubber-hose connection is mounted in the lower left-hand corner of the front. This connection, ⅜ inch in diameter and protruding ½ inch, is used to connect the tester to the engine's intake manifold. The 1½-inch damper valve knob extends from the lower right-hand corner and is used to slow

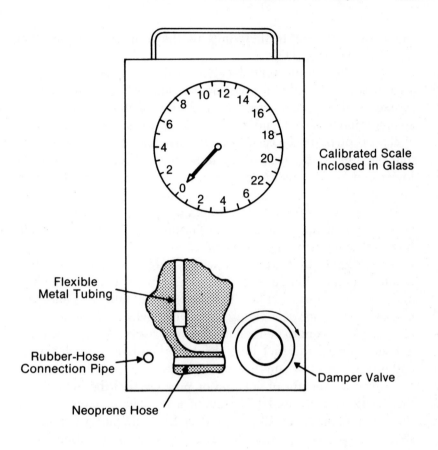

Calibrated Scale
Inclosed in Glass

Flexible
Metal Tubing

Rubber-Hose
Connection Pipe

Damper Valve

Neoprene Hose

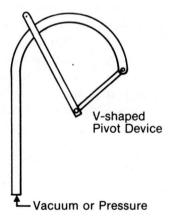

V-shaped
Pivot Device

Vacuum or Pressure

VACUUM-PRESSURE TESTER

down the back-and-forth swings of the indicator needle when a pressure reading is taken.

(4) The sensing unit, located inside the case, consists of a vacuum-pressure tube, a pivot device, and a hose. The vacuum-pressure tube is made from thin, flexible metal tubing and resembles the crooked end of a walking cane. One end of the V-shaped pivot device is connected to the top of the vacuum tube and the other to the base of the indicator needle. Attached to the lower end of the vacuum tube is a neoprene hose, which is fastened at its other end to the interior opening of the cylindrical hose connection. This hose passes through a clamp arrangement at the rear of the damper valve knob. Turning the knob pinches the hose and slows the swings of the needle.

(5) Connecting the tester with a rubber hose to the intake manifold of a running engine creates a partial vacuum in the hose and vacuum-pressure tube. This causes the tube to bend in a clockwise direction, activating the pivot device and allowing the amount of vacuum to be read on the upper scale. When the tester is connected to the fuel line, the tube bends counterclockwise, and pressure is shown on the lower scale.

(6) The amount of vacuum or pressure and the behavior of the needle can be used to diagnose a number of engine conditions. For example, at idling speeds a 15- to 22-inch vacuum and steady needle indicate that the engine is in good operating condition. If, however, the needle occasionally flicks rapidly down and back 4 inches, the engine has one or more sticky valves. A low, steady reading indicates a vacuum leak, and a slightly low, steady reading indicates a retarded ignition. An excessively low pressure reading (for most models of cars 2–4 pounds is normal) indicates a worn fuel pump, whereas an excessively high pressure reading indicates that the pump diaphragm is too tight.

Peter Cataldo

Discussion Questions

1. Does the introduction to this paper meet the requirements presented in the chapter? Explain.
2. Indicate the purpose of these phrases in paragraph 4:
   "resembles the crooked end of a walking cane"
   "the V-shaped pivot device"

3. This paper is accompanied by a cutaway drawing. Why is this type of drawing appropriate?

Clutch Pencil

(1) The clutch pencil is a draftsman's tool that holds drawing lead. It is designed to feed the lead with an assist from gravity when a release button is pressed. In overall appearance, the pencil resembles an ordinary ballpoint pen. It is constructed of plastic, brass, and steel. The components of the clutch pencil are (1) the barrel, (2) the plunger, (3) the tip, (4) the chuck, (5) the spring, and (6) the release button.

(2) The barrel, or main housing, is a hexagonal, pressure-molded plastic tube, which is 4⅜ inches long and ¹¹⁄₃₂ inch wide between opposite surfaces. One end is rounded and externally threaded for a distance of ⁷⁄₁₆ inch. The barrel is bored from the unthreaded end to a diameter of ⁹⁄₃₂ inch and to a depth of 3¾ inches. The remainder of the barrel, which constitutes the round section, is bored through to a diameter of ⁵⁄₃₂ inch.

(3) The tip is a tapered brass tube 1¼ inches long and ¹¹⁄₃₂ inch in diameter at the big end. The outside tapers down to ⁵⁄₁₆ inch over a distance of ⅞ inch and then tapers to ¼ inch at the small end. The ⅞-inch portion is knurled to provide a grip. The big end of the tip is threaded internally to a depth of ⁷⁄₁₆ inch. There is an internal taper at the small end, which has a large diameter of ⁷⁄₃₂ inch and a depth of ³⁄₁₆ inch. The remainder of the tip is drilled through to a ⁵⁄₃₂-inch diameter.

(4) The plunger is a brass tube 4½ inches long with a .145-inch outside diameter and a .100-inch inside diameter. One end is threaded internally to a depth of ¼ inch. Two ferrules of ¼-inch diameter and .040-inch thickness are swaged to the outside of the tube. One is 1¼ inches from the threaded end and the other is ½ inch from the unthreaded end.

(5) The chuck is a steel tube ⅞ inch long which is split into three fingers along ⅝ inch of its length. The split end has a double taper starting at a ⅛-inch diameter and increasing to a ⁷⁄₃₂-inch diameter in ⁵⁄₃₂ inch of its length and then returning to a ⅛-inch diameter in another ⁵⁄₃₂ inch of length. The remainder of the chuck is ⅛ inch in diameter and is threaded for ³⁄₁₆ inch

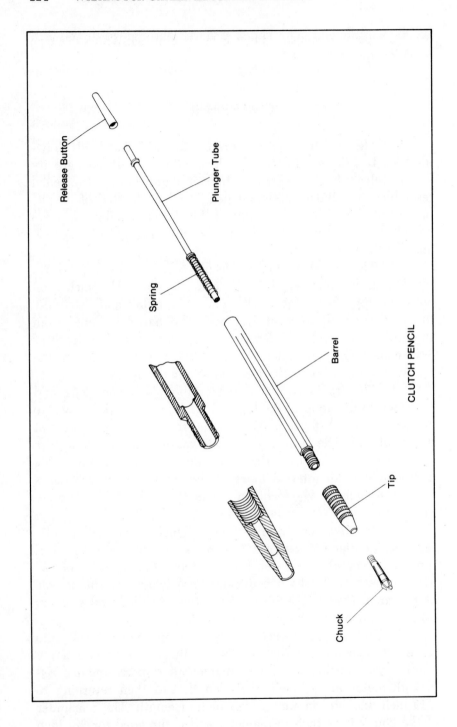

on the unsplit end. The chuck is bored through to a .080-inch diameter.

(6) The spring is #8-gage music wire, has an outside diameter of ¼ inch, 13 coils, and a free length of 1 inch.

(7) The release button is made of brass and is chrome plated. It is ⅞ inch long and tapers from a ¼-inch diameter to a ³⁄₁₆-inch diameter. The button is bored on the large end to a diameter of .145 inch and a depth of ⅝ inch.

(8) The clutch pencil is assembled as follows. Screw the tip onto the barrel, fit the spring over the threaded end of the plunger and the button over the unthreaded end until they seat against the ferrules, insert the plunger and spring into the top of the barrel, insert the small threaded end of the chuck into the tip, and while depressing the button, screw the chuck into the plunger tube. The chuck will now release and grip a piece of drafting lead inserted into it as the button is pressed and released.

student unknown

Discussion Questions

1. The writer gives the overall description of this device in a single sentence but uses six paragraphs to describe the individual parts. Explain this difference in length.
2. Paragraph 8 deals with assembling the pen, a topic not ordinarily part of the description of an object. Why is assembly discussed in this paper?
3. This paper is accompanied by an exploded-view drawing. Why is this type of drawing appropriate?

Suggestions for Writing

Write a paper describing one of the following objects. Develop your paper by following the instructions presented in this chapter.

1. Ball-point pen
2. Baster
3. Bite-wing X-ray film unit
4. Burette
5. Chalkboard eraser
6. Chapstick

7. Crescent wrench
8. Draftsman's compass
9. Filter-tip cigarette
10. Flathead screw
11. Hydrometer
12. Hypodermic syringe
13. Pizza cutter
14. Putty knife
15. Rolling pin
16. Safety pin
17. Screw driver
18. Sparkplug
19. Sparkplug gapper
20. Tire pressure gauge
21. Tire pump
22. T-square
23. X-ray film cassette

8

Letters and Memorandums

Letters and memorandums are by far the most common types of written communication in almost every career field. They are used for countless purposes but especially to ask questions, provide answers, place orders, register or respond to complaints, and give instructions. In this chapter we will discuss the most frequently used types of letters and memorandums, as well as the basic elements common to all. Since well-written, courteous memos and letters materially enhance both your own image and that of your organization, the ability to prepare them is vital to your professional success.

Basics of Business Letters

LETTER FORMATS

There are three standard formats for business letters: modified block (sometimes called balanced block), semiblock, and full block.

In the *modified block format*, the heading, the complimentary close, and the signature start at the center of the page.

All other elements, including first lines of paragraphs, begin at the left-hand margin. The *semiblock format* is identical to the modified block except that the first line of each paragraph is indented from the left, usually five spaces. In the *full block format*, every line in the letter begins at the left-hand margin. The pattern letters on pages 119–121 show these three formats.

PARTS OF THE LETTER

The business letter has six basic parts:

1. heading
2. inside address
3. salutation
4. body
5. complimentary close
6. signature

In addition, a letter may include one or more of the following: attention line, subject line, stenographic reference, enclosure notation, and carbon copy notation. If a letter is longer than a single page, a special heading is required for each additional page (see page 127).

Heading   If you are typing a letter on plain white stationery, the heading consists of your address—street, city, state, and zip code—and the date. Each word of the heading should be spelled out in full. Even the state and the month should not be abbreviated. Here is a typical typed heading:

325 South Michigan Avenue
Big Rapids, Michigan 49307
October 6, 1976

The position of the heading depends, of course, on the letter format. If you are using the full block format, the heading begins at the left-hand margin. With the modified block or semiblock format, it begins at the center of the page.

Business letters often are not written on plain white stationery, however, but on company letterhead. This letterhead is

209 Foster Hall
Case Western Reserve University
Cleveland, Ohio 44106   **(Heading)**
November 15, 1976

Mr. Francis C. Rhyte
Assistant Advertising Manager
Mine Safety Appliances Company   **(Inside Address)**
400 Penn Center Boulevard
Pittsburgh, Pennsylvania 15235

Dear Mr. Rhyte: **(Salutation)**

Thank you for XXXX XXXXXXXXXXXXXXX XXX XX XXXXX XXXXXXXXXXXXXXXX XXX
XXXX XX XXXXXXXX XXXXXXXXXX X XXXXXXXX XXX XXXXXXX XXXXXX XXX
XXXXXXXX XXXXXXXXXXXXX XXXXX XXXXXXXX XXXX XXXXX X XX XXXXXX
XXXXXXXXXXX XXX XXX XXXXXXXXX

I have reviewed XXX XXXX XXXXXXXX XXXX XXXXX XXXXXXXX XXXX ˙XXXXX
XXXXXX XX XXXXXXXX XX XXXX XX XXXXXXXX XXXXXXXXXXXXXX XX XXXXX
XXXX XX XXXXXXXXXXXXX XXXX XXXXXXXXX XX XXXXXX XXXXX XXX XXX X
XXXXXX XX XXXXXXXXX XXXXXX X XXXX XXXXXXXXXXX XX XXXXXXXXXX
XXXXXXXXXXX XXXX XX XXXXXX X XXXXXX XX XXXXXXXXX XXX XXXXXXXXXXXXX   **(Body)**
XXXX XXXXXXXXXX XXXX XXXXX XX XX XXXXXX XXXXXXXXXXXXX XXXXXXXXX
XXX XXXXXXXX XXXXXXX XXXX XXXXXXXXXXXXX

When I have XXXXXXXX X XXXX XXXXXX XXXXX XXXXXXXX XX X XXXXXX
XXXX XXXXXX XXXX XXXXXXXXXXXXX XXX XXXXXXXXXX XX XXXX XXX XXXXXXX
XXX XXXXXXXX XX XXXXXXXXX X XXXX XXXXXX XX XXXX XX XXX XXXXXXXX
XXX XXXXX XX XXXXXXXXXXX XXXXX XXXXXXXX XXXX XXXXXX XXXXXX XXXXXX
XXXX XXXXXXX XX XXXXX XX X XXXXXXXXXXXXXX XX XXXX XXXXX

Your assistance will XXXXXXXXXXX XXXXXX XX XXXXX XX XX XXXXXXXXX
XXX XXXXXXXXXXXXXXX XX XXX XXXX XXX XXXXXXXXXXXXXXXXXX XXXXX
XXXXXXXX

Sincerely yours,   **(Complimentary Close)**

Paul M. Leonelli   **(Signature)**

MODIFIED BLOCK FORMAT

209 Foster Hall
Case Western Reserve University
Cleveland, Ohio 44106   (Heading)
November 15, 1976

Mr. Francis C. Rhyte
Assistant Advertising Manager
Mine Safety Appliances Company   (Inside Address)
400 Penn Center Boulevard
Pittsburgh, Pennsylvania 15235

Dear Mr. Rhyte: (Salutation)

    Thank you for XXXX XXXXXXXXXXX XXX XX XXXXX XXXXXXXXXXXXXXX XXX
XXXX XX XXXXXXXX XXXXXXXXXX X XXXXXXXX XXX XXXXXXX XXXXXX XXX
XXXXXXXXXXXXX XXXXXXXXXXXXX XXXXXXX XXXXXXXX XXXX XXXXXX X XX XXXXXX
XXXXXXXXXXXX XXX XXX XXXXXXXXX

    I have reviewed XXX XXXX XXXXXXXX XXXX XXXXXX XXXXXXXX XXXX XXXXX
XXXXXX XX XXXXXXXXXXX XX XXXX XX XXXXXXX XXXXXXXXXXXXXX XX XXXXX
XXXX XX XXXXXXXXXXXXX XXXX XXXXXXXXX XX XXXXXXX XXXXXX XXX XXX X
XXXXXX XX XXXXXXXXXX XXXXXXX X XXXX XXXXXXXXXX XX XXXXXXXXXX
XXXXXXXXX XXXX XX XXXXX X XXXXXX XX XXXXXXXXX XXX XXXXXXXXXXXXXX   (Body)
XXXX XXXXXXXXXXXXX XXXX XXXXXX XX XX XXXXXX XXXXXXXXXX XXXXXXXXX
XXX XXXXXXX XXXXXXX XXXX XXXXXXXXXXXX

    When I have XXXXXXXX X XXXX XXXXXX XXXXX XXXXXXXX XX X XXXXXX
XXXX XXXXXX XXXX XXXXXXXXXXXX XXX XXXXXXXXXX XX XXXX XXX XXXXXXX
XXX XXXXXXXX XX XXXXXXXXX X XXXX XXXXXX XX XXXX XX XXX XXXXXXXX
XXX XXXXX XX XXXXXXXXXX XXXXX XXXXXXX XXXX XXXXXX XXXXXX XXXXXX
XXXX XXXXXXX XX XXXXX XX X XXXXXXXXXXXXXX XX XXXX XXXXX

    Your assistance will XXXXXXXXXX XXXXXX XX XXXXXX XX XX XXXXXXXXX
XXX XXXXXXXXXXXXXXX XX XXX XXXX XXX XXXXXXXXXXXXXXXXXXX XXXXX
XXXXXXXX

                      Sincerely yours,   (Complimentary Close)

                      Paul M. Leonelli   (Signature)

SEMIBLOCK FORMAT

209 Foster Hall
Case Western Reserve University
Cleveland, Ohio 44106   (Heading)
November 15, 1976

Mr. Francis C. Rhyte
Assistant Advertising Manager
Mine Safety Appliances Company   (Inside Address)
400 Penn Center Boulevard
Pittsburgh, Pennsylvania 15235

Dear Mr. Rhyte: (Salutation)

Thank you for XXXX XXXXXXXXXXXXX XXX XX XXXXX XXXXXXXXXXXXX XXX
XXXX XX XXXXXXXX XXXXXXXXX X XXXXXXXX XXX XXXXXXX XXXXXX XXX
XXXXXXXX XXXXXXXXXXXXX XXXXXX XXXXXXX XXXX XXXXX X XX XXXXXX
XXXXXXXXXXX XXX XXX XXXXXXXXX

I have reviewed XXX XXXX XXXXXXXX XXXX XXXXXX XXXXXXXX XXXX XXXXX
XXXXXX XX XXXXXXX XX XXXX XX XXXXXXX XXXXXXXXXXXXX XX XXXXX
XXXX XX XXXXXXXXXXXXX XXXX XXXXXXXXXX XX XXXXXXX XXXXXX XXX XXX X
XXXXXX XX XXXXXXXXXX XXXXXXX X XXXX XXXXXXXXXXX XX XXXXXXXXXX
XXXXXXXX XXXX XX XXXXXX X XXXXXX XX XXXXXXXXX XXX XXXXXXXXXXXXX   (Body)
XXXX XXXXXXXXXX XXX XXXXX XX XX XXXXXX XXXXXXXXXXXXXX XXXXXXXX
XXX XXXXXXX XXXXXXX XXXX XXXXXXXXXXXX

When I have XXXXXXXX X XXXX XXXXXX XXXXX XXXXXXXX XX X XXXXXX
XXXX XXXXXX XXXX XXXXXXXXXXX XXX XXXXXXXXX XX XXXX XXX XXXXXX
XXX XXXXXXXX XX XXXXXXXX X XXXX XXXXXX XX XXXX XX XXX XXXXXXXX
XXX XXXXX XX XXXXXXXXXX XXXXX XXXXXXX XXXX XXXXX XXXXX XXXXX
XXXX XXXXXXX XX XXXXX XX X XXXXXXXXXXXXX XX XXXX XXXXX

Your assistance will XXXXXXXXXX XXXXXX XX XXXXX XX XX XXXXXXXXX
XXX XXXXXXXXXXXXXXX XX XXX XXXX XXX XXXXXXXXXXXXXXXX XXXXX
XXXXXXXX

Sincerely yours,   (Complimentary Close)

Paul M. Leonelli   (Signature)

FULL BLOCK FORMAT

preprinted with the organization's name and address. The only part of the heading that you have to type is the date. This is positioned, depending on the format you are using, at the left-hand margin or centered, two or three lines below the preprinted address.

Inside Address   The inside address gives the name and address of the organization or person to whom you are writing. The position of the inside address is the same for all three formats. It begins at the left-hand margin, two line spaces below the date in long letters and three to eight line spaces in shorter ones. The shorter the letter, the more space you use.

When writing to an individual, give his or her personal title and full name in the first line.

Mr. Harold L. Calloway
Professor Morris Berger
Miss Jane Fontaine
Mrs. Myra R. McPhail
Ms. Noreen Wyman

"Ms." is an accepted title of address for both married and single women. Unless you know that a woman uses "Miss" or "Mrs." as a personal title, you should address her as "Ms." For rules governing abbreviations of personal titles, see page 304.

The individual's job title, if there is one, should follow the name. It may appear on the same line as the name or one line below it.

Ms. Noreen Wyman, Comptroller
Mr. Harold L. Calloway
Personnel Manager

If you know the job title but not the name of the person you wish to reach, begin the inside address with the title.

Vice-President for Research
Chairman, Board of Directors

In this situation, you can also omit the title from the inside address and include it instead in an attention line (see page 125).

When both name and title are unknown, begin with the organization's name.

Rockland Manufacturing Company

A complete inside address should look like this:

Mr. Mark Thornton
Director of Sales
White-Inland, Inc.
1100 Front Street
Baltimore, Maryland 21202

Except for the personal title, avoid abbreviations in the inside address unless the organization to which you are writing uses an abbreviation such as "Inc.," "Corp.," or "Co." in its official title.

Salutation   The salutation, a formal greeting, begins at the left-hand margin. It is positioned two lines below the inside address. When you write to an individual, the salutation takes this form:

Dear Mrs. Nowicki:
Dear Ms. McCarthy:
Dear Dr. Corelli:

Letters addressed to job titles use the salutation "Dear Sir" or "Dear Madam." Those addressed to organizations use "Gentlemen." Like the above examples, each of these salutations should be followed by a colon.

Body   The body of the letter contains the message you wish to convey. It begins two lines below the salutation, unless a subject line intervenes (see page 125). Ordinarily, the body of a letter is single-spaced, with an extra line space between paragraphs. If the letter contains only one brief paragraph, it may be double-spaced. For letters written in a semiblock format, indent the first line of each paragraph five spaces. The paragraphs of modified block and full block letters begin at the left-hand margin. For easy readability, try to keep the paragraphs short—five or six lines whenever possible.

Complimentary Close   The complimentary close, a formal good-bye, is placed two lines below the last line of the body. In modified block and semiblock formats, it begins at the page's center, and in the full block format, at the left-hand margin. The most common forms are:

> Yours truly,
> Sincerely yours,
> Sincerely,

Other complimentary closes include "Cordially yours," appropriate when you are writing to someone you know well, and "Respectfully yours," used to show special esteem.

Note that in each case only the first word is capitalized. The second word, always lower-cased, is followed by a comma.

Signature   Your typewritten signature appears four lines directly below the complimentary close. If you are writing a letter on behalf of your company, your name should be followed by your title and department. This will enable the person to whom you are writing to reply directly to you.

> James W. Terry
> Manager, Finance Department

A woman may choose to include her personal title in the typewritten signature. This should be enclosed in parentheses.

> (Mrs.) Mary Beeman
> (Miss) Nancy Parker
> (Ms.) Sandra O'Reilly

In the four-line space above the typed signature, sign your name in longhand.

Your company may specify that its legal name should appear

with your signature. This name is then typed in capital letters one line below the complimentary close and four lines above the typewritten signature.

Sincerely yours,
THE MORTON CORPORATION

James W. Terry
Manager, Finance Department

Attention Line   The attention line—only occasionally employed —is useful when you know only the last name or the job title of the person to whom you are writing. It is positioned between the inside address and the salutation, with an extra line space above and below, and it begins at the left-hand margin. Whenever you include an attention line, you omit the recipient's name and title from the inside address and begin with the name of the organization. Since the salutation is determined by the first line of the inside address, the appropriate salutation is "Gentlemen."

White-Inland, Inc.
1100 Front Street
Baltimore, Maryland 21202

Attention: Mr. Thornton

Gentlemen:

Subject Line   The subject line tells what the letter is about. It is used to refer to a specific policy number, file number, invoice number, or the like.

Subject: Your invoice LR-237
Subject: Account number 78-375-162

The subject line is positioned between the salutation and the body, with one space above and below. In semiblock letters, the subject line can be either indented five spaces or centered on the page. In other formats, it begins at the left-hand margin.

Stenographic Reference   The stenographic reference is used when someone other than the writer types the letter. It includes two sets of initials—the writer's, in capital letters, and the typist's, in lower-case letters.

The two sets may be separated by a colon or slash mark, as shown below.

    DLS:crt
    DLS/crt

The reference appears two lines below the last line of the signature and starts at the left-hand margin.

Enclosure Notation   Whenever a brochure, drawing, check, money order, or other document accompanies a letter, an enclosure notation should be typed on the line following the stenographic reference. This can be the word "Enclosure" or the abbreviation "Enc." If more than one document accompanies a letter, it is a good idea to indicate the number of items enclosed.

    DLS:crt
    Enclosure
    DLS/crt
    Enc. 2

Documents of special importance are often specifically named.

    DLS/crt
    Enc. Contract

Carbon Copy Notation   A carbon copy notation is used whenever one or more carbon copies of a letter are sent out. This notation is made up of the lower-case letters "cc" followed by a colon and the name of the person to whom the carbon is being sent. If more than one person is receiving a carbon, type the additional name or names directly below the first name.

cc: Dr. N. R. Prince
cc: Ms. S. L. Johnson
   Mr. N. A. Ames

The carbon copy notation is positioned on the line following the stenographic or enclosure notation.

Headings for Additional Pages   Although most business letters are a single page in length, additional pages are occasionally required. These pages are always typed on plain white stationery, with the same left and right margins as on the first page.

   Each additional page must have a heading, which includes the reader's name, the date, and the page designation. Leave six lines of space at the top of the sheet above the heading. For the heading itself, any of the three styles shown below is acceptable:

Ms. Jennifer Arnett   2   July 23, 1976
Ms. Jennifer Arnett,   July 23, 1976,   page 2
Ms. Jennifer Arnett
July 23, 1976
Page 2

Below the heading, leave two lines of space before starting the continuation of the letter.

PUNCTUATION

Almost all business letters now use open punctuation. This style omits all end-of-line punctuation in the heading, inside address, typewritten signature, and any special part, such as the subject line or enclosure notation. Only when a line ends with an abbreviation is a period used. A colon follows the salutation, and a comma follows the complimentary close. The sample letters in this chapter illustrate open punctuation.

MARGINS

Proper margins enhance your letter's attractiveness and thus the chances that your message will be well received.

   The size of the margins will depend on your letter's length.

The longer the letter, the narrower the margins will be. For a full-page letter (roughly two to three hundred words), use 1-inch side margins and type the first line of the inside address 2½ inches below the top of the sheet. For a shorter letter (one to two hundred words), use 1½-inch side margins and begin the inside address 3 inches below the top of the sheet. For a very brief letter (fifty to a hundred words), use 2-inch side margins and begin the inside address 3½ inches from the top of the sheet. (With certain letterhead stationery, you may have to vary the size of the top margin somewhat.) Bottom and top margins should be roughly the same size. In overall appearance, the letter should resemble a matted picture.

LANGUAGE AND TONE

In writing business letters, strive for an easy, natural tone. Avoid such pompous expressions as "It has come to my attention that . . . ," "Enclosed please find . . . ," and "We wish to acknowledge receipt of . . ." Say instead, "I have learned . . . ," "We are enclosing . . . ," and "We have received . . ." But while avoiding pompous language, also steer clear of slang and overly casual phrasing. Language that is too casual may lead your reader to doubt your sincerity. The language of your letter, in short, should be the same as the language you would use in a business conversation—friendly and courteous.

Courtesy is as important in business letters as it is in face-to-face dealings with others. You can write courteous letters by following a few simple pointers. First, and most obvious, never use insults and sarcasm. These only create ill will. Be sure, too, to avoid expressions that may arouse your reader's resentment. When you say, "We have your letter *claiming* that the oscilloscopes we sold you were defective," you call the reader's honesty into question. When you say, "*It is our position that* our offer is very attractive," you imply that the reader is a quarrelsome person likely to take issue with you. It is a simple matter to rephrase these expressions to convey a friendly, courteous tone.

We are sorry to learn that the oscilloscopes we sold you were defective.

We think you will find our offer very attractive.

Cold impersonality is as destructive to courtesy as are sarcasm and insults. Consider the following letter.

Dear Mr. Furman:

Reference is made to the agreement between you and us dated March 17, 1975, in which you contracted to provide cafeteria catering services for our employees.

In accordance with Paragraph 5(b) of the said agreement, we have elected to discontinue your services. Accordingly, the said agreement is hereby terminated in accordance with its terms without any further obligation or liabilities between the parties.

Sincerely yours,

This letter handles the cancellation in an abrupt, unfeeling manner. The caterer has undoubtedly expended considerable effort in coordinating and developing his services. Common courtesy demands both an expression of regret and an explanation for the action.

Whenever you present information that will be disagreeable to the reader, try to do so in a positive manner. The following example shows the improved tone that results when a negative statement is rephrased as a positive one.

Dear Mr. Furman:

I am very sorry to inform you that we find it necessary to cancel your contract to provide cafeteria catering services. As you know, paragraph 5(b) provides for this cancellation.

Fifteen months ago, when we signed our agreement, we had approximately one hundred more employees in our plant than we have today. Our recent commitment to automated production makes further employee transfers likely in the near future.

Therefore, cafeteria sales would not be high enough to justify any further expense on our part or on yours.

Thank you for the excellent service you have provided. We share your disappointment and wish you every success with your catering services.

Sincerely yours,

By adopting a natural, courteous, and positive tone, you will write letters that reflect favorably on both your organization and yourself.

Letters of Inquiry and Replies

LETTERS OF INQUIRY

A letter of inquiry asks for information. There are numerous situations in which you would write such a letter. You may, for example, wish:

1. more detailed performance data or specifications on a piece of equipment your company might buy
2. a fuller explanation of one aspect of a research project described in a magazine article
3. additional details about a safety program or an employee-rating system developed by another organization
4. clarification of an inadequate or ambiguous set of directions
5. statistical data for a term paper

In writing a letter of inquiry, identify yourself, indicate the general subject, and state clearly that you are seeking information. Be sure to explain why you need or how you plan to use the information you are requesting, for many organizations are understandably reluctant to supply information for unknown purposes. Further, unless in some instance it seems inappropriate to do so, mention why you are writing to that particular individual or organization rather than to another. This gives your reader a greater sense of your purposefulness and also affords you an opportunity to make some favorable comment that will increase your chances of gaining the information you desire.

> I read with interest your article in the November 1975 issue of *Health* magazine, in which you mention your survey of smoking regulations in Michigan hospitals.

> I am a college student on a trainee assignment, and I would like to conduct a similar survey of hospitals in our state. Would you be kind enough to help me by answering the following questions?

Once you've explained the reason for the inquiry, list the actual questions or points you wish answered. This section should be planned so as to inconvenience the reader as little as possible. Keep questions to a minimum, make them brief, and whenever possible word them so they can be answered in a few short sentences. If you ask three or more questions, set them up in a numbered list. Numbering the questions will make it less likely that the reader will accidentally fail to answer one. Finally, indicate that you'll welcome any additional comments the reader can provide.

To increase your chances of a favorable response, give careful thought to possible ways you can repay your reader for the help provided. If, for instance, you want information for use in a survey, you might offer a copy of the survey when it is completed. Sometimes, of course, it will not be possible for you to repay the reader.

Close the letter with an expression of appreciation. A simple "Thank you for any help you can give me" or "Any information you can provide will be appreciated" would be an appropriate closing. Never use the phrase "Thank you in advance for your help," which sounds pompous and suggests there's no chance you'll be turned down. Some readers may interpret this as a pressure tactic and therefore refuse your request.

Letters asking that directions be supplied or clarified follow a pattern somewhat different from other letters of inquiry. Begin by stating your problem and the inconvenience it has caused and then follow with your request for the directions. Conclude by asking that the reader respond as quickly as possible. Maintain a courteous tone throughout the letter.

REPLIES TO INQUIRY LETTERS

Replies to letters of inquiry can be favorable or unfavorable. In either case, answer as soon as possible, preferably within one day.

Begin favorable replies by thanking the reader for the inquiry and indicating that you are supplying the requested information or will do so soon. Your opening might look something like this:

> Thank you for your letter of June 15. We are happy to outline our procedure for testing soil samples for their moisture content.

Such a beginning will leave the reader with a favorable impression of your organization. If you must refer an inquiry to another individual or department for an answer, tell your reader you have done so and, if possible, name a date by which the answer can be expected.

If you are supplying the information requested, take up each question in the order asked, answering it as thoroughly as is necessary. If the questions are written in paragraph form, you may have to restate each briefly before answering. If they are presented as a numbered list, number your answers correspondingly. Whenever possible, make your job easier by including brochures, reports, or other materials which contain the desired information. There is no reason to compose lengthy answers yourself when printed materials are available. If you cannot supply an answer, either because you don't know or because the information is confidential, say so and give the reason. Never by-pass a question without comment. If you have additional material that the reader may find useful, end the letter by offering this information.

Letters that respond to customers' requests for directions differ slightly from letters supplying other types of information. Since the reader may have suffered serious inconvenience due to the lack of directions, begin by apologizing for any difficulties that might have been caused. For example:

> I am sorry to learn that our directions for assembling the center tentpole of our Model A37 four-person tent were inadequate. If you follow the steps below, you should have no further trouble.

Note that this apology does not dispute, even indirectly, any charge that the directions may have been inadequate.

In most cases the customer does not send a list of questions but simply asks for clarification of all or part of the directions supplied with a product he or she has purchased. In responding, include as many points as are needed for clarification. Set these up as a numbered list, so that the reader can clearly see the separate steps. As in the longer paper explaining a process (see chapter 5), present these steps in the form of commands and arrange them in the sequence in which they are to be carried out. If two steps must be performed simultaneously, warn the reader at the start of the first step. If there is a chance that the reader will not understand the reason for a step, explain it. If there is a danger that the reader will perform a step improperly, provide a warning.

End the letter as you would any favorable reply to an inquiry —express the hope that the information will prove helpful and offer to provide further help if it is needed.

> I hope this information will help you. If you have any further questions, please don't hesitate to let me know.

Writing a good refusal letter is not easy. Unless you exercise the utmost tact, you are likely to offend your reader. Whatever the reason for your refusal, try to be courteous and helpful throughout.

Begin by thanking the reader for the request. Then, having established a pleasant tone, state your refusal and explain why you cannot comply. Be specific here. Don't, for example, merely say that compliance would violate company policy—point out why it is unwise or impossible. Avoid any suggestion that the reader might misuse the information if it were to be supplied. This would only cause animosity.

Whenever you can, soften your refusal by offering other information or helpful suggestions. Perhaps you can supply articles, bulletins, or reports that will prove useful. Or maybe you can suggest another source the reader can turn to. Take some time to consider the possibilities; the good will generated will amply repay your efforts.

The ending of the letter should be as courteous and helpful as the opening. Wish the reader success in the venture that prompted the inquiry and offer to provide assistance in other matters.

STUDENT EXAMPLES

Texas Health and Safety Association
516 Main Street
Houston, Texas 38201

April 20, 1976

Mr. Thomas S. Seeley
Michigan Health Organization
1234 Jones Street
Grand Rapids, Michigan 49504

Dear Mr. Seeley:

I read with interest your article in the November 1975 issue of Health magazine in which you mention your survey of smoking regulations in Michigan hospitals.

I am a college student on a trainee assignment, and I would like to conduct a similar survey of hospitals in our state. Would you be kind enough to help me by answering the following questions?

1. How were the hospitals contacted--by phone or letter?

2. Were all hospitals in the state contacted, or just a representative sample?

3. What did you accomplish by this survey?

Any information you can provide will be appreciated. When I have completed my survey, I will be happy to send you a copy of the results.

Sincerely,

James T. Brown
Field Trainee

MICHIGAN HEALTH ORGANIZATION
1234 JONES STREET
GRAND RAPIDS, MICHIGAN 49504

April 24, 1976

Mr. James T. Brown, Field Trainee
Texas Health and Safety Association
516 Main Street
Houston, Texas 38201

Dear Mr. Brown:

Thank you for your letter of April 20, 1976, requesting information about the survey we conducted to determine if smoking is permitted in hospitals.

We hope the following answers to your questions will be helpful:

1. Hospitals were contacted by letter, addressed personally to the administrator. Each letter included a questionnaire and return envelope. (A sample of each is enclosed.) If a reply was not received within ten days, a follow-up letter was then mailed or a personal contact made.

2. All hospitals in the state were contacted in order to obtain a more complete analysis.

3. Hospitals became more aware of the hazards of permitting smoking around people who were already ill; consequently, many changed their regulations to permit smoking only in specified areas.

Under separate cover we are sending you a complete copy of our survey results and also samples of our smoking literature.

We are pleased that you are planning a similar survey in your state and will be more than happy to receive the results when completed. If we can assist you further, please let us know.

Sincerely,

Thomas S. Seeley

Thomas S. Seeley
Program Director

TSS/cef
Enc. 2

Discussion Questions

1. Are these letters typed in the modified block, semiblock, or full block format? How can you tell?
2. Do these letters meet the main requirements for inquiry letters and favorable responses to such letters? Be specific when answering.
3. The stenographic reference "TSS/cef" appears on Thomas Seeley's letter, but no similar reference appears on James Brown's letter. Explain.

239 Vandercook Hall
Ferris State College
Big Rapids, Michigan 49307
March 18, 1976

Mr. H. C. Fischer
Oak Ridge National Laboratory
Post Office Box X
Oak Ridge, Tennessee 37830

Dear Mr. Fischer:

I am a student in the refrigeration, heating, and air-conditioning
program at Ferris State College. This term I am enrolled in a special
studies course, investigating current trends in the use of solar heating
and cooling for residences. My main interest centers on solar collectors
which employ water as the heat transfer medium and which are used in
conjunction with a heat pump.

Recently, I read of your work on the Annual Cycle Energy System and would
appreciate any information you can supply concerning it. Specifically, I
would like to know:

        1. the layout of the system

        2. how the ice bin and heat pump are sized

        3. the types of controls used

If you wish, I will send you a copy of my report when it is finished.
Thank you for any help you can provide.

Sincerely yours,

Charles E. Putz

Charles E. Putz

OAK RIDGE NATIONAL LABORATORY
POST OFFICE BOX X
OAK RIDGE, TENNESSEE 37830

March 30, 1976

Mr. Charles E. Putz
239 Vandercook Hall
Ferris State College
Big Rapids, Michigan 49307

Dear Mr. Putz:

Thank you for your request for further information on the Annual Cycle
Energy System (ACES). The enclosed paper by H. C. Fischer describes this
Oak Ridge National Laboratory work, sponsored by the Energy Research and
Development Administration and the Department of Housing and Urban Development. It should provide all of the information you requested. Also enclosed
is a reprint of an article in Air Conditioning and Refrigeration News on
ACES and a copy of the ORNL Review featuring ACES. Should you wish to receive the Review on a regular basis (quarterly), a complimentary subscrip-
tion can be arranged at your request.

Our limited supplies of E. C. Hise's report "Seasonal Fuel Utilization
Efficiency of Residential Heating Systems" have been exhausted. This report
is not directly related to ACES, but it may be of interest to you; a copy
of the abstract is enclosed. If you wish to purchase the full report (56
pages), you may order it from:

                National Technical Information Service
                5285 Port Royal Road
                Springfield, Virginia 22161

at a cost of $6.00. Ask for ORNL-NSF-EP-82.

One purpose of the Technology Utilization Program is to identify government-
sponsored research and development work that may be transferred to private
industry. If we can be of any further assistance, please do not hesitate to
contact us.

                    Sincerely,

                    Carol Oen

                    Carol Oen
                    Technology Utilization Officer

CO:rj
Enc. 4

Discussion Questions

1. What format do these letters follow? Cite specific parts of each letter to support your answer.
2. Do these letters conform to the requirements for inquiry letters and favorable responses? Be specific when answering.
3. Explain each of these items:
   Co:rj
   Enc. 4

410 Main Street
Boise, Idaho 83424
November 26, 1976

Aquarium Filters, Inc.
162 South Main
Alhambra, Michigan 48702

Gentlemen:

In October, I ordered your Model R-200 Aquari-Rite under-gravel filter for my home aquarium.

About two weeks ago, the filter stopped bubbling and since that time has not worked properly. To prevent the water from becoming dirty and the fish from dying, I have had to change the water every few days.

Because the literature you supplied with the filter does not tell how to correct this problem, please supply me with directions for doing so.

I would appreciate a reply as quickly as possible, as the problem has resulted in serious inconvenience.

Sincerely yours,

John Beebe

John Beebe

Aquarium Filters, Inc.
162 SOUTH MAIN
ALHAMBRA, MICHIGAN 48702

December 3, 1976

Mr. John Beebe
410 Main Street
Boise, Idaho 83424

Dear Mr. Beebe:

We are sorry to hear that the Aquari-Rite under-gravel filter you purchased from us is not bubbling. Please don't be alarmed. Occasionally bacterial growth will plug the air hose leading to the filter. Here are several simple steps to clear the clog without removing the filter from your aquarium.

1. Separate the air hose from the air pump.

2. Suck on the hose until the water in the tank has risen halfway up the hose. You may or may not see the clog at this point.

3. Now blow forcefully into the air hose until you see bubbles coming from the filter. Repeat steps two and three if you can't see any.

4. If this procedure does not work, the small stem on the filter is probably clogged, and you can open it by running a wire through it.

I hope this will solve your difficulty. If you have any further problems, please call us collect at (717) 635-1424 between 8 A.M. and 5 P.M. Again, we are sorry for the inconvenience you have suffered.

Yours truly,

Thomas Waun

Thomas Waun
Customer Relations Department

TW:net

Discussion Questions

1. Do these letters conform to the requirements for inquiry letters requesting directions and the replies to such letters? Cite specific evidence in each letter when answering.
2. Why does John Beebe use the salutation "Gentlemen" in his letter?
3. Is it appropriate for Thomas Waun to end as well as begin his letter with an apology?

Order Letters

Letters are often used to order tools, equipment, or other supplies. Such letters must be carefully drafted to insure that the supplier ships the right goods at the right time and in the right manner.

Order letters must be brief and to the point. Begin by saying, "Please send . . . ," "Please ship . . . ," or something similar. Then identify the goods by name, model or catalog number, size, weight, color, finish, or whatever else is needed to prevent mixups. If you are ordering a single item, the letter may be written in paragraph form. Otherwise, list the items you are ordering. Note how many items of each sort you need, the cost of a single item, and the total cost of the order. To avoid misunderstanding and possible delay in processing your order, don't fail to mention any discounts to which you are entitled. Tell when you wish to pay and how—by check, money order, or credit card. If payment is enclosed, say so in the letter and be sure to include an enclosure notation in the lower left-hand corner.

If important, specify the means of shipment (truck, rail freight, railway express, air express, parcel post), the route to follow, and when you would like to receive the order. Provide any special instructions necessary to insure proper delivery.

STUDENT EXAMPLES

ACME AUTO DIAGNOSTIC SERVICE
18 Ninth Street
Lowden, Iowa 52255

November 3, 1976

Nekoma Automotive Supply Company
239 Eisenhower Street
Seabrook, Kansas 66604

Gentlemen:

Please supply the following merchandise as listed in your current catalog:

1	Model KL-20 30-Ampere Charger for 6- and 12-volt batteries. Unit price: $99.95	$99.95
2	Model FJ-3 Floor Jack. Unit price: $259.95	519.90
1	Model SA-9 Sequential Analyzer. Unit price: $117.99	117.99
1	Model EM HC-CO Emission Meter. Unit price: $299.99	299.99
	TOTAL	$1,037.83

Ship the order collect by truck freight to the above address on or before November 20, 1976. Deliver to door 3 at the south end of the building. Payment will be by check.

Sincerely yours,

Jacques Wilson

Jacques Wilson
Service Manager

JW/nm

NONE-BETTER METAL FABRICATION
273 Bell Street
Rudyard, Montana 59540

July 15, 1976

Machine Tool Industries, Inc.
14 First Avenue
Stahlman, Tennessee 37201

Gentlemen:

Please ship me one Model 241 three-speed metal-cutting band
saw with enclosed capacitor motor and floor stand. This unit
is listed in your April 1976 advertising circular at a special
discount price of $359.95, including shipping.

I am enclosing a money order for this amount.

Sincerely yours,

Albert C. Nowicki

Albert C. Nowicki
Shop Manager

ACN/rl
Enc. Money order

Discussion Questions

1. Do these letters conform to the requirements for order letters? Support your answer with specific evidence.
2. Why does Albert Nowicki mention that the price he is quoting is a special discount price? Why hasn't he included delivery instructions in his letter?
3. Why does "Money order" follow the enclosure notation in Nowicki's letter?

Claim Letters and Replies

CLAIM LETTERS

Writing claim (complaint) letters is an unpleasant but necessary task in any organization. Claims arise in many ways. Orders may be improperly filled, packed, or shipped. Merchandise may be damaged or substandard. Disputes may arise over terms of payment or pricing. The purpose of the claim letter is to point out the error and have it corrected.

Courtesy—important in any business correspondence—may require a special effort when you prepare a claim letter. Faced with a costly, time-consuming mistake, you may well feel anger and resentment, but you must not let these feelings show. Remember your aim—to obtain a satisfactory settlement of your problem. By showing malice, you succeed only in arousing antagonism. With a tactful letter you are more likely to gain your ends and also keep the reader's good will.

Begin your letter by discussing the problem as fully as is necessary. Tell exactly what happened and when, citing sizes, colors, model numbers, finish, or whatever else the reader must know to investigate and make an adjustment. If you have suffered serious inconvenience, mentioning it may help to generate a sympathetic response.

Having presented the problem, state clearly the adjustment you wish. Back your position with whatever supporting arguments are likely to sway the reader. Possible adjustments may include replacement of all or part of the merchandise, a partial or total refund, a discount, or new terms of payment. You may also wish to set a date for the settlement.

End courteously, perhaps by expressing hope for a speedy settlement or offering any further information needed to reach one.

REPLIES TO CLAIM LETTERS

Replies to claim letters, like those to inquiry letters, may be favorable or unfavorable. In either case, answer the letter quickly, within one day if possible, so that your reader knows the problem indeed concerns you. Your reply must have a pleasant tone. Never express anger, and try to avoid terms like "complaint" and "claim." These suggest that the reader is being a nuisance or the request is unjustified.

In writing a favorable reply to a claim letter, the first thing you must do is apologize for the trouble. Then explain exactly what you will do to clear up the problem, and, if appropriate, discuss its causes. You obviously don't want to say that the mix-up was caused by an irresponsible stock clerk, but if there is a valid reason—the company is in the process of switching to a computerized order-filling or invoicing system, for example—by all means explain. This information will help reassure the reader that the problem won't happen again. The goal of your letter is to preserve or reestablish a friendly relationship with the reader, so it is important to end on a positive note. Tell the reader how highly you value your business relationship, express a willingness to deal with any future problems that might arise, or repeat your apology.

Gracefully refusing a claim presents a greater challenge than perhaps any other writing task. Your reader naturally hopes for good news, but the news that you must convey is just the opposite. You must draft your letter carefully to retain the reader's good will. A carelessly written response will almost certainly create resentment.

Try to strike a harmonious note in your opening sentences. For example, you may thank the person for writing, express regret that there's been a problem, or agree with some statement in the original letter. Be careful, however, not to give the impression that you will grant the adjustment.

Next, turn to the situation that prompted the claim and discuss, in whatever detail and manner are appropriate, why it is necessary for you to refuse. It is important that you justify your position. For example, many claims involve supposedly faulty merchandise which investigation shows was improperly used or cared for. In such cases, note the findings and tell the reader how to prevent the trouble from recurring. To avoid suggestions of blame, which will only antagonize the reader, steer clear of expressions like "faulty care," "misused," and "improperly maintained." Unwarranted claims for discounts, special credit terms, or refunds can be countered by reminding the reader that granting them would involve extra expense and be unfair to other customers.

Conclude the letter as you began—pleasantly and, if possible, helpfully. Sometimes you will be able to grant a partial adjustment or provide some special service, thus softening the blow. Offers of future help are also effective. If you follow these suggestions, your letter may disappoint the reader, but it will go a long way toward eliminating resentment.

STUDENT EXAMPLES

Saint Lawrence Hospital
410 Saginaw Street
Lansing, Michigan 48914

April 20, 1976

William B. Jenkins, M.D.
Butterfield Clinic
809 South Hodges
Grand Rapids, Michigan 49503

Dear Dr. Jenkins:

On March 5, I sent you my completed registration form and check in the amount of $15 to cover registration fee and meal expenses at the Annual Fall Respiratory Disease Seminar held at the Hospitality Motor Inn, Grand Rapids, on April 10, 1976.

After talking with several participants, I now understand that since I was involved as a discussion leader I should not have paid any fee at all. Therefore, I am requesting that the amount of $15 be reimbursed at your convenience. If you need any information in order to expedite this matter, such as my cancelled check, please let me know.

I would like to add that I thought the seminar was very well conducted, and I thoroughly enjoyed participating as a discussion leader.

Sincerely,

John W. Potter

John W. Potter, RRT
Chief Respiratory Therapist

JWP/paf

BUTTERFIELD CLINIC

809 South Hodges
Grand Rapids, Michigan 49503

April 22, 1976

John W. Potter, RRT
Chief Respiratory Therapist
Saint Lawrence Hospital
410 Saginaw Street
Lansing, Michigan 48914

Dear Mr. Potter:

We have received your letter of April 20 requesting reimbursement of registration fee and meal expenses.

I apologize for any misunderstanding you may have regarding the fees paid by participants in the seminar. However, as has always been the case at our lectures and seminars, the main speakers are the only persons who are not charged registration fees or meal expenses.

As you know, our seminars are not money-making ventures but educational services to both lay and professional people. We would prefer to charge no fee, but it is nevertheless necessary to charge something to defray actual costs.

We certainly appreciated your help in making the Annual Fall Respiratory Disease Seminar a success, and I hope that the misunderstanding about the fees will not cause you to refuse should we need your services in the future.

If I can be of any further assistance to you, please do not hesitate to contact me.

Sincerely,

William B. Jenkins, M.D.
Committee Chairman

WBJ/tfk

Discussion Questions

1. Does John Potter provide Dr. Jenkins with enough details for Jenkins to evaluate his claim? Give specific evidence to support your answer.
2. Cite several examples of the ways Potter achieves a courteous tone in his letter.
3. Does the reply by Dr. Jenkins conform to the requirements for letters refusing claims? Support your answer with specific points.

2520 South Main Street
Lansing, Michigan 48904
July 23, 1976

American Electronics Company
281 Center Street
Grand Rapids, Michigan 49503

Gentlemen:

On June 26, 1976, I sent your company a check for $99.50, along with
a purchase order for a solid state multi-band AM/FM radio, Model
#61H2435. A copy of the order is enclosed.

Today I received in the mail a solid state AM/FM radio without the
multi-band channel, Model #61F3526, listed in your catalog at $39.95.
Not only is this the incorrect radio, but the tuning knob is cracked.

The radio I ordered was to have been a graduation present for my son,
who will be leaving on a trip in about a week and a half. Therefore,
I would appreciate any measures you could take to correct this order
so that I will have the right radio for my son before he leaves.

I would be pleased to hear from you as soon as possible.

Sincerely,

John K. Jones.

John K. Jones

Enc.

AMERICAN ELECTRONICS COMPANY
281 Center Street_____
Grand Rapids, Mlichigan 49503 _____

July 25, 1976

Mr. John K. Jones
2520 South Main Street
Lansing, Michigan 48904

Dear Mr. Jones:

Thank you for your letter of July 23, 1976, regarding the multi-band
radio that you ordered. We apologize for the mixup and are taking
immediate steps to correct it.

We have recently opened up a centrally located warehouse to handle
all of our mail orders. Since this is a new venture for our company,
we still have a few bugs to eliminate from our procedure, including
the training of new employees in our shipping department. Within a
few weeks, however, we expect the warehouse to be operating with full
efficiency.

Since you stated that you need the radio as soon as possible, I am
having it sent under separate cover via Special Delivery. I trust
that you will return the incorrect order as soon as it is convenient
for you.

I regret this inconvenience and hope that our mistake will not stop
you from ordering from American Electronics in the future.

If you have any further problems, please let me know.

Congratulations on your son's graduation. I hope that he will have
many pleasurable hours with his new radio.

Sincerely yours,

Robert S. Conrad

Robert S. Conrad
Director of Purchasing

RSC/cef

Discussion Questions

1. Has John Jones discussed in sufficient detail the problem that
   prompted his letter? Support your answer with specific evidence.
2. Has Jones presented an effective case for a quick adjustment?
3. Point out how Robert Conrad has created a friendly, courteous
   tone in his reply to Jones.

Memorandums

A memorandum, or memo, is essentially a short letter used to present data, announce meetings, suggest policy changes, request action, ask for recommendations, explain procedures, give directions, and the like. Memos are perhaps the most common form of business and technical writing. They are the primary means by which members of a company or other organization keep one another informed. Because both your coworkers and your superiors will judge your professional ability partly by the memos you write, it is vital to your career that you learn to write them properly.

Although memos usually stay within the writer's own organization, occasionally they may pass between two or more organizations that are involved in a joint enterprise. Thus, when an advertising campaign is being developed, memos often circulate between the client company and the advertising agency.

Memos range from highly formal to very informal, depending on their purpose and the relationship between the writer and reader. In writing a memo, follow the rules that apply to any business letter. Be courteous and natural. Keep your message brief, and make it as readable as you can. Use short sentences and paragraphs, and stick to nontechnical terms whenever possible.

Most memos deal with matters requiring immediate action. Generally, the topic is quite narrow. For example, memos would be used to announce meetings held during the course of a research project, but probably not to present the research results.

Memos provide a flow of information among persons and departments of like rank (horizontal communication) as well as among those occupying different positions in the organizational chain of command (vertical communication). The design engineer who asks the testing laboratory for tensile strength data on a new copper-alloy wire is communicating horizontally. The company president who announces a more liberal vacation policy is communicating vertically, as is the superintendent who informs the president that a new assembly line is now in operation.

Besides conveying information, memos provide a permanent record of actions and decisions. Thus, they greatly reduce the number of oversights and misunderstandings that can occur in day-to-day business operations. The employee who must carry out a procedure containing several steps is much less likely to make an error if the instructions are presented by memo rather than orally.

Because memos are so widely used, most large and medium-sized organizations provide printed memo forms. A common size is 5½ by 8½ inches, although many other sizes are also used. A memorandum consists of two main parts: the heading and the body. Ordinarily, the heading includes spaces for the names of the sender and receiver, the date, and the subject, as shown below:

To: _____

From: _____

Date: _____

Subject: _____

Some forms also have spaces for the department or building of the sender and receiver, the sender's phone number, and the names of persons receiving copies. When a memo runs to two or three pages, as occasionally happens, the headings for the additional pages are identical to those used for any business letter (see page 127).

The body of a memorandum contains the message to the reader. If the reader is not familiar with the subject of the memo, begin with a brief introduction explaining why the memo is being written. For example:

> Recently, some personnel have not followed the proper procedures for taking water samples. As a consequence, test results have been grossly in error, forcing us to repeat tests at the cost of considerable time and expense. In the future, please observe very carefully the following procedures.

In many instances, though, the reader is familiar with the situation prompting the memo, and the subject line of the heading provides all the background information that is required.

A paragraph format is appropriate for most memos. However, when you write a memo giving directions or explaining new procedures, present the information as a numbered list. This format will enable the reader to separate the different steps and carry them out one by one. The steps—like the steps in all process explanations—should be written in the form of commands and presented in the order that the reader is to perform them. Be sure to alert the reader if two steps must be carried out at the same time. If it is possible for the reader to misunderstand the reason for a step or perform it incorrectly, explain the reason or warn of the consequences.

Depending on the topic of the memorandum, a brief conclusion may be needed. If you must have a response by a certain date or if a procedure must go into effect on a specific date, note this at the end of the memo.

Unlike the usual business letter, a memorandum omits the complimentary close and typed signature. The writer may, however, initial or sign the memo at the end.

STUDENT EXAMPLES

To: Water Quality Control Department

From: James H. Mitchell, President

Date: November 27, 1976

Subject: Appointment of Water Quality Control Department Head

I would like to announce the appointment of Mr. George A. Fleisher
to head our Water Quality Control Department. Mr. Fleisher comes to
us from the Environmental Protection Agency, where he has worked as
area coordinator in Maryland for the past three years. He holds an
M.S. degree in marine biology and a Ph.D in limnology. These qualifications, in addition to fourteen years' experience in the field,
ensure that he will be a great asset to the department.

I know that each of you will do everything possible to assist Mr.
Fleisher in assuming his new responsibilities.

Discussion Question

1. Is this memorandum an example of horizontal or vertical communication?

To: Nate Johnson, Plant Superintendent

From: Robert Burtch, Safety Engineer

Date: December 21, 1976

Subject: Use of Defective Vehicles

On December 13, 1976, while making a delivery in Westville, Michigan, one of our drivers passed through the Michigan State Police Vehicle Inspection Point. The police found that the brake lights on the truck were defective and issued a citation. A memorandum reporting the defective lights was then relayed to you and to John Anderson, head of Vehicle Maintenance. However, due to the unavailability of parts and our shortage of trucks, the vehicle was kept in service.

On December 20, 1976, this vehicle was involved in an accident at the east end of the intersection of Oak and Maple in Westville. While the vehicle was traveling east on Oak, a car pulled out of a parking place and into its path. To avoid an accident, our driver slammed on the brakes and stopped. Because the brake lights did not work, the driver behind did not react soon enough and collided with our truck. The damage to the truck was estimated at $500, and the car was totally wrecked. We are fortunate indeed that no one was injured.

To prevent similar occurrences, I suggest you issue a directive informing all drivers that operating a defective company vehicle is forbidden. If our own maintenance personnel are unable to repair the vehicles, then we should contract with an outside automotive repair shop. By taking these steps, we can prevent accidents of the sort described above.

Discussion Questions

1. Does this memorandum represent a horizontal or vertical flow of information?
2. Two paragraphs are devoted to presenting background information and one short paragraph to presenting the writer's recommendation. Explain.

To: Accounting Department Employees

From: Jan Morgenstern

Date: September 3, 1976

Subject: Operation of Yashiki Calculator

A number of you have mentioned that you find it hard to understand
the operation of the memory-bank feature of our newly purchased
No. 40761 Yashiki calculators. The following instructions may be
helpful.

    1. Be sure that all information is cleared from the calculator
       by pressing the C (clear) and MC (memory clear) buttons.

    2. Punch the number that you wish to put into the memory bank.

    3. Enter this number into the memory bank by pressing the M^+
       (memory record) button. This number will remain stored in
       the memory bank until it is called for, as long as the
       calculator is not shut off. Shutting the calculator off
       clears everything from the machine.

    4. To bring the number out of memory-bank storage, simply
       press the MD (memory display) button.

    5. When you wish to clear a number from the memory bank, press
       the MC button. A new number can then be entered into the
       memory bank.

Should any further questions or problems arise, please do not
hesitate to see me.

Discussion Questions

1. The subject heading does not indicate that this memorandum will
deal only with the operation of the memory-bank feature. How can
this omission be justified?
2. In the concluding sentence the writer says, "please do not hesitate
to see me." What function is served by the phrase "do not hesitate"?

To: All Technical Personnel

From: Arnold G. Forbes, Vice-President for Research

Date: April 3, 1976

Subject: New Antibiotic

On March 25, 1976, our company introduced commercially a new oral
broad-spectrum antibiotic called Larocin (anoxicillin). Larocin, an
analog of ampicillin, is a semisynthetic drug. Chemically, it is a
2-amino-p-hydroxybenzyl penicillin trihydrate.

Larocin is similar to ampicillin in its action against susceptible
bacteria during the active multiplication stage. The product acts
against many strains of Gram-negative and Gram-positive organisms.
Susceptible Gram-negative organisms include Hemophilius influenzae,
Escherichia coli, Proteus mirabolis, and Neisseria gonorrhoeae. Among
the susceptible Gram-positive organisms are Streptococcus faecalis,
Diplococcus pneumoniae, and nonpenicillinase-producing staphlococci.

The new product is stable in the presence of gastric acid and may be
given without regard to meals. It diffuses readily into most body
tissues and fluids. Most of the Larocin is excreted unchanged in the
urine, and the product is not protein-bound.

Larocin is available in capsules containing 250 mg and 500 mg apiece,
in oral suspensions containing 125 mg or 250 mg per 5 milliliters, and
in a pediatric formulation containing 20 mg per milliliter.

I know all our employees will share my feeling of pride in this new
and important addition to our line of human health products.

Discussion Question

1. What evidence is there in the memorandum that it is intended for a
   technical audience?

Suggestions for Writing

1. Write a letter of inquiry requesting:

   a. More detailed information concerning the procedures used in a project reported in a magazine or newspaper article.

   b. Additional details concerning a safety program, employee-rating program, inspection system, time-study system, or traffic-routing system developed by another organization.

   c. Performance data or specifications on a piece of equipment your organization might buy.

   d. Clarification of an inadequate or ambiguous set of directions.

   e. Detailed information concerning the pricing, credit, and discount policies of a company with which your organization might do business.

   f. Information and data for a student research project or term paper.

Write a reply to your own letter of inquiry, either supplying the information or refusing the request.

2. Write a letter ordering:

   a. One or more pieces of furniture, household appliances, items of clothing, garden implements, or automobile accessories.

   b. One or more tools, machines, pieces of office or shop equipment, or laboratory devices.

3. Write a claim letter calling attention to one of the following and requesting an adjustment:

   a. An order that was improperly or incompletely filled.

   b. An order that was delivered late.

   c. Merchandise shipped by the wrong carrier or route.

   d. Merchandise damaged in transit because of improper packing.

   e. Improper billing for a recent order.

Write a reply to your own claim letter, either granting or refusing the adjustment.

4. Write a letter explaining how to:

   a. Connect a tape deck to a stereo set.

   b. Collect a potable water sample.

   c. Turn an angle in surveying.

    d.   Test the resistance of an electrical resistor.

    e.   Convert rectangular coordinates to polar coordinates on an electronic calculator.

    f.   Trigger an oscilloscope.

    g.   Package some delicate device.

    h.   Change the setting of a torque wrench.

    i.   Gap spark plugs.

    j.   Perform some other task in your own field of study.

5. Write a memorandum:

    a.   Announcing a meeting to discuss a new research project, advertising program, building project, or similar activity that will soon get under way. Outline several points that the meeting will cover and ask those attending to come prepared to talk about them.

    b.   Recommending that employee lunch hours be staggered to prevent congestion in the cafeteria. Point out some of the problems congestion has caused.

    c.   Summarizing the results of a meeting to discuss ways of coping with high employee absenteeism. Ask for employee comments.

    d.   Reporting that a procedure is being carried out incorrectly by employees. Point out the error and explain how the procedure should be performed.

    e.   Announcing a change in the procedure for testing a particular material or product. Explain the new procedure and tell why the changes were made.

    f.   Asking the recipient to inventory the laboratory stockroom, note any items that are out of stock, and order them. Ask the recipient to report by memo the results of the inventory.

    g.   Summarizing safety violations in some organization or department and suggesting ways of correcting them.

    h.   Announcing a meeting to discuss some production, inspection, or shipping problem that has arisen. Explain why the problem is serious, give several possible solutions, and ask those attending the meeting to come prepared to discuss them.

    i.   Recommending that your organization change a policy. List specific changes and tell why you think each is desirable.

    j.   Summarizing for a new employee the duties involved in a particular job. List the various tasks and explain how each is to be carried out.

9

Proposals

Proposals are written for one of two reasons: (1) to offer to carry out a particular project or (2) to suggest that others undertake a project or adopt a course of action.

Proposals of the first sort are sent to actual or potential customers and offer to perform some kind of work for them. Depending upon your organization's business, your proposal may offer to construct an office building, paint a water tower, overhaul a heating system, survey viewers' tastes in TV programs, conduct a time-motion study, prepare a service manual, analyze the workflow pattern in a manufacturing facility, carry out a market survey, or perform any one of an almost endless variety of other tasks.

Proposals of the second sort may originate inside or outside the organization to which they are directed. You may, for example, suggest that your company carpet its offices, liberalize its vacation policies, establish a comprehensive safety program, reroute traffic within the plant, undertake a particular piece of research, or change a work procedure. Likewise, you may ask your city council to establish a mosquito-control program, the officials of the local power company to install precipitators in their smoke stacks, or a beverage manufacturer to abandon the use of disposable bottles.

These proposals seek primarily to change attitudes, not to sell products or services.

Because proposals are among the most important types of writing you will do in the course of your career, the procedure for preparing them deserves close attention.

There is considerable variation in the length and format of proposals. The length depends upon the action suggested or requested. The more complicated the project, the longer the proposal is likely to be. A proposal to erect a prefabricated garage, for example, could probably be written in one or two pages. At the opposite extreme, a proposal to construct a large apartment complex or completely reorganize a large company's marketing operation could require many dozens of pages.

Proposal formats differ considerably in the number, type, and arrangement of their captions. Many private and governmental agencies issue bulletins specifying in great detail the format that must be followed in any proposal they receive. However, for most short proposals—the kind you are most likely to write—the format discussed in this chapter will prove entirely satisfactory. It includes five parts:

1. heading
2. introduction
3. body
4. list of supplementary materials
5. conclusion

Proposals originating outside the target organization and recommending a new policy or course of action often omit many of the features discussed below, concentrating instead on the reason the proposal should be adopted and the benefits that will result. The student example on page 169 follows this pattern.

Heading

The heading consists of the title of the proposal, the names of the receiver and the sender, and the date. The title should be brief, yet it should describe the proposal clearly. Here is an example.

**PROPOSAL TO SUPPLY DRAFTING TABLES
FOR TECHNICAL ILLUSTRATION LABORATORY**

Submitted to: Richard Bartlow, Chairman, Technical Illustration
              Department
By: Ann Lundborg, for Drafting Supplies, Inc.
Date: August 1, 1976

Introduction

The first sentence of the introduction should state what is being proposed and the cost of carrying it out, unless the cost isn't known or isn't a consideration. For clarity, costs are first spelled out and then given as figures, in parentheses. To continue with the preceding example:

> Drafting Supplies, Inc., proposes to install twenty (20) new drafting tables in the Technical Illustration Laboratory of Adams Technical Institute for the total sum of two thousand two hundred fifty dollars ($2,250.00).
>
> *Ann Lundborg*

Whenever necessary, tell why your proposal should be adopted. Proposals offering to build homes, install furnaces, or perform similar jobs seldom need justification. The prospective customer has generally solicited the proposal and is well aware of the need for the work. Proposals suggesting new courses of action are another matter. Often, these proposals are written in response to some problem—high employee absenteeism, a faulty work procedure, or the like. In such cases, you should define the problem, perhaps briefly trace its history, indicate the need for a solution, and show how your proposal will solve the problem.

Do not neglect to explain the advantages of what you are proposing. These will vary depending upon the specific situation. In proposing that a technical institute install new drafting tables, you might point out the rugged, lightweight construction and smooth, durable surface of your company's tables. In proposing that a surveying company replace its transits with a more accurate type, you might stress the added features and greater accuracy of the new instrument. In still other cases, you might emphasize low installation costs, savings in materials and equipment, ease or economy of operation, or increased productivity.

If there is a chance the reader may doubt the feasibility of your proposal, offer reassurances. This is generally necessary only if the proposed project is unusual or nonroutine. Reassurances may consist of laboratory findings, a brief discussion of a similar project that has proved successful, or any verified data that will convince your reader of the proposal's practicality.

Be sure, also, to present any pertinent fact concerning the project, including when it can be started, how long it will take to complete, and any limitations. For example, if you are proposing to construct a home but do not intend to finish the woodwork, make sure the proposal points this out clearly. Noting limitations is very important, for unless the reader knows just what the project will and will not include, misunderstandings and hard feelings are likely to result.

A good way to end the introduction is with a brief statement designed to create a favorable impression. You may mention your firm's excellent reputation, note your employees' exceptional skills, or the like. The following is an example of a complete introduction.

The J and J Construction Company proposes to construct a home at 290 Loudon Street, Cleveland, for Mr. and Mrs. Anthony Powers at a total estimated cost of thirty-seven thousand six hundred forty dollars ($37,640), not including the lot. The house will have three (3) bedrooms, one and one-half (1½) baths, a living room, a dining L, and a full unfinished basement. The price includes all lighting and bathroom fixtures; a dishwasher, electric stove, and garbage disposal unit for the kitchen; and all interior painting except for the woodwork, which will be left unfinished. The house will be Cape Cod style, with a dormer in the back to enlarge the upper floor. It will be constructed in forty-five (45) days, barring complications, and construction can start within ten (10) days after formal agreement is reached.

Our company has been in the home construction business for over a quarter century, and our original designs have won several regional awards. We are confident that you will be very pleased with our product.

Mark Jensen

Body

The body of the proposal presents several kinds of information, much of it in tabular form. Depending upon the proposal, you may include:

a list of materials, equipment, and supplies needed
a cost breakdown
a list of personnel required
a job schedule
a discussion of the method employed to carry out the work

The listing of materials, equipment, and supplies often contains brief descriptions of some or all of the items. For example, an air conditioner might be described as Electra, 24,000 BTU, Model EK. Do not include too much detail in the listing. If your reader requires further information—as is often the case—you can supply pamphlets, specifications, and the like. When the list includes a very large number of items, it should be presented as a supplement rather than as part of the report. The listing of items required for the construction of a house, for example, should be handled in this way. When the listing is presented separately, tell your reader in the body of the proposal.

The cost breakdown must include every expense that will be incurred in carrying out the proposed work. Depending upon the particular proposal, this breakdown would state the cost of such items as materials, equipment, supplies, labor, transportation, fees and permits, inspections, and room and board. Be sure not to overlook any anticipated cost. To do so is to invite hard feelings and possibly even legal trouble later.

A list of required personnel is ordinarily included only when the project will be carried out within the writer's own company by its own employees. The section should indicate the number of employees that will be involved in the project and their departments. Frequently, key personnel are mentioned by name. This information allows management to evaluate the effects of the personnel shift and to compensate for it. When newly installed equipment will require operators, their number and qualifications should also be given so that management knows in advance of the need for additional personnel.

The schedule should state exactly when each phase of the work will be carried out. This information allows your customer to plan around your activities and minimize disruptions and slowdowns. The schedule for a proposal to inventory the farms of an agricultural corporation might read, in part, as follows:

First week	Inventory farm equipment and spare parts
Second week	Inventory fertilizers
Third week	Inventory seed potatoes, corn, and wheat

Dennis Hadden

For one-day jobs, the schedule is sometimes omitted from the proposal. However, if the work is likely to disrupt the customer's operation in any way, be certain that the proposal includes a schedule.

Whenever the methods that will be employed in the work are likely to be unfamiliar to your reader, discuss them. Generally, such discussion is required only when proposing special research projects, time-motion studies, market surveys, and the like. In your discussion, consider each step in detail and explain why it is necessary. Discuss any testing or analytical procedures in the same fashion. If designs, blueprints, flow charts, and similar materials will be prepared, give details.

The following example, part of a proposal to install room air conditioners in a hotel, incorporates many of the elements discussed above.

Materials

Air conditioner	Electra, 24,000 BTU, Model EK
Wiring	Three-lead plug and box
Frame	6-inch aluminum
Refrigerant	R-12

Costs

30 Electra air conditioners ($480.00 each)	$14,400
Labor (160 man-hours at $7.00/hour)	1,120
Material (frames, wire, refrigerant)	300
Delivery charges	150
Fees and permits	50
Inspection	30
Total costs	$16,050

Daily Schedule

(6 units installed per day for 5 days)

7:00 A.M.–12:00 P.M.	Cut walls, connect wiring, and refinish
12:30 P.M.–2:00 P.M.	Install frames and units
2:00 P.M.–3:00 P.M.	Complete installation
3:00 P.M.–3:30 P.M.	Clean up

Craig S. Sherwood

List of Supplementary Materials

This section informs the reader of the printed or other separate materials accompanying the proposal. These may include blueprints, pamphlets, specification sheets, price lists, and the like. If, because of its length, the list of materials, equipment, and supplies is being attached to the proposal as a separate item, be sure to mention it in this section. You may also want to provide the reader with evidence of your firm's capabilities. Such evidence —reports describing similar projects successfully completed or testimonials from satisfied customers—would be part of the supplementary material. If reports and testimonials are unavailable, then names and addresses of customers can be supplied instead. The following example is from a proposal to construct a house.

Accompanying this proposal you will find a detailed floor plan of the house, complete sets of specifications for both the house and the appliances to be installed, a listing of quantities and types of materials needed for construction, an artist's rendering of the finished house, and several testimonial letters from former customers.

Mark Jensen

Conclusion

The conclusion to your proposal can include a number of elements. When the proposal states a price for the work, it is desirable to mention in the conclusion exactly how long the price will remain in effect. This information will prevent future misunderstandings, and—if costs are to rise soon—it may speed the proposal's acceptance. The conclusion may also briefly review the importance of the project, the advantages of your proposal, or your organization's qualifications for carrying out the project. If it seems desirable, you may offer to discuss the proposal personally. End by expressing your assurance that the work will prove satisfactory, offering to provide any further information, and perhaps thanking the reader for considering the proposal. Here are two student examples, the first written for a prospective customer, the second for the management of the writer's own company.

The prices in this proposal will remain in effect until October 31, 1976, at which time they will be lowered to twelve thousand five hundred sixty dollars ($12,560.00) for the off-season, which lasts until January 1, 1977. Our schedule is filled until June 8, but after that date we can begin work at your convenience.

We are confident that you and your customers will be well satisfied with the dependable Electra air conditioner and also with the work of Thomas Heating and Cooling, for we have been servicing the Minneapolis–St. Paul area for 50 years.

Craig S. Sherwood

As stated before, last year's inventory saved us 15 percent in materials, supplies, and equipment costs as compared with the previous year's costs. The net savings amounted to $65,000. Without a doubt, a new inventory will allow us to repeat these savings, perhaps even increase them. Martin and Hall Associates, who conducted our last inventory, have informed me that they can begin work within one week after receiving final authorization. I suggest we contact them immediately.

Dennis Hadden

Proposals Without Captions

Sometimes proposals are written in the form of a letter, with no captions in the body. Proposals recommending action that does not involve the writer's own organization—for example, the previously mentioned letter to the city council asking for a mosquito-control program—are often written this way. Ordinarily, though, proposals have captions and follow the format described in this chapter.

A Note on Clarity

Clarity is important in all the writing you do—and especially so in proposals. If your proposal is not clearly written, your reader is likely to conclude that you do not clearly understand the project. In such a case, the reader is not likely to consider the proposal very seriously.

You must strive, then, in writing a proposal to make your meaning immediately apparent. The best way to achieve such clarity is to use short sentences and paragraphs and to steer clear of unnecessarily technical terminology. Unless the proposal is very short, it should not be written in a single sitting. Spreading the writing out over several sessions will prevent your language from growing stale and fuzzy. Once your first draft is completed, wait at least a day before polishing it. Then, when you are satisfied with the proposal, ask one or more people not connected with the project to read and criticize it. On the basis of their comments, you may want to revise the proposal again before submitting it for consideration. By following this procedure, you will greatly increase your proposal's clarity and thus its chances of being adopted.

STUDENT EXAMPLES

PROPOSAL TO STOP PRODUCTION OF
NONRETURNABLE BEVERAGE BOTTLES

Submitted to: J. Lucien Smith, President, Banner Beverage Company
By: Robert Ewigleben, Jr., Environmental Consultant
Date: July 6, 1976

(1) As a concerned citizen and environmentalist, I propose that the Banner Beverage Company stop using nonreturnable soft-drink containers and begin using returnable bottles again. The nonreturnable container represents a blatant misuse of our resources and constitutes a major litter problem. For these reasons, I feel my proposal should be adopted.

(2) A recent study conducted by the Oregon State Highway Department found that bottles and cans account for 62 percent of highway litter. These bottles and cans offend the eye and are costly as well. The Michigan Department of State Highways and Transportation estimates that the state spends between $600,000 and $700,000 yearly to pick up discarded containers along state trunklines, U.S. routes, and freeways. This cost doesn't take into account cleanup costs incurred by local groups.

(3) Presently in the United States we face a growing problem in energy production. Our energy supplies are dwindling, and we must cut back and conserve energy. The production of disposable beverage containers consumes much larger quantities of energy than would be required if returnable bottles were used. For example, the production of 10 bimetallic cans consumes 2.5 times as much energy as the production of one 10-trip returnable bottle. Therefore, returnable bottles will reduce energy consumption by Banner Beverage Company.

(4) There are many other benefits from using returnable containers. They reduce the amount of waste in landfills, slow the depletion of our metal resources, and save the consumer money. With regard to the latter, an EPA study of beverage prices showed that the cost of a beverage in a returnable bottle was

less than the cost of the same amount of the beverage in a nonreturnable container.

Data for two large food chains are shown below.

Delmar . . . . .24.8¢ (12 oz. nonreturnable can)
                          20.8¢ (12 oz. returnable bottle)
Monterey . . . . .24.9¢ (16 oz. nonreturnable can)
                          22.4¢ (16 oz. returnable bottle)

(5) I urge that your company phase out over a one-year period the production of nonreturnable containers. This plan will obviously call for the retooling of many plants, the construction of local distribution and collection centers, and improved methods and expansion of cleanup procedures.

(6) Costs to the company will be substantial, but I believe they will be offset in two ways. First, energy savings will reduce production costs. Second, your demand for raw materials will decrease and your profit margin increase.

(7) I feel that with an effective advertising campaign Banner Beverage Company can actually increase profits if my plan is adopted. Stopping the production of nonreturnable containers will show the consumer that Banner is concerned about environmental quality. Since it is one of our largest bottling companies, Banner can set an example for the rest of the industry to follow. Most important, if such a plan is adopted, you will have the satisfaction of knowing that you have made a major contribution to cleaning up our environment.

Discussion Questions

1. What economic arguments does the writer use to show that Banner Beverage Company should stop the production of nonreturnable containers, and where in the proposal do these arguments appear?
2. What is accomplished by the inclusion of the last sentence in paragraph 5 and the clause that begins paragraph 6?
3. How do the arguments used in the conclusion differ from those presented earlier?

PROPOSAL TO CONSTRUCT POWERS' HOME

Submitted to: Mr. and Mrs. Anthony Powers
By: J and J Construction Company
Date: February 14, 1976

Introduction

(1) The J and J Construction Company proposes to construct a home at 290 Loudon Street, Cleveland, for Mr. and Mrs. Anthony Powers at a total estimated cost of thirty-seven thousand six hundred forty dollars ($37,640), not including the lot. The house will have three (3) bedrooms, one and one-half (1½) baths, a living room, a dining L, and a full unfinished basement. The price includes all lighting and bathroom fixtures; a dishwasher, electric stove, and garbage disposal unit for the kitchen; and all interior painting except for the woodwork, which will be left unfinished. The house will be Cape Cod style, with a dormer in the back to enlarge the upper floor. It will be constructed in forty-five (45) days, barring complications, and construction can start within ten (10) days after formal agreement is reached.

(2) Our company has been in the home construction business for over a quarter century, and our original designs have won several regional awards. We are confident that you will be very pleased with our product.

Estimated Materials and Labor Cost Breakdown

Excavation	$ 800.00
Basement	2,800.00
Concrete walks and drive—	
materials and labor	900.00
Carpentry	9,600.00
Lumber	6,750.00
Roofing materials	325.00
Windows and doors	2,500.00
Kitchen appliances	
dishwasher	325.00
stove	320.00
garbage disposal unit	85.00
Plumbing—materials and labor	1,775.00
Heating—materials and labor	2,300.00
Wiring—materials and labor	1,010.00
Light fixtures—materials and labor	250.00
Dry wall	600.00
Painting and decorating interior	400.00

Siding—aluminum exterior	1,200.00
Floor coverings—materials and labor	1,600.00
Contractor's profit	3,500.00
Extras: sod	600.00
TOTAL COST	$37,640.00

Supplementary Materials

(3) Accompanying this proposal you will find a detailed floor plan of the house, complete sets of specifications for both the house and the appliances to be installed, a listing of quantities and types of materials needed for construction, an artist's rendering of the finished house, and several testimonial letters from former customers.

Conclusion

(4) The prices indicated will be effective through June 30, 1976. We have a major project scheduled in May, but construction of your house could easily be completed by June 30 if a decision is made within three (3) weeks.

(5) If you have any questions concerning the proposal, please feel free to contact me at 796-7346, and we can meet at a time convenient to you. Thank you for considering J and J Construction.

Mark Jensen

Discussion Questions

1. This chapter deals with two kinds of proposals: those offering to carry out a particular project and those suggesting that others undertake a project or adopt a course of action. Which type does this example illustrate?
2. What information has the writer included to create a favorable impression of his organization and thus increase the likelihood that his proposal will be accepted?
3. It is important that any proposal to carry out a project note clearly just what the project will and will not include. Is it likely any misunderstanding will occur concerning the scope of this project? Give reasons for your answer.

4. Note that the writer of this proposal has not included a detailed schedule for the completion of each phase of construction. Why can this omission be justified?

PROPOSAL TO SUPPLY DRAFTING TABLES FOR TECHNICAL ILLUSTRATION LABORATORY

Submitted to: Richard Bartlow, Chairman, Technical Illustration
              Department
By: Ann Lundborg, for Drafting Supplies, Inc.
Date: August 1, 1976

Introduction

(1) Drafting Supplies, Inc., proposes to install twenty (20) new drafting tables in the Technical Illustration Laboratory of Adams Technical Institute for the total sum of two thousand two hundred fifty dollars ($2,250.00). The tables have lightweight metal frames and extra-large drawing surfaces for large illustrations. Each table has its own individual light, which can be adjusted to suit the needs of the user. The tables will be assembled on the site and positioned according to your directions. Removing the old tables and replacing them with new ones will take one day and can be carried out at your convenience. We feel our tables are of the highest quality, and our workers will do a skilled job of installation.

Construction of Table and Light

Table framework	Welded aluminum
Table drawing surface	Pressed wood with plastic-coated surface. Dimensions: 48 inches by 36 inches.
Light	Clamp-on steel base, double 20-inch flexible gooseneck, 24-inch fluorescent tube in 25-inch-by-4-inch rectangular holder

Costs

20 Tables ($85.00 each)	$1,700.00
20 Lights ($20.00 each)	400.00
Labor (24-man-hours at $5.00/hour)	120.00
Delivery charge	30.00
TOTAL COSTS	$2,250.00

Supplementary Materials

(2) Attached you will find a number of diagrams of rooms with the same dimensions as yours, showing possible ways that the tables can be arranged. Also attached are photographs of the actual tables with the lights in place and specifications for both tables and lights.

Conclusion

(3) The prices stated in this proposal will be effective until September 30, 1976, at which time rising costs will necessitate an increase of five dollars ($5) per table. Our schedule permits us to install your drafting tables any time during August or September. If you need further information, please call me at 823-2776, and I will be glad to see you at your convenience.

Discussion Questions

1. Does the heading of this proposal meet the requirements given in the chapter? Explain.
2. Why does this proposal include a supplementary materials section?
3. Discuss the reasons why the concluding paragraph is effective.

PROPOSAL TO PURCHASE TWO THEODOLITES AND ONE ELECTRONIC DISTANCE MEASURING DEVICE

Submitted to: Jack McNeeley, President, Livonia Civil Engineering

By: Robert Burtch, Surveying Party Chief

Date: February 14, 1976

Introduction

(1) I propose that our company purchase two (2) Acumark Model A theodolites and one (1) Acumark Model C electronic distance measuring device (EDM) before our work load increases this spring. The total cost of the combined purchases will be eleven thousand dollars ($11,000)—three thousand dollars ($3,000) for each theodolite and five thousand dollars ($5,000) for the EDM.

(2) The field survey crews presently need two new instruments. The transits now being used are old and subject to built-in errors. Although we could replace these instruments with new transits, I strongly recommend that we purchase theodolites instead. An Acumark Model A theodolite costs several hundred dollars more than a transit, but this added cost is more than offset by features not present in transits.

(3) For example, each theodolite has an optical plummet that reduces the time needed to set the instrument over points on windy days. Even on calm days, theodolites can be set up much more quickly than transits. A theodolite is also much more accurate. Our present transits can read out only to the nearest 20 seconds, whereas a theodolite can read out to the nearest second. This feature would eliminate many man-hours in the field when closure of a traverse loop is important. The readout is likewise more convenient and faster, for each theodolite is equipped with an additional scope from which the angles are read. For the money, the theodolite is the best possible instrument for our needs. It combines accuracy with speed, allowing the surveyor to achieve better field results within a shorter period of time.

(4) The EDM would also reduce costly man-hours. Although it would not eliminate the tape, it would allow long distances to be measured more accurately and easily, for it eliminates the errors that are inherent in a tape (i.e., sag, plumbing, and expansion). Measurements that would take hours with more conventional methods of taping can be completed within minutes. The EDM is accurate to within 1 foot per 100,000 feet, whereas a tape is accurate to within 1 foot per 5,000.

Supplementary Materials

(5) Attachment #1 is a report by the American Congress on Surveying and Mapping, showing the savings in man-hours that

can be realized by using precision instruments. Attachment #2 compares the cost of the Acumark Model A theodolite with the costs of several available transits.

Conclusion

(6) The purchase of these instruments is long overdue. The time and money they will save and the accuracy they will provide more than justify their use by our firm. Therefore, I strongly urge you to study this proposal before considering the purchase of any other new instruments.

Discussion Questions

1. Which of the two kinds of proposals discussed in this chapter— those offering to carry out a particular project and those suggesting that others undertake a project or adopt a course of action—does this paper illustrate?
2. The writer notes that replacing his organization's old transits with different devices will be more expensive than purchasing new transits. How does he justify the added cost?
3. Discuss how, primarily, the writer achieves clarity in this proposal?

PROPOSAL TO CREATE VAN POOL FOR EMPLOYEES

Submitted to: Wilbur R. Budd, Executive Vice-President
By: Wendell Moore, Personnel Director
Date: May 1, 1976

Introduction

(1) I propose that our company purchase five (5) three-quarter-ton, ten-passenger vans in order to form an employees' van pool. The total cost of purchase will be between twenty thousand two hundred fifty dollars ($20,250) and twenty-one thousand twenty-five dollars ($21,025); the exact amount will depend on the make of vehicle chosen.

(2) I have made a study of the need for a van pool and its

feasibility. The idea of a pool was well received by the employees, and putting the proposal into effect will undoubtedly improve management-employee relations and also help alleviate our parking problem. As you know, our present facilities do not meet state requirements. Finally, a van pool would greatly reduce tardiness, absenteeism, and the disruptions of operations which these cause. Preliminary estimates indicate an annual savings of $10,000 from such reductions. Our studies show that the West Bend Corporation and Sun Company have successfully established similar pools. Once the proposal has been adopted, two weeks will be required to obtain bids from auto dealers and another two weeks to start busing.

Equipment

(3) Five vehicles will be needed. Closed bids will be submitted by Chevrolet, Dodge, and Ford dealers. The vehicles will have power steering, power brakes, a seating capacity of ten (10) exclusive of the driver, and the ability to get not less than twenty-one (21) miles per gallon.

Costs

(4) The estimated cost per vehicle and total cost of all vehicles are given in Supplement A. These costs, less the estimated discount and including taxes and license fees, total $20,250 for the least costly vehicle and $21,025 for the most costly. These figures are only estimates, and bidding should lower them.

(5) Supplement B indicates the weekly gasoline expenses for each vehicle, assuming the proposed pickup routes are adopted, while Supplement B-1 shows total weekly gasoline expenses. Since the routes differ in length, the gasoline costs likewise differ. Total gasoline cost for the vehicles is $10.66 per week.

(6) Supplements C, C-1, and C-2 show the estimated weekly income from the vehicles, both before and after gasoline expenses are deducted. The income after gasoline expenses amounts to $73.34. Supplement C-3 calculates the final yearly income after all expenses have been deducted. This final income comes to $3,213.68.

Method

(7) The county will be divided into five areas, each serviced by a different van. Each area will have a central pickup point with an ample parking lot for employee cars. These lots will be checked hourly by the Sheriff's Patrol, so parked cars will be safe from molestation. The vehicles will be placed in charge of our regular motor-pool personnel, who will maintain a log book containing a record of miles driven, gasoline and oil costs, and other maintenance expenses. Vehicles will be operated by present personnel from our driver pool. Each driver will spend about three hours per day busing employees.

(8) This proposal not only offers the advantages mentioned earlier but will establish our company as a leader in fighting city air pollution and in conserving gasoline.

Supplementary Materials

(9) Accompanying this proposal are detailed cost and income estimates for this project.

Conclusion

(10) The estimated costs for vehicles apply to this year's models only. Late this summer, when the 1977 models come out, costs will undoubtedly rise. I therefore urge quick approval of the proposal. I realize the proposal may generate questions, and I am ready to provide any additional information you may wish. Call me anytime at ext. 275, or if you like I will be happy to meet with you in your office at your convenience.

Supplement A: Vehicle Cost Estimate

Vehicle type	Chevrolet	Dodge	Ford
Requirements met, standard cost	$ 4,250	$ 4,360	$ 4,455
Less estimated discount	200	225	250
Total estimated cost	4,050	4,135	4,205
Number of vehicles purchased	x5	x5	x5
Estimated total cost (tax & license inc.)	$20,250	$20,675	$21,025

Supplement B: Maintenance and Expense Estimate

Vehicle number	1	2	3	4	5
Miles traveled per day	9	14	17	21	24
Days per week used	x5	x5	x5	x5	x5
Total miles per week	45	70	85	105	120
Divided by average mpg	21	21	21	21	21
Total gallons per vehicle per week	2.1	3.3	4.0	5.0	5.7
Average price per gallon	$ .53	$ .53	$ .53	$ .53	$ .53
Gasoline cost per week per vehicle	$1.12	$1.75	$2.12	$2.65	$3.02

Supplement B-1: Total Weekly Gasoline Cost

Vehicle Number 1	$ 1.12
Vehicle Number 2	1.75
Vehicle Number 3	2.12
Vehicle Number 4	2.65
Vehicle Number 5	3.02
	$10.66

Supplement C: Estimated Income Provision

Vehicle number	1	2	3	4	5
Number of passengers	7	8	9	9	9
Cost per week to passenger ($0.40 per day x 5)	$ 2.00	$ 2.00	$ 2.00	$ 2.00	$ 2.00
Gross income per vehicle	$14.00	$16.00	$18.00	$18.00	$18.00
Less gasoline per week	1.12	1.75	2.12	2.65	3.02
Income per vehicle after gas	$12.88	$14.25	$15.88	$15.35	$14.98

Supplement C-1: Total Gross Weekly Income

Vehicle Number 1	$14.00
Vehicle Number 2	16.00
Vehicle Number 3	18.00
Vehicle Number 4	18.00
Vehicle Number 5	18.00
	$84.00

Supplement C-2: Total Net Weekly Income

Vehicle Number 1	$12.88
Vehicle Number 2	14.25
Vehicle Number 3	15.88
Vehicle Number 4	15.35
Vehicle Number 5	14.98
	$73.34

Supplement C-3: Total Net Yearly Income

Weekly income after gasoline expense	$ 73.34
Times 52 weeks per year	52
Total	$3,813.68
Less estimated expenses (oil, antifreeze, maintenance, etc.)	600.00
Final income after deducting all expenses	$3,213.68

Discussion Questions

1. What kinds of evidence does the writer use to support his proposal and where in the proposal is each kind found?
2. This proposal is quite long, yet it is clear and the reader can follow it easily. Point out the ways in which clarity has been achieved.
3. Why is the conclusion of this proposal effective?

Suggestions for Writing

1. Write a proposal offering to:

   a. Design an interdisciplinary course, an advanced placement test, or an independent study course for a college or technical institute

   b. Paint a house

   c. Design a pump, boiler, two-cycle engine, carburetor, or other device

   d. Study the traffic-flow pattern of a town, campus, or industrial plant and suggest improvements

   e. Redecorate an office or a room in a private residence

   f. Install a generator, furnace, or lighting system

   g. Design a sewage or water system for a new subdivision

h. Compare the cost and performance characteristics of two fur-
    naces, drying ovens, refrigeration systems, or other devices or
    systems
i. Run comparative tests on two or more adhesives, coatings, fibers,
    castings, or other materials or products
j. Provide outside secretarial or stenographic services to some
    business firm
k. Design a system to control dust, chemical vapors, noise, or
    radiation in a laboratory or other facility
l. Investigate the effects of water pollution on a lake or stream
m. Conduct a survey to determine public attitude toward a political
    candidate, a product, or an existing or proposed law or regula-
    tion
n. Develop and carry out a sales campaign

2. Write a proposal requesting that:

a. Your company stagger its work hours or change its vacation
    policy
b. Your city council switch to a different type of traffic light, rezone
    a particular section of town, or spray for mosquitoes
c. Your school extend the library hours, change its grading system,
    or make some other needed improvement
d. Your company improve its lighting, reduce the noise level, install
    vending machines, or provide an employee lounge

10

Progress Reports

Progress reports are used to trace the development of a particular project or, at times, the activities of an individual or organization. Depending upon the nature and scope of the project, reports may be issued weekly, monthly, quarterly, annually, at some other set interval, or irregularly. With some exceptions—for example, sales reports, production reports, and annual reports put out by corporations—progress reports are prepared for projects that will be finished at some future time.

Progress reports vary greatly in length and complexity. If the project is simple, they may be issued as letters or memorandums. If the project is more complex, they may extend to many pages, especially if they are issued infrequently. In rare cases, the reports may even be issued as bound volumes. Like the examples in this book, however, most progress reports are likely to be rather brief.

Progress reports are written in every field, for projects of every sort. For example, you may be asked to write reports that summarize:

1. the progress in a laboratory or research project
2. the progress in the construction of a building, dam, bridge, or highway

3. the course of an advertising or public-relations campaign
4. the stages in the remodeling of a building or other facility or in the installation of new machinery or equipment
5. the activities of your organization over a six-month or one-year period

Value of Progress Reports

Progress reports are valuable for several reasons. To begin with, they enable project directors to schedule equipment and supplies so that they are on hand when needed and to start separate phases of a project as soon as preparatory work is completed. Thus, progress reports help keep projects running smoothly and on or ahead of schedule.

Progress reports also allow management to check on the direction and emphasis of a project and change them if necessary. Assume, for example, that a company has discovered an inexpensive way to make a compound that formerly was very costly. Produced at low cost, this compound may now have utility as both a dry-cleaning solvent and a metal-degreasing solvent. The company sets up a six-month research project and budgets $50,000 to investigate each use. Progress reports are issued every two months. The first phase of the dry-cleaning investigation shows that the compound causes some dyes to fade. On the other hand, preliminary evidence indicates that the compound is an even better metal-cleaning solvent than originally thought. Armed with this information, management can stop work on the dry-cleaning application and use the remaining funds to expand work on the metal-cleaning application.

Management may use progress reports to evaluate the work already done on a project in light of what remains to be done and to drop the project if this action seems called for. For example, a large bottling company may budget $5,000—but no more—to determine whether a new adhesive for bottle labels is better than the one presently used. If progress reports show that more than the allotted sum will be needed to obtain the information, the project can be cancelled and the unspent money saved.

Moreover, progress reports can prevent a last-minute crisis that might otherwise develop if a project is delayed. Suppose a college has planned to begin using a new dormitory by the beginning of the fall semester, but a shortage of structural steel has caused a six-month construction lag. By reading progress reports, school officials will become aware of the situation in time to make alternate plans.

Progress reports have value for the writer as well as the receiver. Unless you write periodic reports, there's some danger that you'll waste time on unimportant aspects of the project or perhaps even forget a primary aim. As a result, the project may be delayed, or you may need to repeat part of the work. If you prepare progress reports, however, these problems are less likely to occur, for you must reconsider the aims of the project every time you write a new report.

Parts of Progress Reports

A typical progress report consists of two parts: the heading and the body. The initial report on a particular project also includes an introduction. These parts are discussed below.

HEADING

The heading of a progress report includes the writer's and recipient's names and titles, the name and the number (if any) of the project, and the time period covered by the report. A typical heading might be:

To: John Ashton, General Contractor
From: John Burtch, Site Foreman
Project: Job No. 579-103-074, Construction of "Knoll on the Lake"
         Apartment Complex
Time Covered by Report: December 1975 through January 1976

INTRODUCTION

Ordinarily, an introduction is included only in the first progress report in a series. The introduction presents the background and goals of the project, indicates when the work will be completed, and points out any special requirements that must be met. If, for example, the project involves designing a device meeting certain specifications, then these specifications should be pointed out. So, too, should any special limitations on the scope of the investigation, the test methods to be employed, and the like. If the project involves a small number of people, their names are customarily included in the introduction. As personnel are added to or dropped from the project, changes are noted at the appropriate point in the body of the report. The following introduction illustrates these features.

> A group of students consisting of Christopher Lichty, Kurt Meyers, and Ronald Jones has been assigned to design a pump that meets the specifications set by Professor Kimberley Gillette on January 30, 1976. The pump is to be constructed as an integral unit that is driven by a belt and pulley powered by a small air-cooled engine. Its height must not exceed 10 inches and its weight must be less than 10 pounds. It must be capable of delivering 10 gallons per minute at 550 revolutions per minute (rpm), and its parts must withstand a maximum pressure of 400 pounds per square inch (psi). The pump is to be designed and drawn by April 30, 1976.
>
> *Ronald Jones*

BODY

The body of most progress reports is organized in three sections:

1. work completed—what has been done since the last report
2. present status—where the project stands now
3. work remaining—what will be done next

The complexity of the report will determine whether or not formal headings will be needed for these three sections. If headings will improve the clarity of the report, then they should be included.

Sometimes—for instance, when there are long intervals between progress reports—it is useful for the reader to be reminded of the status of the project at the time of the last report. In such a case, the body of the report may begin with a summary of the previously reported status.

Here is a progress report—on the rebuilding of a snowmobile —organized by time sequence.

Work Completed

We began by disassembling the old sled completely. Every part was taken off, cleaned, and carefully weighed. Because more speed was needed, we reworked a rotor cover so that it could be turned upside down. Doing this allowed us to adapt a set of Mikuni road-racing carburetors for use with the sled. To match the carburetor, we designed a set of pipes which will be fitted and tested when the sled is reassembled. To obtain better stability, we moved the right ski spindle out three inches. An internal-drive track was chosen because of its lighter weight and the better acceleration it provides. A two-gallon gas tank has been fabricated for installation on the left running board below the clutch.

Present Status

At present, every unneeded pound has been removed from the sled, giving us a very fast machine. With the foregoing work completed, the sled is now ready to be reassembled.

Work Remaining

We must hand-make a front drive so that we can use an Arctic-Cat track on our chassis. The "Cat" suspension must be reworked to get the weight transfer needed for sprint racing. When the sled is back together, we will test it to see if the transfer is right. The weight of the reassembled sled will be around two hundred and eighty pounds. The snowmobile should be finished by the second week in January so that we can enter it in the first race.

Daniel Budzynski

This three-part organization works well when the project is a simple one. But some projects involve a number of tasks being carried out simultaneously, sometimes at different locations. When a project is this complex, it is easier to both write and understand the progress report if it is organized according to the various tasks. Thus, a report describing the progress in the construction of a large apartment complex would include such main headings as plumbing, wiring, heating and ventilation, and the like. Within each major section, however, the discussion should be organized in the past-present-future pattern that is used for reports on simple projects.

In most progress reports, it is enough simply to mention the specific procedures you have carried out in connection with the project. If, however, a procedure is likely to be unfamiliar to your readers, you may wish to include some details or refer readers to a separate process explanation. If it seems desirable to change the direction of a project or even to abandon it, do not hesitate to say so. Be sure, though, that you have sufficient evidence on hand before making such a recommendation, for preliminary findings are often contradicted by later work. If additional materials, equipment, or personnel will be required, ask for them. Finally, do not be afraid to make cautious predictions concerning findings, ability to meet the project schedule, and the like, but at the same time avoid hasty promises. Any such information you add should be presented at the appropriate place in the body of the report. For example, if you carried out an unfamiliar procedure, you would discuss it in the work-done section; predictions would come in the work-remaining section.

When a project is finished, the separate progress reports are sometimes gathered together and issued as a single unit. Sometimes, too, an overall report is written based on the information contained in the separate reports. Because of these possibilities, it is important that all the progress reports on a particular project follow the same pattern.

STUDENT EXAMPLES

To: Kimberley Gillette, Professor of Engineering
From: Ronald Jones, Student
Project: Design of Pump No. P10400
Time Covered by Report: January 30, 1976, through February
                        28, 1976

(1) A group of students consisting of Christopher Lichty, Kurt Meyers, and Ronald Jones has been assigned to design a pump that meets the specifications set by Professor Kimberley Gillette on January 30, 1976. The pump is to be constructed as an integral unit that is driven by a belt and pulley powered by a

small air-cooled engine. Its height must not exceed 10 inches and its weight must be less than 10 pounds. It must be capable of delivering 10 gallons per minute at 550 revolutions per minute (rpm), and its parts must withstand a maximum pressure of 400 pounds per square inch (psi). The pump is to be designed and drawn by April 30, 1976.

(2) On February 1, the group decided in a brainstorming session that a positive displacement pump would be adequate to meet the required specifications. Cast 1013 aluminum was selected as the material of construction for most parts because of its low cost and ability to withstand vibration. Two pistons, each with a diameter of 1¾ inches and a 1-inch stroke, will provide an even displacement. The cylinder walls will be ⅛ inch thick—a thickness easily capable of withstanding the 400 psi load specified. Rough sketches of the internal assembly have now been drawn.

(3) Two major parts of the pump must still be designed. Jones will design the type and size of valves needed to produce the correct volume of flow, while Meyers will determine the size of the shaft and its material. Finally, Lichty will design the other parts required. These determinations will be completed by March 5 and further analysis of the design within three weeks thereafter. Final assembly and detail drawings will then be started, and they will be finished by the April 30 deadline date if everything goes as planned.

Discussion Questions

1. Why does this report include a discussion of the project's background?
2. Which sentence deals with the present status of the project? Why is the present status not discussed more fully?

To: John R. Miller, Chief Technologist
From: Glenn Jones, Engineer
Project: No. 900, The Impact of Integrated Circuits on the Electronics Industry
Time Covered by Report: April 1, 1976, through May 31, 1976

(1) On April 2, 1976, a preliminary meeting of the investigation committee was held. At the meeting, it was decided to con-

sider the following three aspects of the impact of integrated circuits: (1) extent of possible use, (2) costs, and (3) problems of utilizing the circuits in electronic equipment.

(2) On April 8, detailed discussions were held with several major manufacturers of integrated circuits during the National Instrument Technologists' Convention in New York City. These discussions revealed that about 70 percent of all existing electronic circuits could be produced in integrated form.

(3) Following the New York meeting, the chief engineers of several major semiconductor manufacturers were contacted and asked to comment on the relative costs of designing and manufacturing integrated circuits. These engineers agreed that design costs were quite high, since any overall design program must include:

1. design of the functional circuit, often in breadboard form
2. design of each individual circuit element and the geometric layout, including the interconnection pattern
3. design of the photomasks required for the oxide-removal stages
4. development of suitable test programs
5. hand assembly of trial test units

Because of the great variety of integrated circuits required for the different types of electronic devices now manufactured, no general development-cost figure is possible.

(4) At present, a 150-item questionnaire concerning the problems of incorporating integrated circuits into electronic equipment and marketing the resultant products is being prepared. Since great care must be taken to phrase the questions properly, the questionnaire will not be completed until late July.

(5) Once the questionnaire is completed, it will be sent to some 200 manufacturers of electronic equipment with the request that it be filled out and returned by August 15. The findings will be analyzed and summarized in the final progress report at the end of September.

Discussion Questions

1. In the discussion at the beginning of this chapter, it was stated that progress reports prevent the writer from forgetting the primary

aims of the project. What evidence is there that the writer of this report has kept the aims in mind?

2. What advantage has been gained by tabulating the individual elements of the design program in a formal list rather than presenting them in a regular sentence form?

3. In which paragraphs does the writer discuss work completed, present status, and work remaining? What devices besides paragraphing are used to distinguish between these three segments of the report?

To: Rodney Marshall, Director, Vassar Recreation Department

From: Robert Bishop, Supervisor of Construction and Maintenance

Project: Construction of New Municipal Tennis Courts

Time Covered by Report: June 1, 1976, through June 14, 1976

(1) Installation of the cement forms for the five new courts was completed on June 1. Two days were needed to install the holding wire for the cement and the poles for the nets. Three courts were poured on June 4 and two on June 7. On June 9, Benson's Asphalt, Inc., surfaced the courts with two inches of rubber-base asphalt. The courts were primed, sealed, and painted on June 10 and 11.

(2) The nets were installed this morning, Monday, June 14. We are presently unloading the ten-foot chain link fence that will enclose the courts. We should have it installed by Monday, June 21.

(3) Once the fence is installed, we will begin digging the holes for the light poles. The lights and poles will be delivered Wednesday, June 23, and we expect to have them installed by Friday, June 25. Scheduled date of completion is Monday, June 28.

Discussion Questions

1. Has the writer provided a proper heading for his report? Support your answer with specific evidence.

2. Why have captions been omitted from this report?

To: James Reich, York College Surveying Department
From: Randy Richards, Student
Project: Triangulation Traverse of Area North of York College
Time Covered by Report: May 10, 1976, through May 26, 1976

Work Completed

(1) On May 10, we began the actual triangulation traverse. As noted in the first report, a reconnaissance survey revealed that the college campus had been triangulated under the Lambert Projection Coordinate System and monuments had been set at various points on campus. Thus, we tied our traverse into the traverse on campus.

(2) To begin, we established a traverse point over a manhole by turning angles to two known monuments, one at the Marymar Street entrance to the campus and the other at the Science Building. We then turned angles to points 87-4, 87-3, and traverse point No. 2, located at the front entrance of the Science Building. By traversing to the top of the hill at the intersection of Chestnut Street and Hill Avenues, we were able to turn angles to points 86-4, 86-3, and 86-2 from one traverse point, TP_3. From here, we traversed to the intersection of Locust Street and Hill Avenue, where we turned angles to TP_5, TP_6, and TP_7.

Present Status

(3) Currently, we are turning the remainder of the angles to all points up to point 84-1, which is located on a manhole cover by the Maple Street bridge. Because of unanticipated road repairs in the surveying area, we are two days behind schedule.

Work Remaining

(4) Once our present activities are completed, we will return to TP_1, measure the distance to all points with an electronic distance-measuring device, and calculate the vertical angles. Finally, we will traverse southward on Ives Street from point 84-2 and pick up any point missed in the northward traverse up Hill Avenue. When the project is finished, we will have established coordinates on all sixteen points from 84-1 through 87-4.

(5) We plan to complete the project on June 11, weather permitting. This will be two days later than anticipated. When we are finished, we will have a second-order-of-accuracy survey. The maximum angular closure per triangle will be 5 seconds. The average angular closure will be 3 seconds. Distances will be accurate to 1 foot in 10,000 feet.

Discussion Questions

1. Why are captions included in this report?
2. Why does the report omit an introduction?
3. The report notes that the project is two days behind schedule and that it will be completed at least two days late. What purpose is served by this information?

To: Jack Powers, Commissioner, Monroe County Health Department
From: Paul Lewis, Sanitarian, Monroe County Health Department
Project: Improvement of Restaurant Inspection Scores
Time Covered by Report: January 1, 1975, through January 1, 1976

Introduction

(1) This is the first progress report on our department's program to improve the overall scores of restaurant inspections. A 1974 survey showed that Monroe County had the worst restaurant inspection scores of any county in New York State. The state average at that time was 30 points, and Monroe County's average was 42.

(2) To correct this situation, the present program was put into effect January 1, 1975. The program aims to lower the average inspection score for the county to 30 and to eliminate all scores over 40 by January 1, 1980. The program involves:

1. inspecting restaurants more frequently and enforcing the food code more stringently
2. establishing mandatory management certification programs for restaurant managers

3. establishing a cooperative board of sanitarians, restaurant owners and managers, and restaurant employees to coordinate the program and deal with any problems that arise

Work Completed

(3) This program has now been in effect for one year. During this period, restaurants were inspected every three months rather than semiannually, as in the past. The average inspection score has been reduced 6 points below the 1974 figure. Much of the improvement is due to the increased strictness of the inspectors, who were instructed to suspend the licenses of any restaurant that scored over 40 points on two successive inspections. Once this fact became known, most restaurant owners quickly complied with the food-service code.

(4) The first mandatory management certification course got under way on June 2, and the first meeting of the cooperative board was held on July 1.

Present Status

(5) The management certification program is off to a good start; over 30 restaurant managers have completed the two-month course. This training has already resulted in the elimination of many food-code violations.

(6) Because of the rapid turnover of restaurant employees, the cooperative board has been without an employee representative for five of the six months it has been in existence. Without the employee voice, the board has become largely a management–health department group. As a result, many employees feel that their opinions are not wanted and refuse to work with the board. A public-relations consultant has been called in to work on the problem.

Future Plans

(7) During 1976, we hope to reduce the average restaurant inspection score by another 3 points. To help achieve this goal, we plan to continue inspecting restaurants on a quarterly basis and to suspend licenses whenever more than 40 points are

scored on two successive inspections. By the end of the year, some 90 restaurant managers—about one-half the total in the county—will have completed the management certification program.

Discussion Questions

1. Has the writer provided a proper introduction for his report? Support your answer with specific evidence.
2. In the discussion at the beginning of the chapter, it was stated that progress reports prevent the writer from forgetting the primary aims of the project. What evidence is there that the writer of this report has kept these aims in mind?
3. At one point, the writer discusses a problem that has arisen in connection with the project. Locate this discussion.

Suggestions for Writing

Write a progress report on:

1. A research or construction project carried out as part of a course
2. The reorganization of the floor plan of some retail business establishment
3. The construction or remodeling of a store, office building, or house
4. The reorganization of a factory assembly line
5. The resurfacing of a section of roadway
6. A sales campaign
7. A public immunization campaign
8. The remodeling of a laboratory or X-ray facility in a hospital
9. A local fund-raising drive
10. The installation of machinery in a shop
11. The installation of a furnace or air-conditioning system in a commercial building or private house
12. The activities of a professional organization
13. An industrial research project
14. The reorganization of a town's traffic-flow pattern
15. A survey being conducted among members of a certain trade or profession
16. The design of a piece of equipment or apparatus
17. Your progress in one of your courses

11

Investigation Reports

The investigation report describes and discusses the results of a test or other investigation carried out in the laboratory, the shop, or the field. It is, in a sense, a continuation of the process description (discussed in chapter 5), for it tells what results were obtained when a particular process was carried out.

You can expect to write investigation reports both for your courses and on the job. In your classes, an instructor may ask you to describe, for example, the results obtained when you checked a water sample for coliform organisms, determined the specific heat of a metal, analyzed a chemical compound for a particular impurity, determined the cylinder pressures in an automobile engine, or ran a soil percolation test. Such a report helps an instructor gauge your progress by showing how well you have mastered the apparatus, procedures, theory, and calculations involved in the work. It helps you by reinforcing what you have learned in the classroom and through your reading, and it familiarizes you with the format you will follow later when you write on-the-job reports.

On the job, investigation reports have a variety of uses. You may have to report and discuss the results of tests showing the properties of some adhesive, coating material, lubricant, or metal alloy; the condition of an air, water, or soil sample; or the best apparatus or procedure for manufacturing a product. The information these reports provide can be used to improve products or procedures, correct undesirable conditions, or take whatever other action is appropriate.

Full-scale reports are rarely required for work that is performed routinely. For such work, forms are usually provided, and the pertinent information is simply filled in. However, when work is nonroutine, a detailed report must be written. Such a report includes the following sections:

1. heading
2. purpose
3. theory
4. procedure
5. results
6. discussion of results
7. recommendations
8. appendix

These sections are discussed below.

Heading

The heading of an investigation report is similar to that of a proposal or progress report. It includes the name and title of the receiver and the sender, the title of the investigation, and the date of the report. A typical heading follows.

To: Marian McCollum, Director, County Health Department
From: Walter Chavez, Sanitarian
MPN–Presumptive Test, Oxbow Lake
Date: September 1, 1976

Purpose

In stating the purpose of your work, be very specific. If, for example, you are describing the results of an automobile oil consumption test, give the engine size, year, and make of the vehicle. Likewise, tell why the test was performed. This part of the paper does not have to be long. Four or five sentences at most should be sufficient. Two statements of purpose follow.

> The purpose of this study was to determine the most probable number (MPN) of coliform organisms present in a sample of water taken from Oxbow Lake in Porter Township. The department conducted the study because several cases of dysentery have recently been reported by persons who own cottages on the lake.
>
> *Walter Chavez*

> This investigation was carried out to determine the mass concentration of suspended particulate matter in the atmosphere of the residential area bordering the Oakland Metal Fabricating Company. Numerous citizens had complained about excessive fly ash.
>
> *Sherry Durren*

Theory

Following the statement of purpose, present the theory if one is needed. The theory is the basic principle or principles that underlie some procedures. Unless the procedure is based on some such clear principle(s), do not give a theory. Generally, reports on procedures in chemistry, physics, or similar well-defined scientific disciplines include a statement of the theory, whereas other types of investigations—for example, to determine the wearability of a particular type of automobile tire or the light-fastness of a plastic material—do not. Here is one example of a theory:

> The coliform group of bacteria are capable of fermenting lactose sugar to form gas. The presence of gas in an inoculated tube indicates that coliform organisms were present in the water sample; the number of tubes showing gas provides a measure of the degree of contamination.
>
> *Walter Chavez*

Procedure

This section of the report tells the reader how the investigation was carried out. In describing the procedure, be brief. Don't try to write an explanation that would enable the reader to carry out the process. Instead, say just enough to give the reader an intelligent idea of what was done. You can usually accomplish this in a few sentences. Here is how the procedure for analyzing furnace flue gas for carbon dioxide might be written:

> Before the test was begun, a one-fourth-inch hole was drilled in the smoke stack between the boiler breeching and the draft regulator. A second hole was drilled in the fire door. The short sampling tube was inserted in the smoke stack; then the analyzer was adjusted to read zero. The sample was taken by depressing the analyzer bulb eighteen times, and the results were read and recorded. This procedure was repeated using a long sampling tube and sampling through the fire door.
>
> *Charles Finnie*

Results

Depending upon the particular investigation, the results may consist of the actual observations, measurements, or readings; they may also include figures derived from the measurements or readings by using a formula, chart, or graph. In a report on an automobile cylinder pressure test, the results are simply the readings obtained with the pressure gauge:

cylinder no. 1—170 pounds
cylinder no. 2—180 pounds
cylinder no. 3—165 pounds
cylinder no. 4—175 pounds
cylinder no. 5—170 pounds
cylinder no. 6—240 pounds
cylinder no. 7—175 pounds
cylinder no. 8— 90 pounds

Leslie Danforth

Sometimes the results of a test are not only the observations but the findings derived from them. Consider, for example, the determination of the most probable number (MPN) of coliform organisms in a water sample. In this test, a series of lactose-broth tubes is inoculated with the water, incubated, and checked to determine the number of tubes in which gas forms. A chart is then consulted to find the most probable number of organisms. The results section of the report would include the observations, the chart, and the findings obtained through use of the chart. For example:

> After this 48-hour incubation period, the tubes were examined for evidence of gas formation. The observations were as follows:
>
>> tube no. 1—gas
>> tube no. 2—no gas
>> tube no. 3—no gas
>> tube no. 4—gas
>> tube no. 5—no gas
>
> The MPN Index was then calculated from the following chart:
>
> | Number of Tubes with Gas | MPN Index/100 Ml. Sample |
> | --- | --- |
> | none | less than 2.2 |
> | 1 | 2.2 |
> | 2 | 5.1 |
> | 3 | 9.2 |
> | 4 | 16.0 |
> | 5 | infinite |
>
> Since only two tubes showed the presence of gas, the most probable number of coliform organisms was 5.1/100 ml. of the water sample.
>
> *Walter Chavez*

When the test findings are determined by use of a formula, the results section includes the measurements or readings, the formula, and the findings. A report on an investigation to determine atmospheric concentrations of suspended particulate matter might have the following results section:

	North Sampling Location	South Sampling Location
Initial weight of filter, grams	3.0969	3.0947
Final weight of filter, grams	3.1896	3.1692
Volume of air sampled, cubic meters	2,218	1,904

The mass concentration of particulate matter was then calculated by use of the following formula:

$$SP = \frac{(W_t - W_i) \times 10^6}{V}$$

where: W_t = final weight of filter, grams
W_i = initial weight of filter, grams
V = volume of air sampled, cubic meters
SP = suspended particulate matter, micrograms/ cubic meter

The results of the calculations are shown below.

	North Sampling Location	South Sampling Location
SP	41.8	39.1

Sherry Durren

Discussion of Results

This section of the report evaluates the test results and discusses their significance. The content will vary according to the investigation and its purpose. If the investigation involved checking a property of some material—say, the specific heat of copper— you would compare the experimental results with the expected value and try to account for any discrepancy. If you tested several materials for possible use in a particular application, you would discuss how well or poorly each meets the requirements. If the purpose of the investigation was to determine whether or not a particular condition exists, your discussion would answer the question or, if the results are inconclusive, point out the need for further work. Here's how two student writers discuss their results:

The test results show the carbon dioxide content of the flue gas to be 1.5 percent below the normal range. The low carbon dioxide content could have several possible causes: the wrong type of fuel oil, an air leak in the furnace, an air shutter open too far, or a defective nozzle. Since neither the oil nor the oil supplier had been changed, the first probable cause was ruled out, and examination of the furnace quickly eliminated the next two. A check of the nozzle, however, revealed that its screen was clogged with a thick, gummy oil deposit.

Charles Finnie

Although the results show an MPN Index of 5.1 coliforms/ 100 ml., this presumptive test indicates only the presence or absence of gas production, not actual colony morphology. It is possible that the gas produced in the tubes was due to some other type of organism capable of fermenting lactose sugar to form gas. Additional and more precise tests are therefore required before a definite conclusion can be reached.

Walter Chavez

Sometimes the pattern of the results or the spread between the highest and lowest values obtained may be significant. If this is the case, not only the results but their pattern or spread should be discussed. For example, with automobile cylinder pressure tests, the pattern of results is very important. If two consecutive cylinders have below-normal pressures, the problem is likely to be a bad head gasket, although it could also be worn rings. If, on the other hand, only one cylinder or several nonadjacent cylinders display low pressures, then a bad head gasket can be ruled out.

Recommendations

Whenever the results will be used to decide some future course of action, the report must include a recommendations section. Student reports written for laboratory or shop courses are seldom used for this purpose, so they usually do not contain recommendations. For on-the-job reports, however, a recommendations section is almost always a requirement.

The specific recommendation will, of course, depend upon the purpose and scope of the test. You might, for example, recommend that another material, procedure, or device be adopted in place of one presently used; that a product be taken off the market; that a piece of equipment be overhauled or repaired; or that certain precautionary measures be taken. If the scope of the test work was limited, you may recommend that further tests be carried out. Here are two recommendations:

> It is recommended that the old nozzle be replaced with a new one.
>
> *Charles Finnie*

> It is recommended that confirmation and completion tests be carried out on samples of the water to obtain positive proof that the gas produced in this test was generated by coliform organisms.
>
> *Walter Chavez*

Frequently cost, as well as test results, determines the recommendation that is made. Assume that a company which manufactures wall paneling is testing several glues as possible replacements for the one it now uses. Test results show that none of the experimental glues provides bonding strengths equal to those now obtained. However, one experimental glue yields only slightly lower strengths and costs 35 percent less. Here, the recommendation might be to switch to the less expensive glue.

Appendix

The appendix contains material that supplements the information contained in the report proper. If there is no supplementary material, the report will have no appendix. Supplementary material may include:

> test data too detailed to include in the body of the report
> mathematical calculations used in preparing the report
> brochures, bulletins, letters, reports
> drawings, graphs, maps, photographs
> field, laboratory, and shop notes
> case histories
> equipment lists
> specifications

When more than one type of information is included in the appendix, group each type in a separate, clearly labeled section. Refer to pertinent information at the appropriate points in the body of the report so that the reader knows when to consult the appendix.

Ordinarily, test data are included in the appendix only when they are too voluminous to be presented in the results section in their entirety. When data consist of many individual measurements, the measurements can be grouped and averaged and the averages presented in the report proper. Thus, 100 readings or measurements might be divided into ten groups of ten, averaged, and the ten average values considered in the results section. All 100 readings, however, would be listed in the appendix.

It is essential that the test data in the appendix be complete, for the pattern displayed by the individual measurements often has an important bearing on the use made of the figures presented in the results section. Suppose the figure 29 represents an average of the following ten measurements: 27, 29, 31, 32, 30, 26, 31, 30, 28, 26. Because of the narrow spread between the highest and lowest figures, the average of 29 reflects quite well the value of the individual measurements. If, on the other hand, the average is 29 but the individual measurements range from a low of 10 to a high of 41, then the validity of the average is much more questionable, and this fact could affect the recommendations made.

STUDENT EXAMPLES

To: William Winkelman, Service Manager
From: James Abbott, Mechanic
Oil Consumption Test
Date: June 15, 1976

Purpose

(1) The purpose of this test was to determine whether the 400-cubic-inch engine in the 1976 Chevrolet Caprice owned by Mrs. Myra Hamilton was burning enough oil to justify engine

repairs under the terms of its warranty. The owner requested the test because she suspected excessive oil consumption.

Procedure

(2) Before the test was begun, the oil pressure was checked, the PCV valve replaced, the engine thoroughly cleaned and checked for outside oil leakage, the oil and oil filters changed, and the mileage noted.

(3) During the next 2,000 miles of driving, the owner brought her car into the service department whenever it needed oil. The required amount of oil was added, and the mileage was noted. When 2,000 miles had been driven, the oil consumption rate was calculated.

Results

(4) The results obtained when the above procedure was followed are shown in the table below.

Mileage	Quarts of Oil Added
2,500	—
2,900	1
3,300	1
3,700	2
4,100	2
4,500	2

Discussion of Results

(5) These results show that the engine burned an average of one quart of oil every 250 miles. According to the engine specifications, however, the oil consumption should not exceed one quart every 300 miles. Consumption is therefore excessive.

Recommendations

(6) It is recommended that the intake manifold gasket, guide valve, and guide valve seals be checked, a wet-dry compression test run, and any faulty condition be corrected under warranty.

Discussion Questions

1. Comment on the adequacy of the heading. Support your comments with specific evidence.
2. Note that this report does not include a statement of theory. How can the omission be justified?
3. Why has the writer of this report omitted an appendix?

To: Marian McCollum, Director, County Health Department
From: Walter Chavez, Sanitarian
MPN–Presumptive Test, Oxbow Lake
Date: September 1, 1976

Purpose

(1) The purpose of this study was to determine the most probable number (MPN) of coliform organisms present in a sample of water taken from Oxbow Lake in Porter Township. The department conducted the study because several cases of dysentery have recently been reported by persons who own cottages on the lake.

Theory

(2) The coliform group of bacteria are capable of fermenting lactose sugar to form gas. The presence of gas in an inoculated tube indicates that coliform organisms were present in the water sample; the number of tubes showing gas provides a measure of the degree of contamination.

Procedure

(3) Five lactose-broth tubes, each containing smaller inverted tubes, were aseptically inoculated with 10 ml. of the water sample. These tubes were then incubated at 35°C for 48 hours.

Results

(4) After this 48-hour incubation period, the tubes were examined for evidence of gas formation. The observations were as follows:

tube no. 1—gas
tube no. 2—no gas
tube no. 3—no gas
tube no. 4—gas
tube no. 5—no gas

(5) The MPN Index was then calculated from the following chart:

Number of Tubes with Gas	MPN Index/100 Ml. Sample
none	less than 2.2
1	2.2
2	5.1
3	9.2
4	16.0
5	infinite

(6) Since only two tubes showed the presence of gas, the most probable number of coliform organisms was 5.1/100 ml. of the water sample.

Discussion of Results

(7) Although the results show an MPN Index of 5.1 coliforms/100 ml., this presumptive test indicates only the presence or absence of gas production, not actual colony morphology. It is possible that the gas produced in the tubes was due to some other type of organism capable of fermenting lactose sugar to form gas. Additional and more precise tests are therefore required before a definite conclusion can be reached.

Recommendations

(8) It is recommended that confirmation and completion tests be carried out on samples of the water to obtain positive proof that the gas produced in this test was generated by coliform organisms.

Discussion Questions

1. Comment on the effectiveness of this report's purpose section.
2. Which data in the results section are the actual test results? What is the purpose of the other information?

To: Malcolm O'Reilly, Director of Research and Development
From: Thomas Gauthier, Test Engineer
Road Testing Radial Highway Tires
Date: April 9, 1976

Purpose

(1) This work was carried out to test the mileage capability of our newly developed Model XT-225 radial highway tire. This study is the first segment of a field-testing program designed to determine whether or not our tire is equal or superior in wearability to the corresponding models made by our three competitors. Laboratory testing had previously shown the XT-225 to be slightly superior in wearability to the others.

Procedure

(2) The National Bus Company was contacted and agreed to participate in the tests. One set of our tires was installed on a bus, and one set each of Ace T-34, Mercury R-29, and All-Grip M-40 tires was placed on three other buses. Each of these buses operated on the same 350-mile run.

(3) The tires were inflated to the manufacturers' recommended pressures, the depth of the tread measured with a dial indicator, and the average depth calculated for each of the four models. After 7,000 miles, the depth of tread was again measured, and the number of miles required to produce each one-thousandth inch of wear was calculated (see Appendix).

Results

Tire	Miles per one-thousandth inch of wear
Rebound XT-225	79.9
Ace T-34	80.1
Mercury R-29	78.6
All-Grip M-40	79.5

Discussion and Recommendations

(4) Test results show our XT-225 tire to be slightly inferior in wearability to the Ace T-34 tire but slightly better than the Mercury R-29 and All-Grip M-40.

(5) It is recommended that the remaining phases of the field-testing program and the safety-testing program, outlined in report 23-597RHT, be carried out. Preliminary market research and pricing studies should also be initiated as soon as feasible.

Appendix

Tire Tread Wear Data

Make of Tire	Tire Number	Original Tread Depths, Thousandths Inch	Final Tread Depths, Thousandths Inch	Difference, Thousandths Inch	Average Difference, Thousandths Inch
Rebound XT-225	1	500	416	84	
	2	500	410	90	
	3	500	412	88	
	4	500	412	88	87.6
	5	500	414	86	
	6	500	415	85	
	7	500	411	89	
	8	500	409	91	
Ace T-34	1	501*	413	88	
	2	499	415	84	
	3	500	416	84	
	4	502	414	88	87.4
	5	503	411	92	
	6	500	413	87	
	7	505	420	85	
	8	501	410	91	
Mercury R-29	1	504	415	89	
	2	501	415	86	
	3	504	411	93	
	4	502	411	91	89.0
	5	497	409	88	
	6	496	404	92	
	7	503	416	87	
	8	501	415	86	

* Variations probably occurred because tires were made in different molds.

Make of Tire	Tire Number	Original Tread Depths, Thousandths Inch	Final Tread Depths, Thousandths Inch	Difference, Thousandths Inch	Average Difference, Thousandths Inch
	1	498	413	85	
	2	498	410	88	
All-Grip	3	497	407	90	
M-40	4	502	411	91	88.1
	5	503	419	84	
	6	497	406	91	
	7	496	407	89	
	8	503	416	87	

Calculation, Miles per One-Thousandth Inch of Wear

Rebound XT-225 $\dfrac{7000}{87.6} = 79.9$

Ace T-34 $\dfrac{7000}{87.4} = 80.1$

Mercury R-29 $\dfrac{7000}{89.0} = 78.6$

All-Grip M-40 $\dfrac{7000}{88.1} = 79.5$

Discussion Questions

1. Comment on the adequacy of the procedure section of this report, citing specific evidence to support your evaluation.
2. Why does this report include an appendix?
3. Do the average values presented in the results section accurately reflect the value of the individual measurements from which they were derived? Support your answer with specific evidence.

To: Andrew Nye, Director, State Department of Public Health
From: Joseph Hibberd, Sanitarian
Percolation Test Report, Victoria Hills Subdivision
Date: June 4, 1976

Purpose

(1) The purpose of this test was to determine whether the soil on lot #17, Victoria Hills subdivision, Highland Township, is suitable for the installation of an on-site sewage disposal system. This test was performed at the request of the Saginaw County Health Department.

Procedure

(2) Six holes were dug at the rear (south) portion of the lot, on the site of the proposed absorption field (see Appendix). Each hole was 6 to 8 inches in diameter and 40 to 42 inches deep. The holes were presoaked for 10 hours, causing the soil particles to swell and simulating conditions during the wettest part of the year.

(3) A nail was placed in the side of each hole six inches from the bottom, and water was poured into the hole up to the nail marker. After 30 minutes the drop in water level was measured and recorded. The holes were refilled to the marker, and the procedure was repeated until eight readings were recorded. The last reading taken in each hole was used to calculate the percolation rate. The temperature during the test was 62° F.

Results

Drop in Inches, Hole No.

Test No.	Time	1	2	3	4	5	6
1	9:30 A.M.	6	6	6	6	6	6
2	10:00	6	6	5½	6	5	6
3	10:30	6	6	5	5¾	4½	5
4	11:00	6	5	5	5	4	5
5	11:30	5½	5	4½	4½	3¾	4½
6	12:00 P.M.	5½	4½	4	4¼	3½	4
7	12:30	5	4½	4	4¼	3	3¾
8	1:00	4¾	4	3½	4	3	3¼

Calculation of Percolation Rate

Hole No.	Drop in Inches, Final Reading	Rate of Drop, Minutes/Inch
1	4¾	6
2	4	8
3	3½	9
4	4	8
5	3	10
6	3¼	9
	Total	50

Average percolation rate 50/6 = 8 minutes/inch

Discussion of Results

(4) This percolation rate meets the requirements of the Michigan Department of Public Health for on-lot sewage disposal systems.

(5) The soil appears to be a loamy sand with approximately 80 percent sand, 10 percent silt, and 10 percent clay. No rock formations, fragipan, or mottled soil were observed; these items would impair the efficiency of the sewage disposal system. There were no surface drainage or slope limitations in the location tested.

Recommendations

(6) The rear of lot #17, Victoria Hills subdivision, is suitable for the installation of an on-lot sewage disposal system. It is recommended that a permit be issued by the Saginaw County Health Department to allow construction of the system.

Appendix: Location of Percolation Test

(7) The accompanying diagram shows lot # 17, Victoria Hills subdivision, and the location of the percolation test holes.

Discussion Questions

1. Comment on the adequacy of the purpose section, supporting your evaluation with specific evidence.

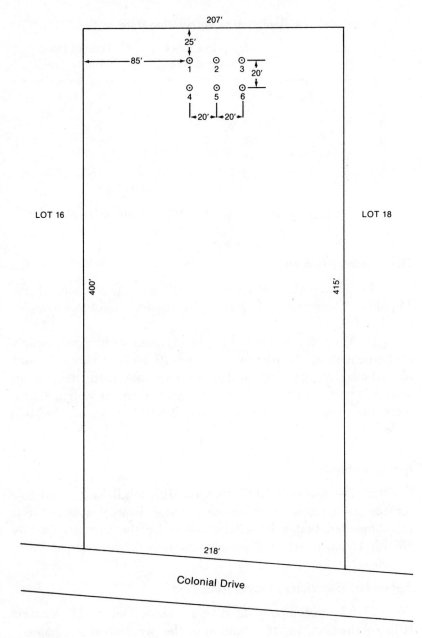

N

LOT 17, VICTORIA HILLS
HIGHLAND TOWNSHIP

2. What kinds of information does the discussion-of-results section include, and what purpose does this information serve?
3. Why does the writer include a diagram showing the location of the test holes?

Suggestions for Writing

Write an investigation report on work carried out to determine:

1. The stability of transistor bias circuits or the effect of a diode in a simple AC circuit
2. The validity of Ohm's Law, the transformer turns equation, or some other equation
3. The concentration of particulate matter in air
4. The specific heat of aluminum, brass, or some other metal
5. The most probable number of organisms in water or a standard plate count on milk
6. The normality of an acid or base, the identity of a chemical compound, or the aspirin content of aspirin tablets
7. The percolation rate or the maximum density and optimum water content value for a soil
8. The acreage of a parcel of land
9. The particle size distribution in fine aggregate for concrete
10. The nitrate and detergent levels in sewage effluent
11. The cylinder pressures, oil pressure, or dwell angle for an automobile
12. The physical characteristics of two or more adhesives, coating, fibers, castings, or other materials or products
13. The performance characteristics of two furnaces, drying ovens, refrigeration systems, or other devices or systems

12

Finding a Job

Writing is a necessary part of the job-seeking process—one you must master if your employment search is to be successful. Many job applicants are not seriously considered because they improperly or inadequately present themselves as candidates. This chapter will show you how to write effective application letters, personal data sheets, and postinterview letters, as well as how to prepare for and handle job interviews.

Job Application Letters

The search for a job can start in several ways. You may meet and talk with a company recruiter who visits your school. Someone—instructor, friend, employee of the hiring company—may tell you of an opening. You may answer an advertisement in a magazine or newspaper. Or you may write an organization to ask whether it has a vacancy in your field. If your first contact is with a company recruiter, a letter of application is not required, although you may write a brief follow-up letter to develop one or two points raised during the interview. In all other cases, however, a letter of the sort described in this chapter will be needed.

A job application letter can be the most important letter you'll ever write. If you're like many job seekers, you have a good idea of the sort of company you'd like to work for, and you have geographical preferences, too. Perhaps you prefer a large organization on the East Coast. Or you may favor a medium-sized company in the South or Southwest. A well-written application letter greatly increases your chances of getting what you want.

Unfortunately, few job seekers know how closely most companies examine the application letters they receive and how ruthlessly they discard those that fail to measure up. Some companies, for instance, automatically reject any letter that does not follow one of the standard business letter formats. Even a single misspelled word or insufficient information about the applicant can send a letter to the "reject" file. Obviously, you must prepare your letter with great care if you hope to compete successfully with other applicants.

Before you write an application letter, it is important to analyze the job you are seeking and your own qualifications for it. A good way to do this is to make a list, itemizing the qualifications required for the job in one column and your own qualifications in another. Although the two columns should be very similar, they need not be identical. If you lack or partially lack one qualification, you may have another that would compensate for it.

Assuming you have the proper qualifications, you are ready to begin your letter. But what should you say to insure that it will have the impact you desire? Since your aim in writing the letter is to sell your services, the best approach is to follow the format of the sales letter. A successful sales letter does three things:

1. It catches the reader's attention.
2. It creates a desire for the product or services by convincing the reader that what is being offered is superior to anything the competition can provide.
3. It causes the reader to take action.

By following the procedure described below, you can achieve these goals.

ATTRACTING ATTENTION

The first thing your application letter must do is attract the reader's attention. Beyond mentioning the position you are applying for and how you heard of the vacancy, the opening paragraph should say something that will interest the reader in considering you for the job. Thus, you should begin your letter by stating the service you can provide the company or by naming one of your outstanding qualifications. There are three types of openings that will achieve your objective: the summary opening, the name opening, and the challenging question opening.

The *summary opening* presents the required information in the form of a direct statement. The following examples illustrate good summary openings.

> I feel my college training in biology and art fully qualifies me for the position of scientific illustrator that you advertised in the July 20 *Detroit Free Press*.

> Because of my training in chemistry and two summers of laboratory work experience, I believe I can successfully fill any opening you may have for a chemical laboratory technician.

As the second example shows, the summary opening can be used to inquire about possible openings as well as to answer advertisements.

If you use the summary opening, be careful not to omit any pertinent information. For example, if you open your letter by saying only, "I wish to be considered for the position of laboratory technician in your firm," you have not presented a qualification or stated a service you can provide. Since it is the qualification or service that attracts the reader's attention, to omit it lessens your likelihood of success.

Above all, never let the employer think you're not serious about wanting the job. If you begin your letter by saying, "I happened to be reading the *Boston Globe* and saw that you are looking for a computer programmer," you will destroy your chances with the very first sentence.

The *name opening* mentions the name of the person who told you about the job. This opening can be especially effective because use of a name suggests a recommendation by that person.

> Ms. Loretta Naegele, head of your firm's drafting department, has told me that you plan to hire two more draftsmen next month. I believe that my "A" record at Newton Technical Insti-

tute and two years of summer employment as a draftsman's assistant would enable me to meet your requirements for this position.

Note that a summary of the writer's qualifications immediately follows the opening sentence.

The *challenging question opening* performs the same function as the other openings but takes the form of a question. It is used most often by persons asking whether an organization has an opening, though it works effectively for advertised jobs also. Here are two typical challenging question openings, the first asking about a possible position and the second inquiring about a position advertised in the newspaper.

> Can your company use someone with two years' experience in designing specialized heating and air-conditioning systems for office buildings?

> Would the mechanical engineer you advertised for in today's *Washington Post* be more valuable to your company if he also had three years' experience as a maintenance technician in the Army?

In both of these openings, the questions are phrased so that they include the writer's general qualifications.

ESTABLISHING SUPERIORITY

Once you have gained your reader's attention, your next goal is to convince him or her of your superiority as a candidate for the position. This is done by expanding upon the qualifications mentioned in the opening paragraph and presenting additional qualifications that make you well suited for the job. Before you begin writing, think carefully about the requirements of the particular job and then stress those aspects of your background that are most relevant and that would interest the employer most. If you are a recent graduate with little job experience, you should first emphasize your course of study and your grades, if they are outstanding, and then discuss any related work experience or extracurricular activities. On the other hand, if you are changing jobs after several years of work experience, you should stress your employment background rather than your educational background.

In discussing your previous employment, it is important that you relate your experiences to the position you are applying for. If you desire a job as a salesperson or a receptionist, for example, you might indicate that your other jobs taught you to deal with the public. If the opening is for an office manager, you might note that your previous work provided experience in supervising others. Even if you have never had directly related work experience, try to think of some aspect of a past job—even a part-time or summer one—that you can relate to the position your are seeking. Because employers prefer candidates who are acquainted with the job, such comments will greatly improve your chances of success.

If you have paid part or all of your educational expenses, held one or more elective offices, or participated extensively in athletics, say so. The first denotes ambition; the second, the ability to lead; and the third, experience with competitive situations—all of which are qualities employers find highly desirable. Mentioning membership in professional organizations shows that your interest in your profession is not just monetary. When writing the letter, do not try to discuss every job or office you have held or to name every sport you have played. Those details that are relevant should go in the personal data sheet (also called résumé) that will accompany your letter. Here is an example of the section of a job application letter that establishes superiority.

> In May 1976, I shall receive a Bachelor of Science degree in environmental quality at Wycoff State College. The Wycoff environmental quality program provides a thorough grounding in sanitary science, public health, and environmental control, as well as training in supervisory and administrative functions. I earned a B+ average in my major field.
>
> In order to pay for my college education, I have worked during both high school and college, holding two jobs in health-allied fields and serving as a summer volunteer at a public clinic. This work has provided me with practical experience in performing the duties of a sanitarian and has taught me to work in harmony with others.
>
> For two years, I participated in intramural athletics and held office in the Wycoff student government. I am a member

of the National Environmental Health Association and the Wycoff Environmental Health Association.

Sally E. Harmon

SUGGESTING ACTION

Few people, if any, are ever hired for a permanent position without first being interviewed, so the closing section of your letter should seek to obtain an interview at the employer's convenience.

If the hiring company is located nearby, you may request an interview directly, as in the following example.

> May I come in for an interview at your convenience? You can reach me at the address given above or by phone at (616) 796-3962.

When the hiring company is a long way off, the expenses of an interview will be high, and there is no tactful way to request one directly. Instead, you can ask if a company representative will be in your area soon, and offer to meet with him or her at that time. Similarly, if you plan to visit the city in which the company is located, you can suggest an interview then. These approaches often lead to interview offers.

Applicants for positions as artists, draftsmen, photographers, journalists, and the like should also offer to let employers see samples of their work.

> Would you like to see copies of the drawings in my portfolio? Just call or write, and I will send them to you immediately.

Again, the result is often an interview offer.

THINGS TO AVOID

Job hunters often damage or destroy their chances of being hired by taking the wrong approach in their application letters. To insure that your letter is favorably received, there are certain things that you must avoid.

To begin, do not be long-winded. People who must read dozens of application letters naturally prefer a letter that is brief.

You will improve your chances of being hired if you keep your letter to a single page.

Never mention in your application letter how badly you need work. Companies are not charitable institutions, and although your appeal may arouse sympathy, it will do little more. If you are unemployed, there is no need to say so. A brief statement to the effect that you can begin work immediately will suffice.

If you are unhappy with your present job, do not so much as hint at this in your letter. The person who airs such grievances is likely to be seen as a malcontent or a troublemaker and receive no further consideration. If you have valid reasons for wanting to change jobs, present these in terms of the positive aspects of the job you are applying for, not the negative aspects of the job you are leaving.

It is rarely a good idea to mention how eager you are to work for the particular organization to which you are writing. Such comments, unless very carefully phrased, tend to sound insincere and create an unfavorable impression. The employer, after all, wants to know how you can benefit the company, not how the company can benefit you.

If you lack on-the-job experience, do not mention this. Such an approach is negative and makes you appear to be wanting in self-confidence. Stress instead how your training has prepared you for the job, and mention the relevant aspects of any part-time or summer work.

It is best to avoid the question of salary until the job interview. By bringing it up in your letter, you run the risk of appearing to be more interested in the pay than in the job itself. If you're answering an advertisement that asks you to state your salary requirements, suggest that the matter be deferred until the job interview.

> My salary requirement is somewhat flexible. May I suggest that the question of salary be deferred until we have discussed the position more fully?

Remember, your goal is to sell your services. Your best approach, therefore, is to ask yourself, "What can I do for this company?"—and then tell your reader as clearly and succinctly as you can.

POLISHING YOUR LETTER

Once your letter is finished, there is one more thing that you must do—carefully proofread and polish what you have written. The letter that you send must not have a single misspelled word or incorrect sentence. After all, the only way the employer can tell that you are a careful, conscientious person is by your application letter.

Be sure, too, that in typing your letter you follow one of the standard business letter formats: the modified block, the semi-block, or the full block. (These formats, and business letters in general, are discussed in chapter 8.) If you know the format used by the company to which you're writing, use that format in your letter. If you don't, it is best to follow the modified block, the most commonly used of the three.

STUDENT EXAMPLES

K-5, East Campus Apartments
Ferris State College
Big Rapids, Michigan 49307
April 27, 1976

Mr. Harold Norman
Personnel Department
Doyle Kelly and Associates, Inc.
2526 State Street
Saginaw, Michigan 48602

Dear Mr. Norman:

Would the surveyor you advertised for in *Civil Engineering* magazine be more valuable to your organization if he also held certificates in civil and electrical engineering?

At present I am enrolled in the surveying program at Ferris State College and expect to receive my bachelor's degree next month. I believe that this program, together with two years of practical experience in surveying and engineering, has prepared me to assume the duties outlined in your advertisement.

I am an associate member of both the Michigan Society of Registered Land Surveyors and the Saginaw Valley chapter of the group. Since last July, I have served on a committee of the society which is revising its publication "Advertising Guidelines for Professional Surveyors." I also hold certificates in civil and electrical engineering.

I can make arrangements to be in Saginaw for an interview any time after May 20. You can reach me at the above address or by calling (616) 796-4396 any weekday.

Sincerely,

Lionel R. Emery

Enc. Personal Data Sheet

Discussion Questions

1. Which of the three types of openings discussed in this chapter does this letter illustrate?
2. The writer mentions his membership in professional societies and his work on a committee to revise a society publication. What do these facts suggest to the potential employer?

209 East Shawnee Street
Nash, Texas 75569
March 24, 1976

Mr. John C. Elliott
Personnel Director
Dalton Drug Company
621 Hall Street
Dallas, Texas 75226

Dear Mr. Elliott:

I have read your advertisement for a sales representative in the March 23 *Dallas Herald* and feel my combined background in business and science offers you special advantages. Please consider this letter my application for the position.

On May 24, 1976, I shall graduate from Ardmore College with the degree of Bachelor of Arts in business administration. My area of concentration is marketing. To prepare for a career in scientific sales, I have supplemented my business education with a number of courses in chemistry and bacteriology. This background will enable me to discuss manufacturing processes and products knowledgeably and thus make me a more effective salesman.

While in college, I have worked three summers in a local drug store. This experience has acquainted me with the day-to-day problems of operating a drug store, as well as with some of the problems and needs of physicians. These insights should enhance my value as a representative of your firm.

The enclosed personal data sheet provides more detailed information concerning my background and qualifications. I am available for an interview at your convenience. You may reach me at the above address or by phone at 796-3965.

Sincerely yours,

James H. Mitchell

Enclosure

Discussion Questions

1. Which of the three types of openings discussed in the chapter does this letter illustrate?
2. What does the writer accomplish by naming his specific area of concentration (marketing) as well as his major field (business administration)?
3. Why doesn't the writer name the drug store where he worked or specify his duties there?

21518 Barton Street
St. Clair Shores, Michigan 48081
March 27, 1976

Mr. Harold Cable
General Manager
Roy O'Brien, Inc.
St. Clair Shores, Michigan 48082

Dear Mr. Cable:

At the Automobile Dealers Association meeting last week, I spoke with Mr. George Weitl of your company. Mr. Weitl informed me that you are opening a new service facility and may be looking for a service manager. I believe my background qualifies me for this position, and I would very much like to be considered for it.

I will receive my bachelor's degree in May, with a major in automotive business management and a minor in automotive service. My program has acquainted me with most phases of automobile service and trained me for a nonengineering position in service, management, or marketing.

I am especially interested in automobile service. Two summers ago, while doing my internship, I served as assistant service manager at a large Chevrolet dealership in South Bend, Indiana. This assignment gave me practical experience with virtually every responsibility of the service manager's position.

I would very much appreciate the opportunity for an interview. I am free Mondays and Thursdays but will gladly arrange to meet with you any day at your convenience.

Sincerely yours,

Peter Cataldo

Enclosure

Discussion Questions

1. Which of the three types of openings discussed in the chapter does this letter illustrate?
2. What is accomplished by the last sentence of this letter?

Personal Data Sheet

Job application letters should be accompanied by a personal data sheet, sometimes called a résumé or vita. A personal data sheet summarizes—generally in two pages or less—the qualifications mentioned in the application letter and presents additional information that the employer will find useful. The data sheet, moreover, allows you to keep your letter brief so that it functions effectively as a sales tool.

The information included in a personal data sheet is ordinarily grouped under six captions: Personal Data, Employment Objective, Education, Employment Experience, Personal and Professional Interests, and References. The arrangement of sections within the data sheet depends upon the stage of the applicant's career. Students and recent graduates, who have had little or no full-time work experience, should put Education before Employment Experience. This is because employers are more interested in such applicants' academic backgrounds. Persons who have worked a number of years, on the other hand, should reverse the order, so that employers can read about their work experience first.

There is no one right style or format for personal data sheets. Several formats are commonly used; two of these are illustrated by the sample data sheets at the end of this section.

To make the best possible impression, your data sheet must be attractive, well organized, and easy to read. You can make it so if you do the following:

1. Underline and/or capitalize headings to make them stand out on the page.
2. Use phrases and clauses rather than complete sentences. Doing so allows more information to be presented in a given space.
3. List your most recent education and employment experience first and work backward. The employer is most interested in what you've done recently and can find the information quickly and easily if it is listed first.

Attractiveness, organization, and readability are only three of the many requirements for a successful data sheet. The other requirements are discussed in the remainder of this section.

HEADING

The heading of the personal data sheet includes your name, address, and telephone number. Generally, this information is centered at the top of the page, although there are other possible arrangements, as shown by the sample data sheets. Do not include a date. If you do, your data sheet will become obsolete much more quickly than it otherwise would.

PERSONAL DATA

Date of birth, height, weight, marital status, number of children, and condition of health are the items commonly listed under Personal Data. Unless you are applying for a job that requires United States citizenship, there is no need to mention nationality. Race, religion, national origin, and sex should also be omitted, for they have no bearing on job performance and cannot be used by an employer as a basis for hiring.

EMPLOYMENT OBJECTIVE

The statement of employment objective indicates your immediate work goal and, if appropriate, the direction you hope your career will take. Here are two examples:

> To learn the duties of a purchasing agent in order to qualify for managerial responsibilities in the purchasing department.

> To gain the experience in analytical techniques that will enable me to become a group leader or research specialist.

Such a statement tells the employer that you are ambitious, have confidence in your ability, and know the avenues for advancement open to you.

EDUCATION

The education section of the data sheet includes both post-high-school and high-school education, in that order. Begin by giving the date of your college or technical school graduation, the degree or certificate you received and your major field of study, and the name and location of the institution.

Especially if you are a new graduate, include, in addition to these basic facts, any other details about your education that will enhance your attractiveness as a job candidate. If your academic record is noteworthy, especially in your major field, be sure to call it to your reader's attention. If you've received any academic honors, these should be mentioned also.

Extracurricular activities likewise help create a desirable image for new job seekers, so don't fail to mention any you've taken part in. Belonging to one or more campus clubs, social and professional organizations, or similar groups stamps you as a person who is outgoing and has a variety of interests. Taking part in intramural or varsity athletics shows that you've had firsthand experience with competitive situations yet know the value of teamwork. Holding office in an organization or serving as a team captain denotes a capacity for leadership. These are qualities that an employer—no matter what the field—looks for in a job applicant.

The education section of a recent graduate's data sheet would look something like this:

May 1976, Associate of Applied Science degree in building construction, Ferris State College, Big Rapids, Michigan 49307

Academic Honors:
Upper 20% of class
3.5 grade point average in major field
3.2 grade point average overall

Extracurricular Activities:
Member of intramural baseball team three years
Member of Pi Kappa Alpha, a social fraternity
Member of Associated Building Construction Technologists, a campus professional organization; treasurer my senior year

Do not list major-field courses unless you are in a new program whose content is not well known to employers. Do, however, list *elective* courses that relate to the job you are applying for. If, for example, your major field is diesel and heavy equipment service but you are applying for a job with an automobile dealership, list or at least mention the courses in automobile repair that you have taken.

If you have very little employment experience to offer, handle high school as you did your post-high-school education. Mention your academic standing if it was high. Then describe relevant extracurricular activities, positions of leadership, and the like.

EMPLOYMENT EXPERIENCE

The employment experience section should include your full-time jobs and—if you have little work experience—any part-time or temporary jobs you have held. List the jobs in reverse chronological order—most recent first—and separate them clearly from one another on the sheet. Begin each description by telling when you held the job and then give the job title and the name and address of the organization.

If a previous job had duties similar to those of the job you're applying for, specify them as concisely and accurately as possible. Otherwise, just provide a job title or brief job description. For example, if you are applying for a position as a highway technologist, there is no need to discuss the duties of such jobs as a gas station attendant or supermarket checkout clerk.

If your job performance has earned you substantial raises or bonuses, mention them. Promotions likewise indicate superior performance and should be mentioned.

Here is an example of the employment experience section of a data sheet.

January 1965 to June 1967	Project Engineer, Gyro Transport Systems, Inc., 9036 Winnetka Street, Northridge, California 90329. Job involved designing specialized motorcycles and gyro-stabilized vehicles of all types. Before becoming designer, worked six months as draftsman. Starting salary, $800/month; final salary, $1,100/month.

James M. Avery

Although military service can be discussed in a separate section or included under Personal Data, it is more convenient to treat it under Employment Experience at the appropriate place in the chronology. When describing military experience, give the dates, the branch of service and your specialty, and the places you served. Discuss your specific duties if they relate to those of the job you're applying for. Since military promotions, like those in civilian life, indicate satisfactory performance, be sure to note your rank upon discharge. If you supervised others, mention this also.

PERSONAL AND PROFESSIONAL INTERESTS

Here you should list memberships in technical and professional societies, participation in civic activities and organizations, and hobbies. Such information tells employers a great deal about you. Membership in one or more professional groups shows that your interest in your profession extends beyond your earnings. Belonging to civic organizations and participating in civic activities indicates a community concern and an interest in meeting other people. All of these are qualities that employers find attractive.

As a rule, it is best not to mention partisan political activity in your data sheet. Like religion, politics should play no part in the employment process.

REFERENCES

Ordinarily, references are included in the data sheet. However, there may be occasions when you won't want to include them. You may, for instance, be answering a "blind" advertisement (one that gives no company name but asks you to send your reply to Box —). In such a case, you probably will not want your references to be contacted until you learn more about the company and the position. Even when you do know the company, you may want to be absolutely sure you are interested in the job before your references are contacted. In either of these cases, simply indicate, under the heading, that you will furnish references on request.

Common courtesy requires that you obtain permission to use a person's name *before* you list it in your data sheet. A good letter of reference is hard to write. Anyone unexpectedly asked to supply one might well resent the request and either refuse to comply or do a slipshod job. Moreover, you will want to make sure that the people you wish to list as references will speak well of you.

No less than three and no more than five references should be included. A smaller number might cause the employer to question your character or ability. A larger number is not likely to uncover any important additional information.

For each reference, list name, title, and address, including zip code. If you know the phone number, be sure to give this also. The employer can then call the reference, a procedure that is convenient for both parties and allows the employer to pursue any line of questioning that seems desirable.

The references you give can be of several types. In addition to former employers, you might also include instructors, coworkers in responsible positions, clients or customers, or prominent people in your community who know you. Some employers may specify the types of references they wish. If so, be sure you include only those types.

STUDENT EXAMPLES

Marie Kowalski
1239 Sunningdale Street
Philadelphia, Pennsylvania 19141
Telephone (215) 545-3194

PERSONAL DATA

Date of birth: November 4, 1955
Height: 5' 3"
Weight: 110 pounds
Marital Status: Single
Health: Excellent

EMPLOYMENT OBJECTIVE

To work in a large hospital and thereby gain firsthand experience with every phase of inhalation therapy.

EDUCATION

May 1976, Associate of Arts and Sciences degree in inhalation therapy, Pierce Junior College, Philadelphia, Pennsylvania 19102

Academic Honors:
Received honors in English and humanities
3.75 grade point average in inhalation therapy and science courses

Extracurricular Activities:
Student leader for Physical Education Department
Member of women's varsity swimming team
Member of Alpha Gamma Delta, a social sorority

June 1973, graduated from Cannon High School, South Park, Pennsylvania 15102

Academic Honors:
3.5 grade point average

Extracurricular Activities:
Member of swimming team four years and debate team two years
Member of Yearbook Committee and Ski Club three years

EMPLOYMENT EXPERIENCE

Summers of
1974 and 1975

Operating room technician, Bon Secours Hospital, 468 Creston Street, Creston, Pennsylvania 16630
Supervisor: Miss Eugenia Van Hoye, R.N.
Provided surgeons with necessary equipment to perform major or minor surgery. Saw to it that all instruments were sterile and in good working order.

March 1972
to
September 1973

X-Ray department secretary, part-time, Mercy Hospital, 328 LaBree Boulevard, South Park, Pennsylvania 15102
Supervisor: Mrs. Joan Biggs
Duties included typing, booking X-ray appointments, and answering the telephone.

Other work experience prior to this time was volunteer. Worked as a "Candy Striper" (aide to the nurses' aide) at Mercy Hospital and as a typist at the Foundation for Exceptional Children, an organization that teaches retarded children.

PERSONAL AND PROFESSIONAL INTERESTS

Member of the Association of Certified Inhalation Therapists. Hobbies include painting, rock collecting, swimming, cycling, volleyball, skiing, camping, and hunting.

REFERENCES

Miss Mary Kinkaid
Associate Professor
Health Services Department
Pierce Junior College
1420 Pine Street
Philadelphia, Pennsylvania 19102
Phone: (215) 545-6400, ext. 319

Miss Eugenia Van Hoye, R.N.
Operating Room Supervisor
Bon Secours Hospital
468 Creston Street
Creston, Pennsylvania 16630
Phone: (814) 866-2183, ext. 510

Mr. Charles E. Allen, R.T.
Chief X-Ray Technologist
Bon Secours Hospital
468 Creston Street
Creston, Pennsylvania 16630
Phone (814) 866-2183, ext. 279

Discussion Questions

1. The writer has had no full-time work experience but includes her part-time employment and volunteer work. What does this information suggest to a potential employer?
2. What do the writer's personal and professional interests suggest about her?

William Revere
57 Clark Street
Dublin, North Carolina 28332
Telephone (919) 862-8479

Personal Data

Date of birth: January 4, 1950
Height: 6' 1"
Weight: 190 pounds
Marital Status: Married, one child
Health: Excellent

Employment Objective

To begin work as a sanitarian and gain experience that will qualify me for a position as chief sanitarian.

Education

August 1975, Bachelor of Science degree in environmental health, Byron Technical Institute, Dublin, North Carolina 28332.

August 1973, Associate in Applied Science degree in the sanitarian assistant program, Byron Technical Institute.

June 1967, graduated from Dublin High School, Dublin, North Carolina 28332, college preparatory program.

Employment Experience

March 1973 to present	Desk clerk, Manor House Motel, Dublin, North Carolina 28332. Worked part-time while attending school.
October 1971 to December 1974	Sorter and loader, Smathers' Bakery, Dublin, North Carolina 28332. Worked during summers and holiday vacations while attending school.
November 1967 to September 1971	Electronics repairman, United States Air Force, Washington, D.C., and Wiesbaden, Germany. Was honorably discharged with the rank of sergeant (E-4).

Outside Interests

Active member of both North Carolina and National Environmental Health Associations. Enjoy hiking, boating, and fishing during my leisure time.

References

Mr. Michael Allen, Instructor
School of Health Sciences
Byron Technical Institute
Dublin, North Carolina 28332
Telephone: (919) 862-8457, ext. 350

Mr. Robert Everin, Manager
Manor House Hotel
Dublin, North Carolina 28332
Telephone: (919) 862-7613

M/Sgt Kenneth Heston, USAF, retired
14123 Palmetto Avenue
Palm Springs, Florida 23110
Telephone: (305) 442-8709

Reverend Charles Knight
29831 Quinkert Street
Dublin, North Carolina 28332
Telephone: (919) 862-1519

Discussion Questions

1. Has the writer provided an adequate references section? Support your answer.
2. When noting his military experience, the writer does not mention his specific duties as an electronics repairman? Why?

The Interview

No matter what job you apply for, before you are hired you can expect to have a job interview. It is possible that the interview will be your first contact with the employer; for example, the interviewer may be a recruiter who visits your school or campus. Usually, however, the interview occurs on the employer's premises after the employer has received and evaluated your letter and personal data sheet. An interview may last from one to several hours and sometimes may involve a number of persons, all of whom you must impress favorably. Obviously, you must plan and execute the interview as carefully as your application letter and personal data sheet.

ADVANCE PREPARATION

Before you appear for your interview, you would be wise to learn as much as you can about the company or organization. The more you learn in advance, the more intelligently you'll be able to discuss your possible role, and the greater will be your chances of being hired.

To begin, go to your school or public library and look the company up in *Dun and Bradstreet, Moody's, Standard and Poor's, Thomas Register,* and any other publication that may be suggested by the librarian. From these publications you can learn the company's credit rating, size, sales volume, and products, as well as the location of its plants, the names and locations of any subsidiaries and affiliates, the names of its chief officers, and the like.

Annual reports can also provide much information about the company. These give financial statements, discuss building programs and other projects, describe new and promising products, and outline the company's plans for the future. You can obtain an annual report by writing to the company's headquarters.

Government agencies and many private institutions are not listed in the publications mentioned above. Quite often, though, such organizations issue pamphlets describing their facilities and services. Your school placement office may have copies of these pamphlets. If not, you can obtain them directly from the organizations.

DRESS AND MANNERS

A job applicant's dress and manners are weighed very carefully during an interview, so strive to make the best impression possible.

Generally, you should dress rather formally and conservatively for an interview. Even if the job you are applying for will never require you to wear a skirt or a coat and tie, you should wear such clothing to the interview. Pay particular attention, too, to the *condition* of your clothes. Their appearance—like the appearance of your application letter and data sheet—is an indicator of the care with which you approach your work. If your clothes are ripped, soiled, or in any way sloppy, the employer will naturally think that your work habits are sloppy too—and there go your chances of being hired. Personal cleanliness is viewed in the same light. If you are well groomed, you will simply make a better impression.

When the interview is held at school or on campus and you must schedule it between shop or laboratory classes, the rules of clothing are often relaxed. In this situation, it is generally acceptable to wear shop or laboratory clothing. Do not, however, wear blue jeans, cutoffs, T-shirts, or the like. Be sure to start the day with fresh clothing so you'll be as neat as possible for the interview.

The employer will also be concerned with your manners during the interview. Once you have been called into the interviewer's office, wait for him or her to shake hands and begin the conversation. Remain standing until you have been offered a seat, and then sit up straight and look directly at the interviewer. You will make a poor impression indeed if you slouch or sprawl in the chair or fuss with items on the interviewer's desk. Never chew gum during an interview, and if you must smoke, wait until the interviewer indicates that it is all right to do so. Try to appear relaxed and confident—without bragging or resorting to wise-cracks—throughout the interview. When it is over, be sure to express your appreciation. Good manners such as these can't help but leave a favorable impression.

ANSWERING QUESTIONS

The problem of how to conduct yourself during an interview is complicated by the variety of approaches interviewers use. Some do almost all the talking while carefully observing how closely and intelligently you listen. Others say almost nothing, forcing you to present your case virtually unaided. Generally, though, the interviewer obtains information by asking questions.

Advance preparation can greatly improve your ability to answer these questions. A day or so before the interview, draw up a list of questions that you might reasonably be asked to deal with. Such a list might include, among others, the following items:

> Why do you wish to work for this organization?
> Tell us something about your family background.
> What special courses have you taken to prepare yourself for a job such as this?
> What jobs have you held in the past and how would the experience prove useful to you in this job?
> Do you work best as part of a team or by yourself?
> What future role do you hope to play in our organization?

Once the list is complete, outline an answer to each item, whenever possible expanding upon information contained in your letter of application and personal data sheet. Familiarize yourself with the answers and then, if a tape recorder is available, record them so that you can hear yourself as the interviewer would. If you are speaking too quickly or too softly, you will hear these flaws and be able to correct them. It is also helpful to have a friend act as interviewer and criticize your performance. Even if the interviewer's questions are phrased differently from those in your list, your efforts won't be wasted, for both sets of questions will concern the same general information.

The way you respond to questions is an important factor in determining whether or not you will be hired. To begin, always wait until the interviewer has finished the question before answering. At times, the interviewer will describe a situation and then ask a question relating to it—a procedure that can take several minutes. When this happens, resist any temptation to begin your answer before the interviewer has finished speaking. Once the question has been asked, take a moment or two to organize your thoughts, then answer. Do not stray from the subject or run on for long periods of time. Say only what you must to answer properly, then stop. At the same time, try to avoid one-word "yes" or "no" answers, which do not allow the interviewer to learn much about you. Do not be afraid to admit that you don't know the answer to a question. Chances are this won't happen frequently, but if it does, an honest "I don't know" is far better than a hastily formulated and perhaps incorrect response.

Interviewers occasionally ask "catch" questions just to see how you'll handle them. If this happens, imagine that the question has been asked by a future customer or client and then phrase your answer in a way that will neither offend the speaker nor contradict your own views. The interviewer might say, for example, "The president is certainly catching a lot of criticism these days, isn't he?" One good response to this question would be, "Yes, but I suppose any president has to expect quite a bit of that." Such an answer would offend neither a supporter nor a critic of the president, and at the same time would not compromise your own position.

ASKING QUESTIONS

Interviewing is not a one-way street. It is as important for you to know that the job, the company, and the community are right for you as it is for the company to know that you are right for it. Therefore, do not hesitate to ask questions that have not been covered by the interviewer. Some of your questions might include:

What opportunities for advancement are open to a person with my background?

Might I expect to be transferred periodically or would I work permanently in this location?

Are the hours I would work likely to be regular or variable?

What fringe benefits does your company offer its employees and their families?

What opportunities for furthering my education are available in the area?

What recreational and cultural activities do the community and surrounding areas offer?

You should leave the interview with your key questions answered so that you will be able to make an intelligent job choice.

DISCUSSING SALARY

At some point during the interview, the subject of salary will come up. Although salary is very important to you, it is best to let the interviewer mention it first. Otherwise, you may appear to be interested only in the money. Sometimes, however, interviewers deliberately avoid the subject to see how you will bring it up. In such a situation, the best advice is to ask directly and without embarrassment, "What is the salary for this position?" An interview is a business transaction and there should be candor on both sides.

Occasionally, an interviewer will ask you what salary you are looking for. This is a difficult situation unless you are very familiar with the range of salaries paid for positions like the one you are seeking. If you can tactfully do so, turn the question back to the interviewer by saying something like, "That's difficult to answer. Can you give me some idea of your company's salary range for the job?" Needless to say, you'll be better prepared for any discussion of salary if you have taken the trouble to learn as much as you can about the prevailing salaries in your field. You can do this by asking your instructors, consulting literature in your school's placement office, and following the classified ads in newspapers and professional publications.

Most companies have an established salary range for each job, and the interviewer will tell you what your starting salary would be. In such a case, unless your qualifications are exceptional, it is unwise to try to bargain for more money. The company knows what a particular position is worth, and your attempt may well lose you the job.

KEEPING A RECORD OF THE INTERVIEW

It is unlikely that you'll receive a job offer at the time of the interview. Instead, the organization will review your qualifications, as well as those of other applicants, and then make a decision. In the meantime, what you've learned can improve your performance in other interviews.

To help you remember each interview, keep a detailed record in a notebook. Record the pertinent information as soon after the interview as you can, while it is still fresh in your mind. Include the names of the interviewers, a description of the job; a summary of the job qualifications, and the salary range. There is always a possibility that you will be called for a second interview, and the information will be very helpful. Note, too, any questions that gave you trouble or any mistakes that you made so that you can correct these weaknesses.

Postinterview Letters

There are four common types of postinterview letters: letter of thanks, job acceptance letter, job refusal letter, and follow-up letter. These are discussed below.

LETTER OF THANKS

A day or two after your interview, send the interviewer a brief note of thanks. Use the opportunity to tell the interviewer once again that you want the job and feel you can handle it. You might write something like this:

> Thank you for my pleasant and informative interview for the position of computer programmer. The job matches my qualifications and sounds most attractive. I hope that you will consider my application favorably.
> I look forward to hearing from you.

Many job candidates neglect to write letters of thanks. Your note, therefore, will set you apart as an especially thoughtful person and increase your chances of winning the job you're after.

If the interviewer has spoken to many other applicants, the note also helps insure that you will be remembered.

JOB ACCEPTANCE LETTER

A job acceptance letter is used to accept a written job offer or to confirm the verbal acceptance of a job offered over the phone. In writing such a letter, show courtesy—even enthusiasm—but don't go overboard in expressing your thanks.

> Thank you very much for offering me the position of marketing assistant with your firm. I am happy to accept, and I am sure I will be able to justify your confidence in me. As you requested, I will report for work on Monday, July 10. In the meantime, if you need to get in touch with me, I will be at my present address until July 7.
>
> I look forward to working for you.

The above letter, though brief, does much more than merely accept the job. It thanks the company for the offer, gives assurance of good future performance, confirms the starting date, tells where to reach the new employee until then, and ends by expressing pleasure. In short, its tone is pleasant, and it says everything necessary.

JOB REFUSAL LETTER

The job refusal letter is harder to write than the other types of postinterview letters. Keep in mind that the organization you are turning down has spent considerable time, effort, and money in corresponding with you, conducting your interview, and reviewing your qualifications before making its offer. It also may have counted heavily on your services. Your refusal letter, therefore, must be especially tactful and courteous.

Begin your letter with a courteous remark about the organization, job, or interview. Follow this with a polite refusal and your reasons for choosing another job. End with another pleasant comment.

> I enjoyed meeting you and discussing the duties of your commercial artist position, and I was gratified to receive your

job offer last Wednesday. I have given the offer serious thought but have finally decided to accept a position with another publisher. As you know from our conversation, I wish to concentrate on scientific illustration. The job I have chosen will allow me to spend full time doing so, while your position would not.

I appreciate the consideration you have shown me. I am sure I would have enjoyed working for your company.

The preceding letter is both pleasant and thoughtful. Though it may disappoint the receiver, it should leave no trace of bitterness or resentment.

FOLLOW-UP LETTER

Ordinarily, you will be hired or rejected within a month of your job interview. If you are rejected, it may be because you lack one or more of the qualifications needed for the position. With medium-sized and large companies, however, there is always a chance that a more suitable opening will occur a few months later. For this reason, if you are still unemployed after several months, you may wish to send a follow-up letter to the companies you've previously interviewed.

On August 15, I was interviewed by Union Carbide Chemicals for the job of chemical laboratory technician. Although I was rejected because I lacked courses in organic analysis, I remember both you and your organization very favorably and hope you will consider me for any current opening that fits my qualifications.

A follow-up note could well lead to a review of your credentials and possibly to a job offer. Without such a note, it is unlikely that your application will be reconsidered.

It is also possible that you are qualified for a job but that another candidate—perhaps one with more experience—is hired instead. If the company has a number of positions like the one you applied for, there probably will be another opening before long. This time, you might be the best candidate to apply. If you are still interested in being considered for an opening of the type you applied for, you might send a follow-up letter such as this one.

Early last summer you interviewed me for a sales position with General Foods. Although I was not hired, you indicated during the interview that I was qualified for the position. General Foods remains in my mind one of the top companies to work for. Should another opening occur in your sales force, I would appreciate your reconsidering my application.

Suggestions for Writing

1. Write a letter applying for a specific job that you have seen advertised or that someone has told you about. Use whichever of the three openings you wish.
2. Write a letter applying for a specific position with a company that may or may not have a vacancy.
3. Prepare a personal data sheet to accompany your application letter. Include references.
4. Write a letter
   a.   thanking an interviewer for interviewing you
   b.   accepting a job offer
   c.   refusing a job offer
   d.   expressing interest in working for a company that has rejected you previously

English Use and Misuse

This section consists of two parts. The first, "English Use," explains the basic elements of grammar, punctuation, and mechanics. The second, "English Misuse," touches upon some of the more common English language errors. Although such a condensed treatment cannot answer every question you might have, the information contained here should help you avoid most errors commonly committed by beginning writers.

ENGLISH USE

Grammar

SENTENCE ELEMENTS

Subject

The subject of a sentence is the word or words that identify the person, place, thing, or idea that sentence is about. A simple subject consists of a noun or noun substitute, while a complete subject consists of a noun or noun substitute plus the words that modify it.

> *Margaret* repaired the faucet. (simple subject)

> *The student sitting over there in the corner* is majoring in industrial hygiene. (complete subject)

In the second example, the simple subject is *student.*

Predicate

The predicate of a sentence is the word or words that make a statement about the subject. A simple predicate consists of a verb, while a complete predicate consists of a verb plus associated words.

> William *died.* (simple predicate)

> Sally *bought a new dress.* (complete predicate)

In the second example, the word *bought* is the simple predicate.

Direct Object

A direct object is the noun or noun substitute that names the person or thing that receives the action of a verb. A direct object normally answers the question "what?" or "whom?"

> The millwright repaired the *lathe.* (Object receives action of verb *repaired* and answers the question "what?")

> The stock clerks chose *John* to represent them. (Object receives action of verb *chose* and answers the question "whom?")

Indirect Object

An indirect object is the noun or noun substitute that tells to whom something is given or for whom something is done.

> Ramona Chavez sold *me* her slide rule. (Indirect object tells to whom slide rule was sold.)

John made *his parents* a table. (Indirect object tells for whom table was made.)

Lend *me* your tape measure. (Subject is not present, but "you" is understood. Indirect object tells to whom tape measure is lent.)

Subject and Object Complements

A subject complement follows a linking verb and is a noun or noun substitute that renames the subject or an adjective that describes the subject.

Lucille is an *architect*. (Complement is noun renaming subject.)

Lucille is *tall*. (Complement is adjective describing subject.)

An object complement is a noun or an adjective that follows the direct object and tells something about it.

The class elected Mary *president*. (Complement is noun.)

She painted the room *green*. (Complement is adjective.)

Appositive

An appositive is a noun or noun substitute, plus associated words, that follows another noun or noun substitute and expands its meaning. Appositives may be restrictive or nonrestrictive. A restrictive appositive sets the person or thing it modifies apart from other things in the same class. It is written without commas.

My sister *Susan* is a professional tennis player. (Appositive distinguishes Susan from other sisters.)

I have just read a book by the novelist *Henry James*. (Appositive distinguishes Henry James from other novelists.)

A nonrestrictive appositive provides more information about someone or something that has been previously identified. When it appears within a sentence, it is set off by commas, and when it appears at the end of a sentence, it is preceded by a single comma.

Mr. Kalinski, *our plumber*, repaired the leaky trap. (Appositive names Mr. Kalinski's occupation.)

Rachel's hobby, *collecting coins*, didn't interest Robert. (Appositive names hobby.)

John is taking a course in botany, *the study of plants*. (Appositive explains the meaning of botany.)

PARTS OF SPEECH

Standard English grammar groups words into eight categories, or parts of speech, based on their function in sentences. These categories are *nouns, pronouns, verbs, adjectives, adverbs, prepositions, conjunctions*, and *interjections*.

Nouns

A noun names a person, place, thing, concept, action, or quality. Nouns can be divided into two main categories: *proper nouns* and *common nouns*.

Proper Nouns

Proper nouns name specific persons, places, things, or events. Here are some typical examples.

France	Christmas
Pacific Ocean	North Dakota
George Washington	*The Last Supper*
Pulitzer Prize	World Series
Spirit of St. Louis	Wyandotte Corporation
Declaration of Independence	Lansing Community College

World War II began when *Germany* invaded *Poland*. (Sentence names one specific event and two specific countries.)

Common Nouns

Common nouns name general classes or categories of persons, places, things, concepts, actions, or qualities. They can be subdivided into *abstract, concrete*, and *collective nouns*.

Abstract nouns name conditions, ideas, qualities—things we cannot see, feel, or otherwise experience with the senses.

arrogance	harmony
envy	liberalism
fear	love
generosity	understanding

His *desire* to win the prize caused him to cheat.

Mary felt great *loyalty* toward her family.

Concrete nouns identify things that can be perceived with the five senses.

man	gauge
bicycle	airplane
building	carton
report	needle
lemon	pen
piston	smoke

The *hammer* had a broken *handle*.

The *atmosphere* was thin at the *peak* of the *mountain*.

Collective nouns are singular in form but denote a group or collection of individuals or things.

assembly	family
class	group
committee	herd
convoy	tribe
crowd	troop

The *jury* filed into the courtroom to announce its verdict.

The *flock* of geese settled onto the lake.

A noun can function in a sentence as a subject, object, subject complement, object complement, appositive, or object of a preposition.

The *committee* approved the budget request. (noun as subject)

He showed *William* the leaking radiator. (noun as indirect object)

The dentist hired the dental *hygienist.* (noun as direct object)

Mr. Herman is the *boss* of this operation. (noun as subject complement)

Her instructors called her a *genius.* (noun as object complement)

John Lindbalm, our new *draftsman,* graduated from Ohio State University. (noun as appositive)

He received the news with *surprise.* (noun as object of preposition)

Nouns change form to show the plural as well as to indicate possession. Most form the plural by adding *s*.

Automobiles are the chief form of transportation in America.

Neville bought two *pounds* of steak for the cookout.

With nouns ending in *s, z, x, ch,* or *sh,* the plural is formed by adding *es*.

Several *bosses* discussed the factors that motivate workers. (plural of noun ending in *s*)

Which *boxes* should we ship to the Acme Corporation? (plural of noun ending in *x*)

Add two *pinches* of oregano to the sauce. (plural of noun ending in *ch*)

The *dishes* were piled in a heap on the sideboard. (plural of noun ending in *sh*)

Nouns ending in a consonant plus a *y* drop the *y* and add an *ies* to make the plural.

The large chemical company merged with two smaller *companies.*

Some nouns that end in *o* form the plurals by adding an *s*, while others add *es*.

The *cameos* made an attractive display in the case. (Plural is formed by adding *s*.)

Fried *potatoes* are a tasty but fattening treat. (Plural is formed by adding *es*.)

Similarly, some nouns ending in *f* or *fe* form the plural by adding an *s*, while others drop the *f* or *fe* and add *ves*.

The *chiefs* of the tribe called for war. (Plural is formed by adding *s* to *chief*.)

The *fifes* struck up a lively air. (Plural is formed by adding *s* to *fife*.)

Martin sold the *calves* when they were six weeks old. (Plural is formed by replacing *f* of *calf* with *ves*.)

Cats have nine *lives*, but frogs croak every night. (Plural is formed by replacing *fe* of *life* with *ves*.)

A few nouns undergo internal change to form the plural, and a few others have identical singular and plural forms.

One *goose* crossed the road; the other two *geese* remained in the farmyard. (Word undergoes internal change to denote plural.)

He sheared one *sheep* on Monday and three *sheep* on Tuesday. (Forms are identical for singular and plural.)

Compound nouns (*father-in-law, commander-in-chief, lady-in-waiting*, and the like) form the plural by adding an *s* or dropping the *y* and adding *ies* to the first word in the compound.

Their *fathers-in-law* do not like each other very well.

The *ladies-in-waiting* served the queen faithfully.

Pronouns

A pronoun is a word that takes the place of a noun in a sentence. As noun substitutes, pronouns can function as subjects, objects, subject complements, appositives, or objects of prepositions. There are eight categories of pronouns: *personal, interrogative, relative, demonstrative, reflexive, intensive, indefinite*, and *reciprocal*.

Personal Pronouns

Personal pronouns are pronouns that refer to one or more clearly identified persons, places, or things.

Subjective	Objective	Possessive
I	me	my, mine
you	you	your, yours
he	him	his
she	her	her, hers
it	it	its
we	us	our, ours
you	you	your, yours
they	them	their, theirs

The personal pronoun forms listed under "Subjective" are used as the subjects of sentences or clauses; the forms listed under "Objective" are used as direct or indirect objects; and the forms listed under "Possessive" are used to show possession. *My, your, her, our*, and *their* always precede a noun, and thus they can be regarded as possessive adjectives. *His* and *its* likewise function as possessive adjectives.

I repaired the lawnmower. (pronoun as subject)

William called *him*. (pronoun as direct object)

William threw *him* the ball. (pronoun as indirect object)

The camera is *hers*. (possessive pronoun as subject complement)

They traded *their* camper for a speedboat. (possessive adjective)

Personal pronouns can be first person, second person, or third person. First person pronouns refer to the speaker(s), second person pronouns refer to the individual(s) spoken to, and third person pronouns refer to the individual(s) or thing(s) spoken about.

First Person	Second Person	Third Person
I, me	you	he, him
we, us		she, her
		it
		they, them

Interrogative Pronouns

Interrogative pronouns begin sentences or clauses that ask questions.

who	what
whom	which
whose	

What is wrong with the dishwasher?

Which of these wrenches fits the bolt?

Relative Pronouns

A relative pronoun is a pronoun that starts a noun clause (see page 272) or an adjective clause (see page 273). Note that the relative pronouns in the first column below can also serve as interrogative pronouns.

who	that
whom	whoever
whose	whomever
what	whatever
which	whichever

The field *that* I plan to major in is heating, air conditioning, and refrigeration.

Harvey Wilson, *whose* printing shop burned last month, is rebuilding in a new location.

Demonstrative Pronouns

A demonstrative pronoun is used to point out or identify something. There are four demonstrative pronouns.

this	these
that	those

That is the lathe to use.

I like *those*.

This and *these* are used to point out things that are close at hand, *that* and *those* to point out things that are farther away.

> *This* T-square and *that* compass belong to Joan. (Compass is farther from speaker than T-square.)

Reflexive and Intensive Pronouns

A reflexive pronoun turns the action of the verb back toward the subject, while an intensive pronoun is used as an adjective to emphasize another noun or pronoun. Such pronouns end either with *-self* or *-selves*.

myself	oneself
yourself	ourselves
himself	yourselves
herself	themselves
itself	

> The machinist cut *himself* on the metal shaving. (reflexive pronoun)

> The manager *herself* answered the customer's complaint. (intensive pronoun)

Do not use a reflexive pronoun as a substitute for a personal pronoun.

> John and *myself* will repair the radiator. (incorrect)

> John and *I* will repair the radiator. (correct)

Indefinite Pronouns

Indefinite pronouns refer to persons, places, or things that are not clearly identified.

each	some	nobody
either	someone	nothing
neither	somebody	none
all	something	one
another	everyone	much
any	everybody	many

anyone	everything	most
anybody	no one	few
anything		

Neither of the students wrote good exams.

I saw *nobody* in the chemistry laboratory.

Reciprocal Pronouns

A reciprocal pronoun is used to indicate an exchange of action between two or more parties. There are two reciprocal pronouns: *each other* and *one another*. *Each other* is used when there are two parties involved in the action; *one another* is used when there are three or more.

Larry and I always help *each other* with chemistry problems. (two persons)

The shop employees congratulated *one another* upon winning the company's safety award. (more than two persons)

In informal speech, *each other* and *one another* are often used interchangeably. However, this practice should be avoided in formal writing.

Verbs

A verb is a word that expresses action or a state of being. It may make a statement, ask a question, or give an order or direction.

Henry *worked* diligently on his mathematics problems. (Verb makes a statement.)

Has the chisel been returned to the tool crib? (Verb asks a question.)

Put that wrench back in the tool kit. (Verb gives an order.)

Verbs may be divided into two classes, with some overlap. These are action verbs and linking verbs.

Action Verbs

An action verb—one that expresses action—may be classified as transitive or intransitive. A transitive verb requires a direct object, which receives the action of the verb and completes its meaning.

The mechanic *installed* the carburetor.

In this example, *carburetor* is the direct object and completes the meaning of the action indicated by *installed*.

An intransitive verb, on the other hand, does not need an object to complete its meaning.

Ellen *resigned*.

Betty *worked* for O'Hara Electronic Corporation.

There are many verbs that can be both transitive and intransitive. Whether a verb is transitive or intransitive depends on the sentence in which it is used.

Jerry *stood* the tripod in the corner. (transitive verb)

Jerry *stood* in the doorway. (intransitive verb)

The verbs in the above sentences all consist of single words. Often, however, one or more other words will be combined with the main verb. These other words that are combined are known as helping verbs.

The mechanic *will install* the carburetor in the automobile.

Betty *will have worked* for O'Hara Electronic Corporation two years this June.

Some common helping verbs are:

has	been	had (to)
have	do	shall
had	does	will
am	did	going (to)
is	used (to)	about (to)
are	may	would
was	might	should
were	must	ought (to)
be	have (to)	can
being	has (to)	could

Several of these words can function not only as helping verbs but also as verbs by themselves. This dual function is illustrated in the following two sentences.

I *have requested* a raise. (*have* as helping verb)

I *have* two jobs. (*have* as a verb by itself)

Linking Verbs

A linking verb expresses a condition or state of being rather than an action. Some linking verbs connect the subject of a sentence or clause to a noun or pronoun that identifies or renames the subject. Others connect the subject to an adjective that describes the subject.

Ms. Kincaid *is* the chief biologist. (Subject, *Ms. Kincaid,* is linked to noun, *biologist,* which identifies or renames the subject.)

His speech *was* excellent. (Subject, *speech,* is linked to adjective, *excellent,* which describes the subject.)

The most common linking verbs are forms of the verb *be* (*is, are, am, was, were, been*). Some other verbs that may be used as linking verbs are *seem, become, appear, remain, feel, look, smell, sound,* and *taste.* When used as linking verbs, words in the second group in effect function as forms of the verb *be.* Thus, in the sentence "The water felt cold," *felt* has the same meaning as *was.* When, however, the words in the second group stand for physical actions, they function as action verbs. For example, in the sentence "The swimmer felt the water," *felt* is an action verb with *water* its direct object.

Like action verbs, linking verbs may be combined with helping verbs.

You *will feel* better soon. (helping verb *will* with linking verb *feel*)

He *does seem* less competent than the others. (helping verb *does* with linking verb *seem*)

Tuesday *may be* the day when Belinda receives a raise. (helping verb *may* with linking verb *be*)

Verb Forms

Verbs undergo changes in form to show time distinctions. All verbs have three principal parts—*present* (*present infinitive*), *past*, and *past participle*. Though not a principal part, a fourth necessary verb form is the *present participle*.

Individual verbs may have as few as three forms or as many as eight forms. Most verbs, however, have four forms, as illustrated below.

	Present Infinitive	Past	Past Participle	Present Participle
I	*talk*	*talked*	talked	*talking*
you	talk	talked	talked	talking
he, she, it	*talks*	talked	talked	talking
we, you, they	talk	talked	talked	talking

In the table, the four forms are *talk, talks, talked,* and *talking*. All regular verbs, those which take -*d*, -*ed*, or -*t* endings, have four forms, as do some irregular verbs, those which undergo internal changes. *Swing* is one such irregular verb; its four forms are *swing, swings, swung,* and *swinging*.

A second group of irregular verbs has five forms.

	Present Infinitive	Past	Past Participle	Present Participle
I	*write*	*wrote*	*written*	*writing*
you	write	wrote	written	writing
he, she, it	*writes*	wrote	written	writing
we, you, they	write	wrote	written	writing

Here, the five forms are *write, writes, wrote, written,* and *writing*.

A very few irregular verbs—*set, hit,* and *hurt,* for example—have only three forms.

	Present Infinitive	Past	Past Participle	Present Participle
I	*hit*	hit	hit	*hitting*
you	hit	hit	hit	hitting
he, she, it	*hits*	hit	hit	hitting
we, you, they	hit	hit	hit	hitting

Hit, hits, and *hitting* are the three forms of this verb.

One irregular verb, *be,* has eight forms: *be, am, are, is. was, were, been, being.*

Tense

Verbs show the time of the action or state of being they represent through tense. There are six tenses: *present, past, future, present perfect, past perfect,* and *future perfect.* The different tenses are formed by using the principal parts of the verb, either alone or in combination with helping verbs.

	Present	Past	Future
I	write	wrote	shall (will) write
you	write	wrote	shall (will) write
he, she, it	writes	wrote	shall (will) write
we, you, they	write	wrote	shall (will) write

	Present Perfect	Past Perfect	Future Perfect
I	have written	had written	shall (will) have written
you	have written	had written	shall (will) have written
he, she, it	has written	had written	shall (will) have written
we, you, they	have written	had written	shall (will) have written

The present tense is used to show present state of being and to state facts that are permanently true; to show general or habitual action; and sometimes, with appropriate adverbs, to denote future action.

Helen *looks* beautiful in her new gown. (present state of being)

Brazil *is* in South America. (permanent truth)

John *lives* on the eighteenth floor. (general action)

I *brush* my teeth each morning. (habitual action)

Monday, I *begin* my new job. (future action)

The past tense indicates that a state of being or an action took place at a particular time in the past.

Robert *was* unhappy with his performance on the test. (past state of being)

Maria *completed* the computer program yesterday. (past action)

The future tense indicates that a state of being or an action will occur in the future.

I *will feel* better after a good night's sleep. (future state of being)

I *will take* the trash out later. (future action)

The present perfect tense is used when a state of being or an action that began in the past, or its effects, continues until the present time.

The players *have been* irritable since they lost the homecoming game. (State of being continues until present.)

Norman *has worked* as a chemical laboratory technician for five years. (Action continues until present.)

William *has repaired* the snow blower. (Effect of action continues until present.)

The past perfect tense shows a past state of being or action that was completed prior to another past state of being or action. It is properly used only when two past times are expressed.

He *had been* sick for a number of years before he died. (Italicized state of being occurred first.)

Michele bought a new typewriter. She *had wanted* one ·for several months. (Italicized action occurred first.)

I *had finished* the experiment before the instructor left. (Italicized action occurred first)

The future perfect tense indicates that a state of being or an action will be completed at a particular time in the future.

The laboratory director *shall have been* with the company ten years next July. (Future state of being will be completed.)

I *shall have completed* all the requirements for my degree by next June. (Future action will be completed.)

The progressive form of the verb is used to show action that is underway. It can be used with all verb tenses.

I *am running.* (present progressive)

I *was running.* (past progressive)

I *shall be running.* (future progressive)

I *have been running.* (present perfect progressive)

I *had been running.* (past perfect progressive)

I *shall have been running.* (future perfect progressive)

Voice

Transitive verbs have two voices: *active* and *passive.* A verb is in the active voice when the subject performs the action specified by the verb.

Teresa *identified* the organic compound. (Subject performs action.)

A verb is in the passive voice when the subject does not perform the action but is acted upon. The noun or pronoun that identifies the performer of the action either appears in a prepositional phrase or is not mentioned at all.

The organic compound *was identified* by Teresa. (Prepositional phrase *by Teresa* identifies performer.)

The organic compound *was identified* as ethyl alcohol. (Performer not identified.)

A passive verb is always made up of a form of the verb *be* followed by the perfect form of an action verb.

A sentence in the passive voice can be converted to the active voice by making the object of the preposition the subject, making the original subject the direct object, and dropping the form of the verb *be*.

Technical and scientific writing commonly employs the passive voice for explanations of processes, where its flat, impersonal tone adds an air of scientific objectivity. Other kinds of writing should, however, avoid the passive voice except where it is desirable to conceal the doer of the action or where the action rather than the actor is important.

Mood

Mood is the form of a verb that shows whether the writer regards a statement as a fact; a request or command; or a condition contrary in some way to fact, wish, or possibility. There are three moods: *indicative, imperative,* and *subjunctive.*

The indicative mood states a real or a supposed fact or asks a question.

William *graduates* from high school tomorrow.

Has the guard been placed on the flywheel?

The imperative mood expresses a command or a request stated in the form of a command.

Leave the room immediately! (command)

Please *turn* the phonograph down. (request)

The subjunctive mood is used (1) in *if, as if,* and *as though* clauses to express a wish, a possibility, or an action or condition contrary to fact and (2) in *that* clauses which express orders, demands, resolutions, proposals, and motions. A few set English expressions (*so be it, come what may, suffice it to say* are examples) retain the subjunctive form.

When expressing a present or a future wish, possibility, or condition in an *if* clause, use the verb *were* with any personal pronoun—*I, you, he, she, it, we, they*—or noun serving as the subject of the clause.

> If only he *were* more forceful! (present wish contrary to fact)
>
> Even if she *were* to explain, Mary wouldn't believe her. (present possibility)
>
> If Stanley *were* wise, he'd switch his major to machine tool. (present condition contrary to fact)

To express a wish, possibility, or condition contrary to past facts, use *had been* or *had* plus the past participle of an action verb.

> If only I *had seen* him before he left. (past wish contrary to fact)
>
> If the instructor *had been* there, the accident wouldn't have happened. (past condition contrary to fact)
>
> Even if she *had explained*, Mary wouldn't have believed her. (past possibility contrary to fact)

When using *as if* or *as though* in clauses to express an action or a condition that occurs simultaneously with the action of the main verb, use *were* with any personal pronoun serving as subject of the clause.

> Arthur is behaving as if he *were* a millionaire. (Condition expressed in clause is simultaneous with present action of main verb *behaving*.)
>
> Arthur behaved as if he *were* a millionaire. (Condition expressed in clause is simultaneous with past action of main verb *behaved*.)
>
> I know Arthur will behave as if he *were* a millionaire. (Action expressed in clause is simultaneous with future action of main verb *behave*.)

To express an action or a condition that occurs before that

of the main verb, use *had been* or *had* plus the past participle of an action verb.

> Arthur acts as if he *had been* a millionaire. (Condition expressed in clause occurs prior to present action of verb *acts.*)
>
> Arthur acted as if he *had been* a millionaire. (Condition expressed in clause occurs prior to past action of verb *acted.*)
>
> They all looked as though they *had swallowed* something very sour and unpleasant. (Action of clause occurs prior to past action of verb *looked.*)

When writing *that* clauses which express orders, demands, requests, resolutions, proposals, or motions, use *be* or the present form of an action verb with any personal pronoun or noun that serves as the subject of the clause.

> I move that they *be* commended for their fine job.
>
> They demanded that the secretary *be* removed because he failed to keep adequate records of the meetings.
>
> The group requested that she *go* to the scene of the accident and *inspect* it personally.

With other *that* clauses, use the appropriate form of the verb *to be* or the action verb.

> I know that they *are* doing a good job.
>
> They heard that the secretary *was* removed because he failed to keep adequate records of the meetings.
>
> I see in the newspaper that the President *leaves* for Europe Monday.

Adjectives

An adjective is a word that modifies a noun or pronoun by describing, limiting, or in some other way making its meaning more exact. There are three general categories of adjectives: *limiting, descriptive,* and *proper.*

A limiting adjective in some way identifies or points out the noun or pronoun it modifies, or it indicates number or quantity. Several categories of pronouns—interrogative, relative, demonstrative, indefinite, and possessive—can function as limiting adjectives, as do numbers and the articles *a, an,* and *the.*

Whose micrometer is on the floor? (interrogative adjective)

The repairman *whose* truck was stolen called the police. (relative adjective)

This shop has the best safety record. (demonstrative adjective)

Some chemists have special training in bacteriology. (indefinite adjective)

She focused *her* microscope on the rod-shaped organisms. (possessive adjective)

Three people applied for the job. (numerical adjective)

They consulted *an* engineer about *the* problem. (article)

A descriptive adjective names a quality, characteristic, or condition of a noun or a pronoun. Descriptive adjectives make up the largest category of adjectives.

The *yellow* car belongs to Robert.

He applied *clear* lacquer to the table top.

The *diligent* foreman improved worker productivity by 10 percent.

A proper adjective is an adjective that is derived from a proper noun.

That building is a fine example of *Victorian* architecture.

An *Italian* restaurant is opening across the street.

Adjectives change form to show comparison. When two persons, places, or things are being compared, the adjective form is called the *comparative* form. When three or more are being compared, the form is called the *superlative* form. Short adjectives usually form the comparative by adding *-er* and the superlative by adding *-est* at the end of the word. Long adjectives usually form the comparative by adding *more* and the superlative by adding *most* before the word.

tall—taller—tallest

productive—more productive—most productive

Some adjectives have irregular comparative and superlative forms.

good—better—best

bad—worse—worst

little—less—least

A few adjectives, because their meaning is absolute, cannot logically be compared at all. Words like *dead, fatal, perfect,* and *complete* fall into this category.

Adverbs

An adverb is a word that modifies a verb, an adjective, another adverb, or an entire clause (or sentence). It answers such questions as "how?" "when?" "where?" "why?" "how much?" and "how often?"

The painter worked *very* rapidly. (Adverb modifies adverb and answers the question "how?")

The package arrived *yesterday.* (Adverb modifies verb and answers the question "when?")

The die maker walked *away* from the bench. (Adverb modifies verb and answers the question "where?")

The tire is *too* worn to be safe. (Adverb modifies adjective and answers the question "how much?")

The secretary is *frequently* late for work. (Adverb modifies adjective and answers the question "how often?")

Accordingly, we rescheduled the entire advertising campaign. (Adverb modifies entire clause and answers the question "why?")

Most adverbs—notably those that answer the question "how?"—end in *-ly.* In fact, most adverbs are formed by adding

-ly to adjectives. Many words may serve as either adjectives or adverbs. A few examples are:

only	deep	well
early	fast	straight
far	right	little
near	wrong	much
late		

Like adjectives, adverbs have comparative and superlative forms. For the comparative of most adverbs ending in *-ly*, the word *more* is added before the adverb, and for the superlative, the word *most* is added.

slowly—more slowly—most slowly

effectively—more effectively—most effectively

Some adverbs that have only one syllable form the comparative and superlative by adding *-er* and *-est*.

high—higher—highest

soon—sooner—soonest

There are also adverbs that have irregular comparative and superlative forms.

well—better—best

badly—worse—worst

Prepositions

A preposition is a word that links a noun or pronoun (its object) to another sentence element by expressing such relationships as direction (*to, into, across, toward*), location (*at, in, on, under*), or time (*before, after, during*).

The drillpress *in* the corner needs overhauling. (Preposition relates object of preposition, *corner*, to *drillpress*.)

We will wait *until* Tuesday. (Preposition relates object of preposition, *Tuesday*, to *wait*.)

There are only about seventy prepositions in the English language. Here are some of the most common.

above	during	on
after	except	onto
against	for	over
among	from	since
at	in	through
before	into	to
below	like	toward
beside	near	under
between	of	with
by	off	without

Prepositions occur in phrases that may serve as adverbs, adjectives, or nouns. Prepositional phrases are discussed more fully on page 269.

Conjunctions

A conjunction is a word that connects words, phrases, or clauses. There are two main types of conjunctions: coordinating and subordinating. Coordinating conjunctions—words such as *and, but, for, nor, or, yet*—connect words, phrases, and clauses of equal rank. Subordinating conjunctions—words such as *although, as, because, if, since, so that, unless, which, while*—link subordinate clauses to main clauses.

> Tom *and* his brother are opening a gas station. (Coordinating conjunction connects nouns.)
>
> Should I call you at home *or* at your office? (Coordinating conjunction connects phrases.)
>
> Bill applied to medical school, *but* he was not accepted. (Coordinating conjunction connects independent clauses.)
>
> The class was canceled *because* the instructor was ill. (Subordinating conjunction connects subordinate clause to main clause.)

Coordinating conjunctions used in pairs are called correlative conjunctions. *Both—and, either—or, neither—nor, not only*

—but also, and *whether—or* are conjunctions of this type. The elements that follow correlative conjunctions must have the same grammatical form; that is, they must be parallel.

> Henry *not only* works full-time *but also* takes courses at night. (Correlative conjunctions connect parallel verbs.)
>
> You can study auto mechanics *either* at Ferris State College *or* at Delta College. (Correlative conjunctions connect parallel phrases.)
>
> The library lends *both* books *and* records. (Correlative conjunctions connect parallel nouns.)

Interjections

An interjection is an exclamatory word that expresses strong feeling or surprise. It has no grammatical relation to the rest of the sentence. An interjection is followed by either an exclamation point or a comma.

> *Hey*! That's my coat you're taking. (strong interjection)
>
> *Oh*, is it time to leave already? (mild interjection)

PHRASES

A phrase is a group of related words that lacks a subject or predicate and that serves as a single part of speech. There are five types of phrases: *verb phrases, prepositional phrases, participial phrases, gerund phrases,* and *infinitive phrases.* The last three are built around gerunds, participles, and infinitives, which are derived from verbs and known as *verbals.*

Verb Phrases

A verb phrase consists of a main verb plus one or more helping verbs.

> Breakfast *will be served* at 7:30. (helping verbs plus action verb)
>
> You really *ought to call* her. (helping verb plus action verb)

I *would have been* happy to approve your shop project. (helping verb plus linking verb)

Words can appear between the helping verb and the main verb of a verb phrase.

William is *always* studying when I call. (*Always* interrupts phrase *is studying.*)

Prepositional Phrases

A prepositional phrase is made up of a preposition, one or more objects of that preposition, and any words associated with the object. Prepositional phrases can function as adjectives, adverbs, or nouns.

The student *at the microscope* is examining a fly's wing. (prepositional phrase as adjective)

I smelled smoke *in the laboratory.* (prepositional phrase as adverb)

After the meeting is the best time to talk to the lecturer. (prepositional phrase as noun)

When serving as nouns, prepositional phrases, like regular nouns, can function as subjects, direct objects, appositives, and subject complements.

Participial Phrases

A participial phrase is made up of a participle plus associated words. Participles are verb forms that function as adjectives and thus modify nouns or noun substitutes. There are two types of participles—present and past. A present participle ends in *-ing* and indicates an action being carried out by the noun or noun substitute it modifies. A past participle usually ends in *-ed, -en, -t, -n,* or *-d*, and indicates that the noun or noun substitute it modifies has been acted upon or has carried out an action.

The typesetter *operating the linotype* is my sister. (present participial phrase)

Mr. Wilson, *disturbed by the noise,* called the police. (past participial phrase)

The typewriters, *worn beyond repair,* are being replaced. (past participial phrase)

Finished with the operation, the surgeon removed her gloves. (past participial phrase)

Participial phrases may be restrictive or nonrestrictive. The purpose of a restrictive participial phrase is to distinguish the person or thing modified from others in the same class. A nonrestrictive participial phrase provides more information about someone or something that has previously been identified. The differences between restrictive and nonrestrictive elements are discussed more fully on pages 287–288.

Gerund Phrases

A gerund phrase is made up of a gerund plus associated words. Gerunds are verb forms that—like present participles—end in *-ing* but serve as nouns rather than as adjectives. Like ordinary nouns, gerund phrases can function of subjects, direct objects, indirect objects, subject complements, appositives, and objects of prepositions.

Running the X-ray spectrograph requires specialized chemical training. (gerund phrase as subject)

John enjoys *swimming in the ocean.* (gerund phrase as direct object)

Felice gave *writing the report* her full attention. (gerund phrase as indirect object)

Henrietta's hobby is *collecting stamps.* (gerund phrase as subject complement)

Henrietta's hobby, *collecting stamps,* has made her many friends. (gerund phrase as appositive)

He devoted every spare moment to *overhauling the car.* (gerund phrase as object of preposition)

Infinitive Phrases

An infinitive consists of the word *to* plus the present form of a verb, and an infinitive phrase is made up of an infinitive plus associated words (objects and modifiers). Both infinitives and infinitive phrases can function as adjectives, adverbs, or nouns.

> The student had a project *to complete* by Friday. (infinitive phrase as adjective)

> Lenore worked *to earn money for college*. (infinitive phrase as adverb)

> Her goal was *to major in environmental health*. (infinitive phrase as noun)

A gerund can often be substituted for an infinitive, and vice versa.

> *To identify the chemical compound* took two hours. (infinitive phrase as subject)

> *Identifying the chemical compound* took two hours. (gerund phrase as subject)

At times, the *to* in an infinitive may be omitted following verbs such as *make, dare,* and *let.*

> He made the engine (*to*) *run again.* (*To* is omitted but understood.)

> She didn't dare (*to*) *challenge the instructor's statement.* (In this sentence, *to* can be kept or omitted.)

CLAUSES

A clause is a group of related words containing a subject and a predicate and functioning as part of a sentence. There are two types of clauses: *independent* and *dependent* (also called subordinate).

Independent Clauses

An independent (main) clause expresses a complete thought and can stand alone as a sentence.

> *Marion replaced the light switch.* (independent clause serving as complete sentence)

When the term ended, *Andrew left for New York.* (independent clause following a dependent clause in a complete sentence)

Sue cleaned the oven, and *Roger defrosted the refrigerator.* (two independent clauses in one complete sentence)

Dependent (Subordinate) Clauses

A dependent (subordinate) clause has a subject and predicate, but it does not express a complete thought and therefore cannot stand alone as a sentence. It functions within a sentence as a noun, adjective, or adverb.

Noun Clauses

A noun clause is a dependent clause that functions as a noun. Thus it may serve in any of the ways that other noun substitutes serve.

What I am working toward is a degree in avionics. (noun clause as subject of sentence)

I'll award first prize to *whoever has the highest average in my course.* (noun clause as object of preposition)

His greatest hope, *that he would graduate with high honors,* was not realized. (noun clause as appositive)

Noun clauses normally begin with one of the following words:

who	what	when
whom	whoever	why
whose	whomever	where
that	whatever	how
which	whichever	whether

The words in the first two columns are relative pronouns; the words in the third column are subordinating conjunctions. The relative pronoun *that* at the beginning of a dependent clause is sometimes left out when the clause is used as a direct object.

She hoped (*that*) *she would graduate with honors.* (Relative pronoun *that* is omitted but understood.)

Adjective Clauses

An adjective clause is a dependent clause that functions as an adjective.

Mr. Martin, *who now works as a mechanic*, used to sell insurance. (Adjective clause modifies subject.)

She made a small fortune from the wrench *which she invented*. (Adjective clause modifies object of preposition.)

He entered Hanson's supermarket, *where he bought meat for dinner*. (Adjective clause modifies direct object.)

Adjective clauses usually begin with one of the following words:

who	when
whom	where
whose	why
that	after
which	before

The words in the first column are relative pronouns; the words in the second column are subordinating conjunctions. Some adjective clauses are restrictive; that is, their purpose is to distinguish the person or thing being modified from others in the same class. Other adjective clauses are nonrestrictive; that is, they merely provide more information about someone or something that is already clearly identified. Restrictive clauses are not set off by commas, but nonrestrictive clauses are. (Restrictive and nonrestrictive elements are discussed more fully on pages 287–288.) When an adjective clause is restrictive, the relative pronoun at the beginning can sometimes be omitted.

The woman (*whom*) *he hired as a bacteriologist* has her master's degree. (Relative pronoun *whom* is omitted but understood.)

The parts (*that*) *we ordered six weeks ago* have not arrived. (Relative pronoun *that* is omitted but understood.)

Sometimes a preposition is used before the relative pronoun.

The gauge *with which Norman measured the pressure* was faulty. (Preposition *with* is used before relative pronoun *which*.)

Adverb Clauses

An adverb clause is a dependent clause that functions as an adverb; thus it may modify a verb, an adjective, another adverb, or an entire clause (or sentence). An adverb clause answers such questions as "how?" "when?" "where?" "why?" "under what conditions?" or "to what extent?" about whatever it modifies.

You may go *whenever you wish*. (Clause modifies verb and answers question "when?")

The shop looked cleaner *than I had ever seen it before*. (Clause modifies adjective and answers question "to what extent?")

She worked rapidly *so that she could leave early*. (Clause modifies adverb and answers question "why?")

Unless everyone cooperates, we have little chance of success. (Adverb clause modifies entire main clause and answers question "under what conditions?")

Some words that commonly introduce adverb clauses are listed below, according to the questions that the clauses answer. The words that signal adverb clauses are always subordinating conjunctions.

When?	Why?
while	because
when	since
whenever	as
as	so that
as soon as	now that
before	
after	**Under What Conditions?**
since	if
until	once
Where?	unless
where	though
wherever	although
How?	provided that
as if	**To What Extent?**
as though	than

AGREEMENT OF SUBJECTS AND VERBS

A verb should agree in number with its subject. If the subject is singular, the verb should be singular. If the subject is plural, the verb should be plural.

Sometimes the subject is separated from the verb by a prepositional phrase, a participial phrase, or an adjective clause. In this situation, be sure that the verb agrees in number with the subject of the sentence, not a noun in the phrase or clause.

> Our supply of nails *was* inadequate. (Verb agrees with singular subject, *supply*)
>
> Several courses required for my major *are* not being offered this term. (Verb agrees with plural subject, *courses.*)
>
> The map which accompanied your directions *was* very helpful. (Verb agrees with singular subject, *map.*)

Phrases beginning with words such as *along with, as well as, in addition to, like,* and *with* that follow the subject do not affect the number of the verb. The verb agrees with the subject of the sentence.

> Mr. Jones, along with his son and daughter, *operates* a repair shop. (Verb agrees with singular subject, *Mr. Jones.*)
>
> The walls, as well as the ceiling, *were* freshly painted. (Verb agrees with plural subject, *walls.*)

Singular subjects joined by *and* require a plural verb, whereas singular subjects joined by *or* or *nor* require a singular verb.

> The drafting board and T-square *were* initialed by the owner.
>
> A doctor or a nurse *is* always on duty.

When one singular subject and one plural subject are joined by *or* or *nor*, the verb agrees in number with the subject that is closer to the verb.

> Neither the secretaries nor the office manager *was* there. (Verb agrees with singular subject, *manager*, which is closer to the verb.)

Neither the office manager nor the secretaries *were* there. (Verb agrees with plural subject, *secretaries*, which is closer to the verb.)

When the following pronouns are used as subjects, they take singular verbs:

each	anyone	someone
each one	anybody	somebody
either	anything	something
either one	everyone	no one
neither	everybody	nobody
neither one	everything	nothing

Somebody *has* stolen the car.

Neither *was* told about the meeting.

The antecedents *all, some, most*, and *more* may require either a singular or a plural verb. If the *of* phrase preceding the verb specifies a mass or bulk of something, a singular verb is required. If the phrase specifies a number of things or persons, a plural verb is required.

Most of the honey *has* crystallized. (Phrase specifies bulk or mass; singular verb is needed.)

Some of the tools *were* missing from the kit. (Phrase specifies numbers; plural verb is needed.)

The verb of an adjective clause is singular or plural depending upon whether the noun or noun substitute the clause modifies is singular or plural.

I like a book *that has large type.* (Singular verb, *has*, of adjective clause agrees with singular noun, *book*, which the clause modifies.)

I like books *that have large type.* (Plural verb, *have*, of adjective clause agrees with plural noun, *books*, which the clause modifies.

Fred is one of those people *who are always in debt.* (Adjective clause modifies plural noun, *people*; therefore, the verb of the clause, *are*, is plural.)

Celia is the only one of the group *who has an accounting degree.* (Adjective clause modifies singular noun substitute, *one*; therefore, the verb of the clause, *has*, is singular.)

A collective noun takes a singular verb when it refers to the group as a single unit. When the noun refers to the group as a collection of individuals, it takes a plural verb. In most instances, collective nouns are regarded as single units.

The class *is* in the library. (*Class* is considered a unit.)

The class *are* giving their reports on famous explorers. (*Class* is considered a collection of individuals.)

With sentences beginning with *there is* or *there are*, the writer must look ahead and see whether the subject is singular or plural before choosing the verb.

There *are* several ways of checking the acidity of a solution. (Plural verb agrees with plural subject, *ways.*)

There *is* no battery in that flashlight. (Singular verb agrees with singular subject, *battery.*)

A linking verb agrees with its subject, not with the subject complement that follows it.

My favorite fruit *is* bananas. (Verb agrees with singular subject, *fruit.*)

Bananas *are* my favorite fruit. (Verb agrees with plural subject, *bananas.*)

AGREEMENT OF PRONOUNS AND ANTECEDENTS

The noun or noun substitute that a pronoun refers to is called its antecedent. The pronoun should agree in number with the antecedent. If the antecedent is singular, the pronoun should be singular. If the antecedent is plural, the pronoun should be plural.

Singular pronouns are used to refer to such antecedents as:

each	anyone	someone
each one	anybody	somebody
either	anything	something
either one	everyone	no one
neither	everybody	nobody
neither one	everything	nothing

Anyone who has finished *his* test may leave.

Neither of the salesmen had met *his* quota.

At present, the use of *his or her* is becoming more common when the gender of the antecedent is unknown, as in the first sentence above.

Anyone who has finished *his or her* test may leave.

Sometimes, in order to avoid a ridiculous result, it may be necessary to use a plural pronoun with a singular antecedent if the meaning of the antecedent is obviously plural.

Everybody told me about the accident, but I didn't believe *him.* (ridiculous)

Everybody told me about the accident, but I didn't believe *them.* (logical)

The antecedents *all, some, most,* and *more* may require either a singular or a plural pronoun. If the *of* phrase following the pronoun specifies a mass or bulk of something, a singular pronoun is needed. If the phrase specifies a number of things or persons, a plural pronoun is needed.

Some of the trees had lost *their* bark. (Phrase specifies number; plural pronoun is needed.)

Some of the cola had kept *its* carbonation. (Phrase specifies bulk or mass; singular pronoun is needed.)

All of the women had finished *their* tasks. (Phrase specifies number; plural pronoun is needed.)

Most of the wool had kept *its* luster. (Phrase specifies bulk or mass; singular pronoun is needed.)

When two or more antecedents are joined by *and*, a plural pronoun is required.

> His car and boat were left in *their* usual places.

> Harold and Norman finished *their* presentation ten minutes early.

When two or more singular antecedents are joined by *or* or *nor*, a singular pronoun is usually required.

> Neither Margaret nor Jane has completed *her* task.

Sometimes, awkward or ridiculous results occur if the above rule is applied. In such cases, it is all right to use the plural rather than the singular pronoun.

> Neither Sharon nor Roger has written *his* or *her* thank-you note. (awkward)

> Neither Sharon nor Roger have written *their* thank-you notes. (acceptable)

In such cases, however, it is usually possible to rephrase the sentence and avoid the problem.

> Sharon and Roger have not written their thank-you notes.

> Neither Sharon nor Roger has written a thank-you note.

If one singular and one plural antecedent are joined by *or* or *nor*, the pronoun agrees in number with the closer antecedent. Generally, it is necessary to write the antecedents in one particular order to express the desired meaning.

> Neither the superintendent nor the workers recognized *their* peril. (Pronoun agrees with plural antecedent *workers*.)

> Neither the workers nor the superintendent recognized *his* peril. (Pronoun agrees with singular antecedent *superintendent*.)

Notice that the meaning is different in these sentences. In the first, the peril is to everyone; in the second, the peril is to the superintendent only.

CASE

The case of a noun or pronoun depends upon its function in a sentence. There are three cases in English: the subjective, the objective, and the possessive. The first of these is used for subjects of sentences, the second is used for direct and indirect objects, and the third is used to show possession.

Nouns and most indefinite pronouns undergo changes in form only for the possessive case.

John knows *Douglas. Douglas* knows *John.* (Forms are identical in both subjective and objective cases.)

John's college program is very difficult. (Add *'s* to *John* to show possession.)

Six of the most common pronouns have different forms for each case, and choosing the proper form can sometimes present problems.

Subjective	Objective	Possessive
I	me	my, mine
he	him	his
she	her	her, hers
we	us	our, ours
they	them	their, theirs
who	whom	whose

There are several rules for the proper use of case. To begin, an appositive is always in the same case as the noun or noun substitute it identifies.

The superintendent selected two people, Loretta and *me*, to receive merit increases. (Pronoun is appositive of noun functioning as direct object.)

We, Loretta and *I*, received merit increases. (Pronoun is appositive of pronoun functioning as subject.)

Pronouns directly preceding nouns should take the subjective case if the noun functions as the subject of the sentence. They should take the objective case if the noun serves as the object.

We managers must set a good example for the employees. (Pronoun precedes subject of the sentence.)

The guide took *us* visitors through the nuclear installation. (Pronoun precedes object of sentence.)

Pronouns in compound subjects of sentences should be in the subjective case. Those in compound objects should be in the objective case.

Sam and *I* plan to work in public health. (Pronoun is in compound subject.)

The school awarded Marcia and *her* certificates of excellence in drafting. (Pronoun is in compound indirect object.)

In dependent clauses, a pronoun serving as the subject *within its clause* must be in the subjective case, and a pronoun serving as an object within its clause must be in the objective case. This rule holds true regardless of the function performed by the clause itself.

The recruiter will see all students *who* request a job interview. (Pronoun *who* is the subject of its clause and is therefore in the subjective case, even though the clause itself functions as an object in the sentence.)

Whom we should invite is the really difficult question. (Pronoun *whom* is the direct object within its clause and is therefore in the objective case, even though the clause itself functions as the subject of the sentence.)

In sentences making comparisons and using the expressions *than* or *as—as*, the pronoun may be in the subjective case or the objective case. If it is the subject of an unstated verb, it takes the subjective case. If it is the object of an unstated verb, it takes the objective case.

She is taller than *I* (am tall). (Pronoun is subject of unstated verb *am*.)

She likes you as much as (she likes) *me*. (Pronoun is object of unstated verb *likes*.)

She likes you as much as *I* (like you). (Pronoun is subject of unstated verb *like*.)

A pronoun directly preceding a gerund should take the possessive case.

I don't understand *his* failing the course.

I didn't like *their* leaving without saying goodbye.

The subjective case should always be used for the complement of the verb *to be* in formal writing (although this rule is widely ignored in conversation and informal writing).

It is *I*.

That is *he* assaying the ore sample.

The person who put us over our sales was *she*.

Punctuation

APOSTROPHES

Apostrophes are used for three purposes: to show ownership or possession; to mark the omission of letters or numbers in a word or date; and to form plurals of letters, figures, symbols, and words referred to as words.

Possession

The way possession is shown depends upon whether a noun is singular or plural and upon its ending. Singular and plural nouns that do not end in an *s* or *z* sound are made possessive by adding an apostrophe and an *s*.

The *carpenter's* level was stolen. (singular noun)

The *children's* toys are outside. (plural noun)

Plural nouns that end in an *s* or *z* sound form the possessive by adding only an apostrophe at the end.

The *workers'* lockers were moved. (lockers belonging to more than one worker)

All the *ladies'* shoes were covered with mud. (shoes belonging to more than one lady)

Singular nouns ending in an *s* or *z* sound form the possessive by adding either an apostrophe alone or an apostrophe and an *s*, whichever the writer desires.

James' (or *James's*) safety helmet saved him from a severe head injury. (Either possessive form is suitable.)

Many writers prefer an apostrophe alone if adding an *s* would result in an awkward series of *s* sounds.

Moses' followers entered the Land of Promise. (*Moses's* is awkward, so apostrophe alone is added.)

To show joint ownership by two or more individuals, use the possessive form for the last noun only. To show individual ownership, use the possessive form for each noun.

Ben and *Martin's* project took them a month to complete. (joint possession)

Madeline's and *Mary's* notebooks were lying on the laboratory bench. (individual possession)

Do not use apostrophes with the possessive pronouns *his, hers, its, ours, yours,* and *theirs*. The following indefinite pronouns, however, do require possessive apostrophes:

anyone's	one's	everybody's
everyone's	anybody's	nobody's
no one's	somebody's	another's

Contractions

Contractions of words or numbers are formed by omitting one or more letters or numerals. The omission is shown by placing an apostrophe exactly where the omission is made.

Isn't our report longer than theirs? (contraction of *is not*)

I *don't* think *you're* qualified for the job. (contractions of *do not* and *you are*)

I'm a University of Delaware graduate, class of '76 (contractions of *I am* and *1976*).

Plurals

For the sake of clarity, the plurals of letters, numbers, symbols, and words referred to as words are formed by adding an apostrophe and an *s*. In addition, an apostrophe is often used to form the plurals of abbreviations.

Mind your *p's* and *q's*. (plurals of letters)

Your *2's* and *3's* are hard to tell apart. (plurals of numbers)

Your *&'s* should be written as *and's*. (plurals of symbol and word referred to as word)

The furnace has a capacity of 250,000 *Btu's*. (plural of abbreviation)

When there is no danger of confusion, however, an *s* alone is sufficient.

The turbine was installed in the *1960s*.

The President gave a reception for the returning *POWs*.

COMMAS

Commas are used to separate or set off main clauses in compound sentences joined by coordinating conjunctions; introductory elements in sentences; items in a series; coordinate adjectives; nonrestrictive clauses, phrases, and appositives; geographical items and dates; and certain other expressions inserted in sentences.

Compound Sentences

A compound sentence is one made up of two or more independent clauses which are joined by a coordinating conjunction (*and, but, or, nor, for, yet, so*). Coordinating conjunctions used to join the parts of a compound sentence are preceded by a comma.

The side of the heater cracked, *and* Elise stood staring glumly at the ruined experiment.

Alvin is majoring in electronics, *but* his sister is studying dental hygiene.

Writers sometimes omit commas between short independent clauses, but it is safer to avoid this practice because the reader may be at least temporarily confused.

No one spoke *but* the instructor appeared surprised.

No one spoke but the instructor . . . (initial confusion)

No one spoke, but the instructor appeared surprised. (confusion eliminated by comma)

They wished to go *for* the play was highly rated.

They wished to go for the play . . . (initial misreading)

They wished to go, for the play was highly rated. (confusion eliminated by comma)

When independent clauses are joined by a conjunctive adverb, a semicolon rather than a comma is used between the clauses. Examples of such sentences are given in the section on semicolons, page 290.

Do not mistake a simple sentence with a compound predicate for a compound sentence.

Harry washed the dishes, and Doreen sliced the carrots. (compound sentence)

Harry washed the dishes and sliced the carrots. (simple sentence with compound predicate)

Note that in the second sentence the part following the *and* has no subject and cannot stand alone.

Introductory Elements

Introductory elements separated by commas include phrases, clauses, and interjections. When an introductory phrase or clause is very short and there is no chance the sentence will be misread, the comma can be omitted. Otherwise, a comma should be used.

In all, the task was not a difficult one. (short introductory phrase)

By 1869 they reached California. (short introductory phrase)

After changing the oil and checking the tire pressure, Albert started his journey. (long introductory phrase)

Whenever she finished a laboratory report, Pamela treated herself to a sundae. (introductory clause)

To earn an A on the exam, José studied six hours each night for a week. (introductory phrase)

Well, the problem is not very serious. (interjection)

If you decide to apply, Morris will hire you. (introductory clause)

Commas are placed after introductory elements to increase clarity. Before omitting a comma after an introductory element, be sure the sentence will be just as clear and easy to follow without the comma.

Items in Series

The items in a series that are separated by commas include words, phrases, and clauses.

Tom, Manuel, and *Roberta* earned two-year degrees in television servicing. (words in series)

He walked *through the door, down the hall,* and *into the engine room.* (phrases in series)

The employment director said *that his company had openings for chemists, that it was actively recruiting,* and *that a representative would visit the school soon.* (clauses in series)

Sometimes the comma before the last item is omitted, but it is best to avoid this practice because it can result in a confusing sentence.

He bought a slide rule, a notebook with dividers and a table of logarithms.

Without the comma, it is unclear whether the table of logarithms is part of the notebook or a separate item. To avoid such confusion, it is best always to use a comma before the last item.

> He bought a slide rule, a notebook with dividers, and a table of logarithms.

Coordinate Adjectives

Commas are used to separate coordinate adjectives—adjectives that modify the same noun or noun substitute and that can be reversed without changing the meaning of the sentence.

> He was a *quick, efficient* repairman.
>
> He was an *efficient, quick* repairman.

When the word order cannot be reversed, the adjectives are not coordinate, and no comma is used to separate them.

> *Many advanced* models of computers were on display.

In this sentence, *many* and *advanced* cannot be reversed without making the sentence meaningless.

A second way of testing whether or not adjectives are coordinate is mentally to insert an *and* between them. If the meaning does not change when *and* is inserted, the adjectives are coordinate.

Nonrestrictive Clauses, Phrases, and Appositives

Adjective clauses are of two types, restrictive and nonrestrictive. A restrictive clause is a clause that distinguishes the person or thing it modifies from other persons or things in the same class. Restrictive clauses are never set off with commas. A nonrestrictive clause merely provides additional information about somebody or something that is already clearly identified. Nonrestrictive clauses are always set off with commas.

> Any chemist *who can't use a slide rule* is at a serious disadvantage. (Restrictive clause distinguishes chemists who can't use slide rules from other chemists.)

Mary, *who never went to college,* has written nine books. (Nonrestrictive clause merely adds the information that Mary, whose identity is already understood, never went to college.)

Nonrestrictive clauses are not essential to the basic meaning of the sentence. Note that the clause in the second sentence above can be removed without changing the sentence's basic meaning. Restrictive clauses, on the other hand, are nearly always essential to the meaning of the sentence. When such a clause is removed, the meaning changes, and the sentence often makes no sense, as would be the case if the clause in the first sentence above were removed.

In certain sentences, clauses may be either restrictive or nonrestrictive, depending on the idea the writer wishes to express.

The carpenter *who was working on the roof* dropped his hammer. (More than one carpenter was present, and the one working on the roof dropped his hammer.)

The carpenter, *who was working on the roof,* dropped his hammer. (One carpenter was present, he was working on the roof, and he dropped his hammer.)

Like clauses, phrases and appositives may be either restrictive or nonrestrictive.

The inspector, *engrossed in her work,* did not hear the fire alarm. (nonrestrictive phrase)

Graduates *interested in professional advancement* should join one or more professional societies. (restrictive phrase)

Dr. McKay, *our laboratory director,* will address the seminar. (nonrestrictive appositive)

My friend *Henry* earned a certificate in welding. (restrictive appositive)

Note that these phrases and appositives are set off by commas according to the same rules that apply to restrictive and nonrestrictive clauses.

Geographical Items and Dates

Geographical items requiring commas include mailing addresses and locations. The sentences below show where commas are used.

> Sherry Davis, 230 Archer Boulevard, Morristown, Oklahoma, won the grand prize.

> I shall vacation in Paris, France, this summer.

In these examples, commas appear after the street designation and the city, state, and country. Commas are not used, however, to set off zip codes.

> My home address is 2107 Jenkins Drive, Midland, Michigan 48640.

> Dates are punctuated as shown in the following example.

> On Sunday, June 15, 1975, Henriette will receive her degree in environmental health.

Here, commas are inserted after the day of the week, the day of the month, and the year.

Commas may be left out of dates that include only the month and the year. Both examples below are correct.

> In September 1971 the school began offering a major in pharmacy.

> The last time I saw him was in April, 1975.

Other Expressions Inserted in Sentences
(Parenthetical Expressions)

Commas are used to set off many other expressions that are inserted in sentences. Usually these expressions are words or phrases that interrupt the flow of the sentence; as with nonrestrictive clauses and phrases, these expressions could be omitted and the sentence would still read smoothly and logically without any significant change of meaning. For that reason, such expressions are sometimes called "parenthetical," even though they are not set off in parentheses. Examples of such expressions are phrases that add emphasis or link a sentence to the one before it, *not*-phrases, and names of persons being addressed directly.

> John planned to study electronics. William, *on the other hand,* intended to study philosophy. (Expression links sentence to one before it.)

> It's true, *of course,* that I am disappointed by my lack of advancement in this company. (Expression adds emphasis.)

> Mathematics, *not home economics,* was her favorite high school subject. (*not*-phrase)

> I think, *Joyce,* that you'd make a wonderful teacher. (name of person being spoken to)

SEMICOLONS

Semicolons have several uses in sentences. One use is to separate independent clauses that are not joined by a coordinating conjunction.

> John apologized for being late; he said he had been caught in rush-hour traffic.

A second use for the semicolon is to separate independent clauses joined by a conjunctive adverb. Some of the more commonly used conjunctive adverbs are:

nevertheless	accordingly	hence
consequently	moreover	otherwise
furthermore	therefore	subsequently
however		

> Noreen didn't want to be chairperson; *however,* she agreed to accept the position.

> He refused to write a term paper; *hence,* he failed the course.

Note that a comma is used after the conjunctive adverb.

Sometimes a coordinating conjunction is used together with a conjunctive adverb between two independent clauses. In this case, a comma (*not* a semicolon) is employed before the co-ordinating conjunction, and the comma following the conjunctive adverb is omitted.

> He did not want to change jobs, *but nevertheless* he was forced to.

A third use for the semicolon is to separate independent clauses joined by transitional phrases. A transitional phrase differs from a conjunctive adverb only in that it consists of more than one word. The examples below are common transitional phrases.

on the other hand	for example	in other words
on the contrary	that is	in the first place
for instance	in fact	in addition

> The president of the college did not oppose vocational education; *on the contrary*, he strongly favored it.

> Nearly all our graduates find jobs; *for example*, 93 percent of this year's printing technology students have found jobs with newspapers or book publishers.

A comma follows a transitional phrase just as it follows a conjunctive adverb.

It is important to remember that the conjunctive adverbs and transitional phrases listed above may also be inserted *within* clauses or sentences as "parenthetical" expressions (see page 289). Since they do not then separate independent clauses, they are set off by two commas rather than by a semicolon before and a comma after.

> Marsha, *for instance*, felt very confident. Dick, *however*, was nervous and uncertain. (Parenthetical expression links sentence to one before it.)

A fourth use for the semicolon is to separate two or more series of items in a sentence.

> The closets contained carpenters' saws, hammers, and planes; draftsmen's T-squares, drawing boards, and triangles; and machinists' calipers and micrometers.

The semicolons mark the end of each series of items. As a result, the sentence is much clearer and easier to read.

Similarly, semicolons are used when an item (or items) within one series already contains commas.

> The meal included steak, which was cooked to perfection; spinach, my favorite vegetable; and baked potatoes.

Used this way, the semicolons help to show where each of the items in the series ends.

A fifth use for the semicolon is to separate independent clauses joined by a coordinating conjunction when one or both of the clauses contain commas.

> The short, serious student wanted to explain the experiment; but the visitor, nervous and impatient, would not stay to listen.

Ordinarily, of course, independent clauses joined by coordinating conjunctions are separated by commas. The use of the semicolon when commas are present makes it easier to distinguish the two main divisions of the sentence.

COLONS

Colons are used after sentences that introduce appositives, formal lists, and formal explanations.

> All her efforts were directed toward one goal: earning a degree in civil engineering. (appositive)

> Four occupations were represented by those in attendance: electrician, carpenter, plumber, and sheet-metal worker. (formal list)

> To determine if the product is suitable, do as follows: (1) select random samples of six-inch angle irons, (2) mount each sample in the testing machine, and (3) test for deformation tensile strength. (formal explanation)

Note that in each case a complete sentence precedes the colon.

A colon is often used instead of a comma following a phrase

or sentence that introduces a long, formal quotation, particularly if the quotation consists of more than one sentence.

> The candidate arose, faced his audience, and said: "Ladies and gentlemen, we are living in troubled times. Millions of Americans are out of work, food prices are soaring, our cities are facing bankruptcy, and our streets are stalking grounds for muggers and other criminals. The present administration is doing nothing to solve these problems. We need new leadership."

When one independent clause follows another and the second directly illustrates or expands upon the first, the two clauses are often separated by a colon.

> Any large organization is confronted with two separate, though related, information problems: it must maintain an effective internal communication system, and it must see that an effective overall communication system is maintained. (Second clause expands upon first.)

Colons have other functions. They separate hours from minutes in numerals showing time (6:15), a title from a subtitle (*The Careful Writer: A Guide to English Usage*), the salutations of business letters from the remainder of the letter (Dear Mr. Barker:), the chapter from the verse in Biblical references (Job 3:27), and numbers indicating the ratio of one amount to another (a 3:2:2 ratio).

DASHES

Like colons, dashes are used to set off appositives, lists, and explanations, although they are employed in less formal situations.

> Only one person could be guilty of such an oversight—William! (appositive)

> The workroom was very sparsely equipped—a workbench, a small tool cabinet, and a single lathe. (list)

> There's only one plausible reason why your level has disappeared—it was stolen. (explanation)

A sudden break in thought is generally set off by a dash.

Her car's transmission—it was a 1971 Ford, wasn't it?—was overhauled yesterday.

Dashes also set off parenthetical expressions that contain commas.

The physical therapist—poised, articulate, and well informed—made a pleasing impression on the audience.

Finally, dashes are employed to set off comments following a list.

A set of crescent wrenches, pliers, and a screwdriver—these are what he bought.

In typing, a dash consists of two hyphens, one after the other, with no space between them and the words that come before and after.

HYPHENS

Perhaps the most widespread use of hyphens is to separate words that function as single adjectives and come before nouns. The use of these hyphenated, or compound, adjectives is very common, allowing a wide range of ideas to be expressed. Two typical examples of hyphenated adjectives are:

The *deep-blue* sea was beautiful.

The *cane-shaped* tube measures both vacuum and pressure.

Note that the meaning of the first sentence would change if the hyphen were replaced with a comma or simply omitted. With the hyphen, we are referring to a sea that is deep blue in color. If the hyphen were replaced with a comma, we would be referring to a sea that is deep and blue. With neither a hyphen nor a comma, there would be no way to tell which is deep, the color blue or the sea itself.

When the first word of the compound is an adverb ending

in *-ly* or when the compound adjective comes after the noun it modifies, the hyphen is omitted.

The *deeply* embarrassed man apologized for his comment.

The sea was *deep blue.*

In a series of two or more compound adjectives that all have the same term following the hyphen, the term following the hyphen need not be repeated throughout the series. It is often briefer and smoother to use the term only at the end of the series. However, the hyphens preceding omitted parts are retained:

Several *six-* and *eight-cylinder* engines were overhauled yesterday.

The third-, fourth-, and fifth-floor rooms are being repainted.

Hyphens are also used in two-word numbers from twenty-one to ninety-nine and in fractions when these are written out.

Alma has served *twenty-three* years as an assistant director of this laboratory.

The company's *seventy-eighth* year saw its sales exceed $80 million.

Three-fourths of the class will receive C's.

Prefixes and suffixes are words or groups of letters attached to words to expand or change their meaning. A prefix is attached at the beginning of the word it is used with; a suffix is attached at the end of the word it is used with. Although most prefixes are not hyphenated, the prefixes *ex-, self-, all-,* and the suffix *-elect,* are set off with hyphens.

The founder of our business is a *self-made* woman.

Norbert is *president-elect* of the machinists' local.

The *ex-governor* gave a speech.

A prefix used before a term that begins with a capital letter is always hyphenated.

The senator was accused of being *un-American*.

The *pro-SST* speaker received little applause.

Hyphens are also employed to prevent misreading of certain words that would look like other words if they were not hyphenated.

The *un-ionized* salt precipitates from the solution. (Without the hyphen, the word, meaning not ionized, might be misread as *unionized*.)

The worker *re-covered* the exposed pipe. (Without the hyphen, the word might be misread as *recovered*.)

Finally, when a word must be split between two typed or printed lines, a hyphen is placed at the end of the first line to show the division. The word is always broken, and the hyphen inserted, between syllables. Any good dictionary shows the syllable divisions of each word it includes.

PARENTHESES

Parentheses are used to enclose numbers or letters used with formal listings in sentences and to set off examples and other supplementary information or comments that would interrupt the main sequence of ideas.

Each paper should contain (1) an introduction, (2) a number of paragraphs developing the thesis sentence, and (3) a conclusion.

Some vocational programs (auto service, for example) are filled months before the new semester begins.

John's first promotion came as a surprise. (He had been with the company only three months.) But his second promotion left all of us astounded.

Parentheses deemphasize the material they enclose. Where emphasis is desired, use dashes.

BRACKETS

Brackets are used in quoted material to enclose words or phrases that have been added for clarity and also—with the word *sic*—to identify errors in the material being quoted.

> "The founder of the school [Woodbridge Ferris] also served as governor of Michigan." (Name is added to original.)

> "The accused man dennied [*sic*] all charges." (Word is misspelled in original.)

As the second sentence illustrates, when a writer notices an error in material being quoted, he or she inserts the word *sic*, in brackets, directly after the error. The reader who sees this knows that the error was not made by the writer but is being accurately reproduced from the original.

Brackets are also used for parentheses within parentheses.

> (This story was reported by a number of newspapers [see, for example, the *New York Times*, April 19, 1976, p. 3] and magazines, as well as by the television networks.)

PERIODS

Periods are used to end sentences which state facts, make requests that are not in the form of questions, or give instructions.

> Monty works for Northgate Tool and Die Company. (Sentence states fact.)

> Please lend me your protractor. (Sentence makes request.)

> Do your assignment before you leave. (Sentence gives instruction.)

Periods also follow common abbreviations, such as:

Mr.	Dr.	A.D.	c.o.d.
Mrs.	Jr.	A.M.	Ave.
Ms.	B.C.	P.M.	Inc.

Today, periods are often omitted after abbreviations for the names of organizations or governmental agencies. Some abbreviations commonly written without periods are:

AFL-CIO	VA	CBS	PTA
ROTC	TVA	FBI	NAACP
FDIC	IBM	FHA	CIA

A series of three spaced periods is used to indicate that material has been omitted from quoted passages. These periods are called an *ellipsis mark*. If the ellipsis mark comes after the end of a complete sentence in the quoted material, the period at the end of the sentence is retained.

In his speech to the graduates, the senator said: "These are . . . difficult times for us all. . . . But you are prepared to meet the challenge."

QUESTION MARKS

A question mark is used after a whole sentence or a part of a sentence that asks a question.

Will you show me how to focus this laser beam? (Whole sentence asks question.)

Have you checked the oil? cleaned the windshield? replenished the battery water? (Series of parts asks questions.)

Mrs. Kendall—wasn't she your teacher once?—has retired after thirty-five years of service. (Interrupting clause between dashes asks question.)

The inspector asked, "Why is the guard missing from this gear box?" (Quotation asks question.)

Question marks in parentheses are used to indicate a writer is not certain of some piece of information. The question mark immediately follows the material in doubt.

He reached America in 1768(?) and settled in Boston.

EXCLAMATION POINTS

Exclamation points are used after words, phrases, or clauses to denote a high degree of fear, anger, joy, or other emotion.

> William! It's been years since I've seen you!
>
> Walter! Get back to work immediately!
>
> Ouch! That hurts!

Do not overuse the exclamation point. If you do, it will soon fail to produce the intended effect.

QUOTATION MARKS

A direct quotation repeats a person's written or spoken comments in his or her own words. A direct quotation, when brief, is set off by quotation marks.

> The placement director announced, "The Aeolian Heating and Air Conditioning Corporation's recruiter will be on campus this Thursday." (spoken comments)
>
> The final report concluded that "Epoxy Glue No. 143 provides 80 percent more bonding strength than the one presently used in our panels but costs only 15 percent more." (written comments)

In typewritten copy, quotations that are five or more lines long are not placed in quotation marks. Instead, the quoted material is indented five spaces from both the left and the right margins, and the first line of each quoted paragraph is indented an additional five spaces. Long quotes are single-spaced, while the remainder of the copy is double-spaced.

Quotation marks are used in dialogues to set off the exact words of each speaker. Each exchange, no matter how short, is treated as a separate paragraph.

> "Sit down," the instructor said. "I'd like to talk to you."
>
> "Thank you," Ann replied, settling herself in the chair beside his desk.

Notice that, when the quotation comes before an expression such as *he said*, the comma is inside the quotation marks.

Commas and periods that come at the end of quoted material are always inside the quotation marks, as the above dialogue shows. Semicolons and colons, on the other hand, are always outside the quotation marks.

> He said, "I want to study drafting"; however, his placement test indicated a low aptitude for that field.

> She called the following "egghead reading": the Bible, Chaucer, and Shakespeare.

A question mark or exclamation point may be placed either inside or outside the quotation marks, depending on what it applies to. If it applies only to the quoted material, it goes inside. If it applies to an entire sentence containing quoted material, it goes outside.

> He asked, "When will your laboratory project be finished?" (Quoted material, not whole sentence, asks question.)

> Why did Irma suddenly announce, "I've quit my job"? (Whole sentence, not quoted material, asks question.)

> William's mother shouted, "Come in this house immediately!" (Quoted material, not whole sentence, expresses strong emotion.)

Besides setting off written and spoken quotations, quotation marks also are used to denote titles of magazine articles, essays, short stories, other short pieces of writing, chapters and sections of books, poems, songs, and television and radio programs.

> The article was entitled "Results of Testing Willow Creek for Coliform Organisms." (article)

> Did you see "All in the Family" last night? (TV program)

> Next week we will discuss chapter 8, "Letters and Memorandums." (chapter of a book)

Words, letters, numerals, and symbols referred to as such are sometimes set off by quotation marks.

In England, the word for wrench is "spanner."

Your "G's" and "&'s" are hard to tell apart.

Usually, however, such expressions are written in italics (see page 304).

Mechanics

CAPITALIZATION

The first word of any sentence and the pronoun "I" are always capitalized. In addition, capitals are used for proper nouns; words derived from proper nouns; certain abbreviations; personal titles preceding a name; and important words in titles of books, periodicals, articles, literary works, and films.

A proper noun is a noun that refers by name to one specific person, group of persons, place, or thing. Such names are capitalized, whereas common nouns—those that refer to any of a class of things—are not. Proper nouns include names of the following:

persons

organizations and institutions

racial, national, political, and religious groups

countries, states, cities, streets, and buildings

days and months (but not seasons)

trademarks

languages

historical events and eras

He attends *Ferris State College*, a college that has pioneered in offering health-related programs.

She spent ten years working in *San Francisco*.

Lolita Martinez, our class valedictorian, was born in *Matamoras, Mexico*.

Next *Sunday, June* 5th, I begin work as a supervisor.

Note that in the first sentence the name of the specific college is capitalized, but the word *college*, which refers generally to the type of school, is not.

Adjectives created from proper nouns, like the proper nouns themselves, should be capitalized.

> Lolita Martinez, our class valedictorian, is of *Mexican* ancestry.

Abbreviations are capitalized if the words they stand for would be capitalized; otherwise, they are not.

> Stanley Kolinski is an *FBI* agent.
>
> His mother just became a district sales manager for *IBM* Corporation.
>
> The shaft revolved at 1,500 *rpm*. (The abbreviation *rpm* is not capitalized because "revolutions per minute" would not be.)

A personal title that immediately precedes a name is capitalized. A personal title not followed by a name is left lowercase.

> The banquet for graduating chemical technologists was addressed by *Dean* Arthur Swanson.
>
> The *dean* of our Special Education Division, *Dr.* Helen McConnell, was asked to serve as an advisor to. *President* Carter.

When writing titles of books, newspapers, magazine articles, reports, films, and the like, capitalize the first and last words and all the words between them except for *a*, *an*, and *the* and conjunctions and prepositions of fewer than five letters.

> Our course textbook will be *The Basics of Industrial Hygiene*. (Short preposition *of* is not capitalized.)
>
> He used a study guide, *Solving Problems in Chemistry and Physics*, when he did his homework. (Short preposition *in* and conjunction *and* are not capitalized.)

ITALICS

Italics are used for (1) titles of separate publications, such as books, newspapers, magazines, journals, bulletins, and long reports; (2) titles of movies, plays, paintings and sculptures, long musical works, and long poems; (3) proper names of individual airplanes, ships, trains, and spacecraft; (4) foreign words and phrases; and (5) words, letters, numerals, and symbols referred to as such. In handwritten and typed papers, underlining indicates italics.

Following are examples of italics used for titles of separate publications.

Ann's favorite novel is Tolstoy's *War and Peace*, yet she never misses an issue of *True Romances*. (book, magazine)

His paper included quotations from the *New York Times*, the *Journal of Business Education*, and a U.S. Office of Education bulletin entitled *Business School Enrollments, 1965–1975.* (newspaper, journal, bulletin)

Following are examples of italics used for titles of movies, plays, and works of art.

Have you ever seen Picasso's *Guernica*? (painting)

West Side Story, which had great success both as a Broadway musical and as a film, was based on Shakespeare's *Romeo and Juliet*. (musical, movie, play)

John Milton's sonnet "On His Blindness" is one of the greatest short poems in English, but his masterpiece is surely *Paradise Lost*. (short poem in quotes, long poem in italics)

Proper names of individual airplanes, ships, trains, and spacecraft are italicized (but not their model designations, such as DC-7 or Boeing 747).

He flew to Oslo on the *Star of the North*. He sailed back on *Queen Elizabeth II*. (plane, ship)

Many foreign words and phrases have made their way into English over the centuries. At any one time there are many that have not been completely absorbed, and these are italicized.

He committed a terrible *faux pas* (social blunder).

I have a strange feeling of *déjà vu* (a sensation that something has been experienced before).

When a foreign word is completely absorbed into the English language, the italics are dropped. For example, the word *employee*, originally a French word, used to be italicized but no longer is.

Italics are also used to indicate words, letters, numerals, and symbols referred to as such.

The English word *thou* is related to the German word *du*.

My handwriting is hard to read because each *r* looks like an *s*, and each *4* looks like a *9*.

As previously mentioned, quotation marks are sometimes used instead of italics for words, letters, numerals, and symbols.

ABBREVIATIONS

Mister, doctor, and similar titles of address are always abbreviated when they immediately precede a name.

Mr. John Williams and *Mrs.* Sandra Barkon operate a small medical testing laboratory.

He spoke to *Dr.* Mandell about his standing in the class.

Junior, senior, esquire, and degree titles are abbreviated when they immediately follow proper names.

The company was founded by Anthony Cappucine, *Jr.*

The sign on the office identified its occupant as Elizabeth Williams, *M.D.*

Some organizations or agencies are commonly referred to by their initials. The following are typical abbreviations of this kind.

| FBI | AMA | CIA |
| GOP | UN | ACLU |

Certain Latin terms are always abbreviated. These abbreviations include *i.e., e.g., etc.,* and *et al.* Certain other terms, mostly Latin, are abbreviated when they occur with dates or numerals. These abbreviations include B.C., A.D., P.M., and A.M.

Science and technology make use of many terms of measurement. When one or more of these terms occur repeatedly in a single article or report, they are generally abbreviated. Whenever the meaning of the abbreviation might not be known to every reader, the term is written out the first time it is used and its abbreviation, in parentheses, put immediately after it.

The heater was a 250,000 British thermal unit (Btu) model.

The viscosity of the fluid measured 15 centistokes (cks.) at room temperature.

A period is sometimes used after the last letter of the abbreviation. To an increasing extent, however, periods are being omitted unless the abbreviation has the same spelling as some other word (for example, in., gal., and fig. for inch, gallon, and figure).

NUMBERS

Numerals (figures) are usually used for numbers higher than one hundred; numbers smaller than one hundred are usually written as words. This is not a hard and fast rule, however, and some writers prefer to spell out numbers through nine and use figures for all others. Whichever general practice is followed, there are several specific exceptions.

Numbers in a series should be written in the same way, regardless of their size.

We have *150* salesmen, *52* research engineers, and *7* laboratory technicians.

In dates which include the year, figures are always used.

January 3, 1975 (not January 3rd, 1975)

When the year is not given, either numbers or figures are correct.

August 5

August 5th

August fifth

the fifth of August

the 5th of August

In business and technical writing, figures are used for units of measurement; for decimals, percentages, and other mathematical expressions; and for expressions of time with P.M. or A.M.

The metal is *0.135* inch thick.

The project has been *35* percent completed.

This constant, multiplied by *3*, gives *12.424*.

The plant's work day starts at *9* A.M. and ends at *4:30* P.M.

Figures are also used for numbers in street addresses and for page numbers of publications.

Her photographic studio is located at *139* Powell Street.

The diagram is on page *223* of the text.

Any number beginning a sentence should be spelled out. If this would require too many words, the sentence should be rewritten so that the number occurs within it and numerals can be used.

Forty people attended the safety meeting.

A crowd of *115,394* persons attended the game. (If this number began the sentence, eight words, an excessive number, would be needed to write it out.)

Ordinarily, fractions are spelled out unless (1) they occur in a mathematical expression or with a unit of measurement, or (2) they have denominators larger than 10.

Of the students in highway technology, *three-fourths* have received job offers.

Multiply $\frac{3}{4}$ by $\frac{3}{16}$ to obtain the answer. (mathematical expression)

A $\frac{5}{16}$-inch crescent wrench is needed for the bolt. (unit of measurement)

The new machine performs the operation in $\frac{1}{20}$th the time required by the old. (denominator larger than ten)

When two numbers occur one immediately after the other, spell out the first one and use numerals for the second one. Exception: if the first number is larger than 100, use numerals for the first one and spell out the second one.

The parts are held together by *six* 2-inch bolts.

Hanson's Hardware sold *125 sixty*-watt light bulbs last week.

ENGLISH MISUSE

Faulty Pronoun Reference

A pronoun reference is faulty if the pronoun refers to more than one antecedent, to a hidden antecedent, or to no antecedent at all.
The following sentences contain pronouns that refer to more than one antecedent.

Take the radio out of the car and sell *it*. (Which is to be sold, the radio or the car with the radio removed?)

The supervisors told the sheet-metal workers that *they* were doing a good job. (Who were doing a good job, the supervisors or the workers?)

This type of fault can be corrected in a number of ways, as shown below.

Take the radio out of the car, and then sell the car. (noun substituted for pronoun)

The supervisors complimented the sheet-metal workers on the good job they were doing. (sentence rephrased, to make meaning clear)

An antecedent is hidden if the pronoun refers to a possessive adjective rather than to a noun.

When I removed the table's finish, *it* proved to be oak. (*It* refers to *table's*.)

This fault can be corrected by switching the positions of the possessive adjective and the pronoun, then making whatever changes are needed for correct English form.

When I removed its finish, the table proved to be oak.

A no-antecedent sentence, as the name indicates, is one in which the noun to which the pronoun refers has been left out completely.

The shop is humming with activity because *they* are working hard.

Such a sentence can be corrected by substituting an appropriate noun for the pronoun.

The shop is humming with activity because the *employees* are working hard.

Dangling Modifiers

A dangling modifier is a phrase or clause that is not clearly and logically related to the noun or noun substitute it modifies. Some of the types of constructions that can present this problem are shown below.

Walking to the movie, a cloudburst drenched me. (Present participial phrase appears to modify *cloudburst*.)

After filling my gas tank, a nail punctured my tire. (Prepositional phrase with gerund object appears to modify *nail*.)

When nine years old, my mother enrolled in medical school. (Elliptical adverb clause, with "I was" omitted, appears to modify *mother*.)

To do a good job, instructions must be carefully followed. (Infinitive phrase appears to modify *instructions.*)

Dangling modifiers can be corrected in two general ways. First, the modifier may be left as it is and the main clause rewritten to begin with the term actually being modified.

Walking to the movie, I was drenched by a cloudburst.

To do a good job, a worker must follow instructions carefully.

Second, the dangling part of the sentence can be expanded into a complete dependent clause with both a subject and a verb.

While I was walking to the movie, a cloudburst drenched me.

When I was nine years old, my mother enrolled in medical school.

After I filled my gas tank, a nail punctured my tire.

Misplaced Modifiers

A misplaced modifier is a word, phrase, or clause that is separated from the word that it modifies. Sentences with misplaced modifiers often sound ridiculous.

The hostess served toast to her guest *that was badly burned.* (Guest appears to be badly burned.)

The dealer sold the Mercedes to the town banker *with leather seats.* (Banker appears to have leather seats.)

Misplaced modifiers are corrected by positioning the modifier next to the word it modifies.

The hostess served toast *that was badly burned* to her guest.

The dealer sold the *Mercedes with leather seats* to the town banker.

A "squinting" modifier is a modifier that is located in such a position that it can modify either of two parts of a sentence.

Workers who are tardy *frequently* lose their jobs. (Does the writer mean "tardy frequently" or "frequently lose their jobs"?)

A squinting modifier can be corrected by repositioning the modifier or by rephrasing the sentence so that the modifier can refer only to one thing.

Workers who are *frequently* tardy lose their jobs. (modifier repositioned)

Workers who are tardy lose their jobs *frequently*. (modifier repositioned)

Tardy workers *frequently* lose their jobs. (sentence rephrased)

Nonparallelism

Parallelism is the use of the same grammatical form to express a series of equivalent ideas. Many types of grammatical elements may be used in parallel construction:

William looked in the car, under the bushes, and by the river bank for the lost billfold. (prepositional phrases)

He liked to rise late, to enjoy a leisurely breakfast, and to read the morning newspapers on Sunday. (infinitive phrases)

By carrying extra credits, studying every spare minute, and going to school during the summer, Frank finished college in two years. (gerund phrases)

Anyone talking in a loud voice, cracking chewing gum, or creating any other type of disturbance will be asked to leave the library. (participial phrases)

Harry refused to eat oysters because he disliked their looks and because he had been sickened by them as a child. (adverb clauses)

Stanley believed that he had committed a serious breach of etiquette and that he owed the hostess an apology. (noun clauses)

The police caught the boys who had broken the street lights and who had tipped over the filled garbage cans. (adjective clauses)

Nonparallelism results when different grammatical forms are used to express a series of equivalent ideas. The following sentences show nonparallelism.

We called the meeting *to present* our new vacation policies, *for discussing* last week's accident, and *to review* the status of our XR-1 project. (infinitives and gerund in series)

The physical education teacher *develops* whatever physical skills the child may have and *to aid* the child who has emotional problems. (verb and infinitive in series)

The kit includes directions not only *for removing* the old paint but also *to refinish* the piece. (prepositional phrase with gerund object and infinitive in series)

She enjoys courses *involving mathematics* and *which challenge her intellectually*. (participial phrase and adjective clause in series)

Note the improvement in clarity and smoothness that parallelism provides when the four sentences above are revised.

We called the meeting *to present* our new vacation policy, *to discuss* last week's accident, and *to review* the status of our XR-1 project.

The physical education teacher *develops* whatever physical skills the child may have and *aids* the child who has emotional problems.

The kit includes directions not only *for removing* the old paint but also *for refinishing* the piece.

She enjoys courses *which involve mathematics* and *which challenge her intellectually*.

Faulty Comparisons

A faulty comparison results when two things not of the same kind are compared.

Beth's *photography* is like a *professional*. (Sentence compares photography and professional.)

The *electronics graduates* from Acme College get better job offers than *Apex College*. (Sentence compares graduates and Apex College.)

Faulty comparison can be corrected by changing the sentence so that things of the same kind are compared.

Beth's *photography* is like *that* of a professional.

Beth's *photography* is like *a professional's* (*photography*). (Word *photography* is omitted but understood.)

The *electronics graduates* from Acme College get better job offers than do *those* from Apex College.

Sentence Fragments

A sentence fragment is a part of a sentence written (capitalized and punctuated) as if it were a complete sentence. In order to be considered complete a sentence must pass two tests. First, it must have a subject and verb; second, it must make sense by itself.

If *you decide* to go. (This has a subject and verb but does not make sense by itself.)

A *homerun* in the first inning. (This makes sense but lacks a verb.)

None of the various types of clauses and phrases used to subordinate ideas meets the tests of a complete sentence. In each of the examples below, the sentence fragment is italicized.

The owner went to lunch. *Leaving me in charge of the store.* (present participial phrase)

Jody, a chemistry major, minored in bacteriology. *Hoping to increase her chances of working for a pharmaceutical company.* (present participial phrase)

He bought the car. *Advertised in the paper.* (past participial phrase)

The carpenter bought a sandwich. *To eat at noon.* (infinitive phrase)

That is Mr. Smith. *The principal of Summit High School.* (appositive)

John washed the windows. *And put up the storms.* (second half of compound predicate)

I went to class. *Although I was not prepared.* (adverb clause)

Whenever you ask. He will help you. (adverb clause)

I saw who cheated on the test. *Which really puts me on the spot.* (adjective clause)

Sentence fragments can be corrected in two ways. One way is to combine the fragment with the preceding or following sentence—with or without a comma (or occasionally a dash), depending on the particular sentence and the meaning intended. The other way is to change the fragment itself into a complete sentence by supplying a missing element such as a subject or verb, or both, and sometimes also replacing a subordinating word such as a subordinating conjunction or relative pronoun. Note, in the following sentences, how each of the fragments given above has been corrected. (Some of the fragments could have been corrected in either of the two ways just described.)

The owner went to lunch, *leaving me in charge of the store.* (Fragment is joined to preceding sentence with comma.)

Jody, a chemistry major, minored in bacteriology. *She hoped to increase her chances of working for a pharmaceutical company.* (Fragment is changed into complete sentence by replacing present participle, *hoping*, with subject and verb, *she hoped*.)

He bought the car *advertised in the paper.* (Fragment is joined to preceding sentence; comma is not required.)

The carpenter bought a sandwich *to eat at noon.* (Fragment is joined to preceding sentence; comma is not required.)

That is Mr. Smith, *the principal of Summit High School.* (Fragment is joined to preceding sentence with comma, but note that fragment could also be changed into complete sentence by adding subject and verb, *He is.*)

John washed the windows *and put up the storms.* (Fragment is joined to preceding sentence; comma is not required.)

I went to class, *although I was not prepared.* (Fragment is joined to preceding sentence; comma is not required but is optional for emphasis.)

Whenever you ask, he will help you. (Fragment is joined to following sentence; comma is used for clarity.)

I saw who cheated on the test—*which really puts me on the spot.* (Fragment is joined to preceding sentence; comma is acceptable, but dash is used instead for emphasis.)

Although fragments are seldom appropriate in expository writing, they are commonly used in everyday conversation. The following exchange shows an instance of such usage:

"Where are you going this evening?"
"To Woodland Mall."
"With whom?"
"Maisie Perkins."
"What time?"
"About 6:30."
"What for?"
"To buy some new shoes."
"May I come too?"
"Certainly."

Note that a complete sentence was used at the beginning to establish the framework. Fragments were then enough to continue the dialogue until the final question, when the speaker needed to use a complete sentence once again.

Sentence fragments occur in the writings of many of our best-known authors, where they are used to create special moods or effects. In general, however, writers should avoid them, except in dialogue or for special emphasis.

Run-on Sentences and Comma Splices

A run-on sentence occurs when one complete sentence is run into another without the proper end punctuation and beginning capital letter to separate them. A comma splice occurs when there is only a comma between two complete sentences.

The millwrights voted to strike the electricians decided to stay on the job. (run-on sentence)

The millwrights voted to strike, the electricians decided to stay on the job. (comma splice)

These two types of errors can be corrected in several ways. First, the sentences may be separated by using a period and a capital.

The millwrights voted to strike. The electricians decided to stay on the job.

Second, the sentences may be separated by using a semicolon.

The millwrights voted to strike; the electricians decided to stay on the job.

Third, the sentences may be separated with a comma plus a coordinating conjunction.

The millwrights voted to strike, but the electricians decided to stay on the job.

Fourth, one of the sentences may be changed into a subordinate clause introduced by a subordinating conjunction.

Although the millwrights voted to strike, the electricians decided to stay on the job.

Finally, the sentences can be separated by means of a semicolon and a conjunctive adverb.

The millwrights voted to strike; however, the electricians decided to stay on the job.

The method of correction to use will depend upon the particular statement. When the ideas expressed in the two sentences are not closely related, the first or second method is often preferable unless a choppy effect results. For more closely related ideas, the method chosen should be the one that can best express the relationship between them. If, for example, examination shows one idea to be subordinate to the other, then the sentence expressing it can be converted to a subordinate clause introduced by a subordinating conjunction. In some cases, several or all of the methods may be used interchangeably.

Clichés

Clichés are once colorful expressions that through overuse have become stale and worn out. Habitual use of clichés weakens a writer's power to create fresh images or express exact meanings. The writing that results lacks color and seems careless and hastily done. Here is a small sampling of clichés.

acid test	hit the nail on the head
almighty dollar	honesty is the best policy
apple of his eye	in the last analysis
beat a hasty retreat	innocent as a lamb
better late than never	last but not least
black sheep	make hay while the sun shines
blind as a bat	nipped in the bud
budding genius	no sooner said than done
burn the midnight oil	perfect specimen
chip off the old block	picture of health
clear as a bell	put in an appearance
conspicuous by its absence	rears its ugly head
cool as a cucumber	scrape the bottom of the barrel
doomed to disappointment	set the world on fire
each and every	sick as a dog
easier said than done	slow but sure
exception proves the rule	strike while the iron is hot
fast and furious	when my ship comes in
goes without saying	wine, women, and song
green with envy	worse for wear

Wordiness

Wordiness is a fault especially common with beginning writers. It results in papers that are long-winded, boring, and often difficult to follow. One form of wordiness is often called "deadwood." This term refers to words and phrases that do nothing except take up space and clutter the writing. In the following sentence, the deadwood is enclosed in brackets.

> Responsible parents [of today] do not allow their children [to have] absolute freedom [to do as they please], but neither do they severely restrict the children's activities.

Now consider this rewritten version, in which the deadwood has been eliminated.

> Responsible parents do not allow their children absolute freedom, but neither do they severely restrict the children's activities.

Careful editing has not only reduced the length of the first version by a third—from twenty-seven words to eighteen—but also increased the clarity of the writing.

Gobbledygook, a special form of wordiness, is characterized by the unnecessary use of long words and technical terms. Gobbledygook is usually the result of an attempt to make writing sound impressive or to conceal the lack of anything to communicate. Here are some sentences written in gobbledygook. Revised versions in good, plain English are given in parentheses.

> The fish exhibited a 100 percent mortality response. (All of the fish died.)

> Implementation of this policy will be effectuated on January 2, 1977. (The policy will take effect on January 2, 1977.)

> We have been made cognizant of the fact that the experiment will be terminated in the foreseeable future. (We have learned that the experiment will end soon.)

> Illumination is required to be extinguished on the premises on termination of daily activities. (Turn off the lights at the end of the day.)

Technical terms in writing are justified only if (1) they save words *and* (2) the reader knows their meaning. Biologists, for instance, know that *symbiotic relationship* means "a mutually beneficial relationship between two unlike organisms," and so the term poses no problems in technical journals published for biologists. Such a term should not, however, be employed in an article aimed at nontechnical readers unless it is clearly defined the first time it is used. As a general rule, technical terms should be used very sparingly in articles for general audiences.

Overuse of Passive Voice

A sentence is in the passive voice when the subject receives the action of the verb and in the active voice when the subject performs the action. The following two sentences illustrate the difference.

> The boy *hit* the ball. (Active voice—subject, *boy*, performs action.)

> The ball *was hit* by the boy. (Passive voice—subject, *ball*, receives action.)

The passive voice gives writing a dull, impersonal tone and adds unnecessary words. Consider the following paragraph, written largely in the passive voice.

> Graft becomes possible when gifts are given to police officers or favors are done for them by persons who expect preferential treatment in return. Gifts of many kinds may be received by officers. Often free meals are given to officers by the owners of restaurants on their beats. During the Christmas season, officers may be given gifts of liquor, food, or theater tickets by merchants. If favored treatment is not received by the donors, no great harm is done. But when traffic offenses, safety code violations, and the like are overlooked by the officers, corruption results. When such corruption is exposed by the newspapers, faith is lost in the law and law enforcement agencies.

Note the livelier tone of the rewritten version.

> Graft becomes possible when police officers accept gifts or favors from persons who expect preferential treatment in

return. Officers may receive gifts of many kinds. Often restaurant owners provide free meals for officers on local patrol. During the Christmas season, merchants make gifts of liquor, food, or theater tickets. If donors do not receive favored treatment, no great harm is done. But when officers overlook traffic offenses, safety code violations, and the like, corruption results. When the newspapers expose such corruption, citizens lose faith in the law and law enforcement agencies.

Because of its livelier, more emphatic tone, the active voice is usually more effective. Nonetheless, there are certain situations where the passive voice is better. Occasionally, for instance, it may be desirable to conceal someone's identity. Consider this memorandum from a supervisor to a group of employees who have consistently taken overly long coffee breaks.

At the monthly supervisors' meeting, it was suggested that coffee breaks be suspended permanently unless employees immediately limit them to ten minutes. The suggestion was approved. Please observe the ten-minute limit from now on so that such action will not be necessary.

To prevent hostile comments and harassment, the supervisor deliberately does not name the person who made the suggestion.

Technical and scientific writing commonly employs the passive voice to explain how processes are or were carried out, since in such descriptions it is the action, not the actor, that is important and an objective, impersonal tone is desirable.

To obtain a water sample for dissolved oxygen analysis, a B.O.D. bottle is completely filled and then capped so no air is trapped inside. Next, 2 ml of manganese sulfate solution is added, well below the surface of the sample, and this is followed by 2 ml of alkali-iodide-oxide agent. The bottle is then stoppered carefully, so as to exclude air bubbles, and the contents are mixed by inverting the bottle at least 15 times.

There are times when the passive voice is preferable in everyday writing.

The garbage is collected once a week—on Monday.

The aircraft carrier was commissioned last August.

In these sentences, just as in the scientific example above, what was done, rather than who did it, is the important thing. The passive voice gives the action the necessary emphasis.

Except in these special situations, however, writers should employ the active voice.

Shift in Person

Personal pronouns can be first person, second person, or third person. First-person pronouns refer to the speaker(s), second-person pronouns refer to the individual(s) spoken to, and third-person pronouns refer to the individual(s) or thing(s) spoken about.

Student writers often shift needlessly from one person to another, as in these examples.

> An understanding roommate is one to whom *you* can tell a personal problem. This type of roommate knows when *I* want to be alone and respects *my* wish. (shift from second to first person)

> If an employee works hard, *he* has many opportunities for advancement, and eventually *you* might become a department supervisor. (shift from third to second person)

> After *I* had worked as a cashier for six months, it was nice being promoted to bookkeeper, with *her* own office. (shift from first to third person)

Shifts in person are evidence of hurried, thoughtless writing and should be avoided. Note the improved smoothness and clarity of the corrected examples.

> An understanding roommate is one to whom *you* can tell a personal problem. This type of roommate knows when *you* want to be alone and respects *your* wish. (second person only)

> If an employee works hard, *he* has many opportunities for advancement, and eventually *he* might become a department supervisor. (third person only)

> After *I* had worked as a cashier for six months, it was nice being promoted to bookkeeper, with *my* own office. (first person only)

Shift in Tense

In describing a series of events or a past situation, student writers often make unwarranted and confusing shifts in the tense of verbs, from past to present and vice versa. These needless shifts in tense are especially likely to occur in summarizing the plots of narratives such as plays, movies, and stories. The following paragraph contains two unwarranted shifts in tense.

> When Framton Nuttel first *arrives* at Mrs. Sappleton's home, he *is* greeted by her niece, Vera, who *announces* that she *will* entertain him until her aunt *comes* downstairs. Vera, a compulsive storyteller, *proceeded* [shift from present to past tense] to tell Framton a beautifully tragic but completely false tale about the death of her aunt's husband and two brothers. She *said* that three years before, the three *had gone* hunting, *perished* in a bog, and their bodies *had never been* recovered. Framton *believes* [shift from past back to present tense] her.

To prevent unwarranted shifts in tense, the writer must keep clearly in mind the time frame of the events or situation being described and not shift tense unless the time changes. In the revised paragraph below, the unwarranted shifts have been corrected.

> When Framton Nuttel *arrives* at Mrs. Sappleton's home, he *is* greeted by her niece, Vera, who *announces* that she *will* entertain him until her aunt *comes* downstairs. Vera, a compulsive storyteller, *proceeds* to tell Framton a beautifully tragic but completely false tale about the death of her aunt's husband and two brothers. She *says* that three years before, the three *went* hunting, *perished* in a bog, and their bodies *were never* recovered. Framton *believes* her.

Shift in Number

Pronouns and verbs show number—that is, they are either singular or plural. Unwarranted shifts in number are really a form of agreement error (see pages 275–279) and should be avoided. An unwarranted shift in number is shown in the following example.

The *Red Cross does* much more than give first-aid classes and provide flood relief. *They are* an international organization and *have* literally hundreds of different programs. *It deserves* everyone's support. (shifts in number from singular to plural and back to singular)

Here are the same sentences with the unwarranted shifts in number corrected.

The *Red Cross does* much more than give first-aid classes and provide flood relief. *It is* an international organization and *has* literally hundreds of different programs. *It deserves* everyone's support.

Faulty Sentences for Class Discussion

The following sentences are taken from student papers. Each sentence contains one or more errors. Identify the errors in each case and then rewrite or restate the sentences correctly.

1. The gourmet restaurant and the lunch counter are both styles of eating that I enjoy.

2. Altman played guitar in a rock band and skied in mens downhill races.

3. Ellen and Margot are completely different when comparing their physical characteristics, modes of dress, and life styles.

4. I received good grades from both Mr. Thurman and Mr. Fergus. However, unlike Mr. Fergus, I felt a close personal relationship with Mr. Thurman.

5. Upon entering, the shop looked totally disorganized.

6. The condition of the tables, T-squares, and other drafting equipment at the Harris Company was in excellent shape.

7. Test tubes, petri dishes, and inoculating needles always made a mess of John's bench, in great contrast to the neatness of Harriet.

8. When a person thinks of nursing, they usually regard it as a glamorous profession.

9. There are two basic kinds of jellyfish. The blue manaets and the red manaets.

10. Three different types of psychotics are paranoia, manic depression, and schizophrenia.

11. Having ruled out the other two engines, the Wankel engine is the one we should consider.

12. A machinists work is a type of work that requires a great deal of mechanical ability.

13. After completing introductory organic chemistry, organic analysis must be taken by the chemistry major.

14. Bring the fish chowder to a boil. By doing this, the haddock will be cooked.

15. Make sure the heat is not too intense, otherwise, the popcorn may burn.

16. Swirl the butter around the saucepan using a tablespoon.

17. After washing the dishes, rinsing and stacking in a drainboard; the table, stove, and counter tops must be wiped clean.

18. Place the film with it still on the reel under running water for ten minutes.

19. Adolf Hitler's military forces might have won World War II if he had ordered an attack on Britain during or immediately after France fell to Germany.

20. After treating the stains, the first load of clothing should be placed in the washer.

21. Some games depend very much on the decisions of officials such as baseball.

22. The weight of the screw driver is four ounces and is eight inches long.

23. The object that I will describe in this paper is a single-headed end wrench. It's material is most commonly composed of steel.

24. The length of the lead pencil is 7¼ inches long.

25. The Cigarette is ignited by matches or a lighter and inhaled into the lungs.

26. At it's widest point, the funnel has a diameter of 7 inches.

27. The durability of a silo will withstand a tornado.

28. Take the red wire and connect it to the positive pole of a 12-volt battery.

29. Here are some instructions for the specific problem you mentioned that should correct the problem.

30. These accidents are a serious problem, we must find ways to cut down on the injurys cause by the unsafe machinery.

31. Be sure that the employees understand the importance of precision in their methods and procedures in relation to this device.

32. Customers' complaints are that the threads on the pipe are to deep and have some chips.

33. The wood must be sanded smoothly before starting the finishing process.

34. It has been brought to my attention that panels are being damaged on the assembly line.

35. If the quality of the traverse surveys do not improve, we must take steps to correct the problem.

36. The chief defect of this device is the loss of sample vapors escaping through improperly designed gasket seals.

37. The apparatus used in this test included: a remote starter switch and a ⅝ inch compression bore.

38. The engine was warmed up before performing the test.

39. Two objects are needed to perform this process; a sharp knife and a strong rope at least three feet in length.

40. When the procedure was repeated, a different set of readings were obtained.

41. In the last part of the process silicon dioxide will be added to improve the paints texture.

42. After completing the organization of the line and staff agencies, an assistant city manager will be hired.

43. This job will consist of figuring heat load calculations, proper sizing of equipment, and installing the furnace and ducts.

44. I believe because of my great deal of experience in the field of performing thyroid tests that I am qualified to attend this program.

45. We are confident that our well-designed equipment will be a long-lasting and efficient way to air-condition your home.

46. At the end of fall term, I earned 19 credits.

47. Copper is being replaced with aluminum which is the third best conductor for high temperature service.

48. The switch was attached to the wall with screws just like the wall plate.

49. Once the inside was finished, staining of the outside was done.

50. I was engaged in the repair of various types of railroad cars.

51. I enjoy outdoor activities with a special interest in repairing and riding motorcycles.

52. I have taken such classes as: Management, Marketing, and Economics.

53. During the summer I worked for my father who owns a landscaping service in Blanktown.

Index

Revision Symbols
for Student Papers

Symbol	Problem	Page
ab	improper abbreviation	304–305
adj	wrong adjective form	263–265
adv	wrong adverb form	265–266
agr / pa	faulty agreement of pronoun and antecedent	277–279, 321–322
agr / su	faulty agreement of subject and verb	275–277, 321–322
apos	missing or misused apostrophe	282–284
awk	awkward phrasing	
[ ]	missing or misused brackets	297
cap	capital letter needed	301–302
case	wrong case	280–282
cl	cliché	316
col	missing or misused colon	292–293
com	missing or misused comma	284–290
cs	comma splice	314–316
comp	faulty comparison	311–312
dm	dangling modifier	308–309
dash	missing or misused dash	293–294
ellip	missing or misused ellipses	298
excl	missing or misused exclamation point	299
frag	sentence fragment	312–314
hy	missing or misused hyphen	294–296
ital	missing or misused italics	302–304
lc	lowercase letter needed	301–302
log	faulty logic	